Shakespeare and Ecology

OXFORD SHAKESPEARE TOPICS

Published And Forthcoming Titles Include:

David Bevington, *Shakespeare and Biography*
Colin Burrow, *Shakespeare and Classical Antiquity*
Michael Caines, *Shakespeare and the Eighteenth Century*
Lawrence Danson, *Shakespeare's Dramatic Genres*
Janette Dillon, *Shakespeare and the Staging of English History*
Paul Edmondson and Stanley Wells, *Shakespeare's Sonnets*
Gabriel Egan, *Shakespeare and Marx*
Andrew Gurr and Mariko Ichikawa, *Staging in Shakespeare's Theatres*
Jonathan Gil Harris, *Shakespeare and Literary Theory*
Russell Jackson, *Shakespeare and the English-speaking Cinema*
Douglas Lanier, *Shakespeare and Modern Popular Culture*
Hester Lees-Jeffries, *Shakespeare and Memory*
Ania Loomba, *Shakespeare, Race, and Colonialism*
Raphael Lyne, *Shakespeare's Late Work*
Russ McDonald, *Shakespeare and the Arts of Language*
Steven Marx, *Shakespeare and the Bible*
Robert S. Miola, *Shakespeare's Reading*
Marianne Novy, *Shakespeare and Outsiders*
Phyllis Rackin, *Shakespeare and Women*
Catherine Richardson, *Shakespeare and Material Culture*
Stuart Sillars, *Shakespeare and the Victorians*
Bruce R. Smith, *Shakespeare and Masculinity*
Zdeněk Stříbrný, *Shakespeare and Eastern Europe*
Michael Taylor, *Shakespeare Criticism in the Twentieth Century*
Alden T. Vaughan and Virginia Mason Vaughan, *Shakespeare in America*
Stanley Wells, ed., *Shakespeare in the Theatre: An Anthology of Criticism*
Martin Wiggins, *Shakespeare and the Drama of his Time*

Oxford Shakespeare Topics

GENERAL EDITORS: PETER HOLLAND AND STANLEY WELLS

Shakespeare and Ecology

RANDALL MARTIN

OXFORD
UNIVERSITY PRESS

OXFORD
UNIVERSITY PRESS

Great Clarendon Street, Oxford, OX2 6DP,
United Kingdom

Oxford University Press is a department of the University of Oxford.
It furthers the University's objective of excellence in research, scholarship,
and education by publishing worldwide. Oxford is a registered trade mark of
Oxford University Press in the UK and in certain other countries

First edition published in 2015

Published in the United States of America by Oxford University Press
198 Madison Avenue, New York, NY 10016, United States of America

British Library Cataloguing in Publication Data
Data available

Library of Congress Control Number: 2015931554

ISBN 978–0–19–956702–7 (hbk.)
ISBN 978–0–19–956701–0 (pbk.)

For Stanley Wells

Acknowledgements

Ecology is an interdisciplinary subject, and this book's efforts to cross-fertilize knowledge in early modern history, science, and Shakespearian drama with evolutionary biology and environmental politics have benefited from friends and colleagues in these and other fields who have generously shared ideas and information. Sincere thanks to: Jennifer Andrews, John Clement Ball, Lynne Bruckner, Rachel Bryant, Lowell Duckert, Hillary Eklund, Edward Geisweidt, Joanna Grossman, Chris Guglielmo, Kristie Heard, Grace Ioppolo, MJ Kidnie, Sean Lawrence, John Leonard, Sharon O'Dair, Ross Leckie, Julia Reinhard Lupton, Jonathon Macfarlane, Scott Maisano, Linda McJannet, Steve Mentz, Yolanda Morbey, Simon Palfrey, James Purkis, Andrea Sella, Edith Snook, Steve Sohmer, Graham Thompson, Rebecca Totaro, Bryce Traister, and Paul Werstine.

I would also like to thank the librarians and staff of The British Library, The Bodleian Library, The Canadian Centre for Architecture, The Huntington Library, Helen Hargest and Anais Vanian-Cooper of The Shakespeare Birthplace Trust, The Shakespeare Centre Library, The University of New Brunswick Library, and Western University Libraries for their valuable research assistance.

Madeline Bassnett, Steve Heard, and Deanne Williams kindly read drafts of the entire book. I am very grateful for their improving suggestions and corrections. Any remaining gaps in scientific and Shakespearian knowledge are my own.

Finally, at Oxford University Press I want to thank Jacqueline Baker for her initial encouragement and continual support, her colleagues Michelle Morton and Rachel Platt, two anonymous OUP readers for their stimulating suggestions, my copy-editor Phil Dines, and above all the series editors, Peter Holland and Stanley Wells, for their wise and inspiring guidance.

July 2014
London Ontario

Contents

List of Illustrations

Ecological Modernity in Shakespeare: an overview

The story of how The Globe (1599) was rebuilt from the reused oak timbers of The Theatre (1576) is well known. Less familiar is the environmental crisis that prompted this thrifty recycling. Shakespeare's company, the Chamberlain's Men, were in danger of losing The Theatre because the lease had expired. The landlord, Giles Allen, was threatening to pull down the playhouse and put its wood and timber to other uses. The leaseholders, Richard and Cuthbert Burbage, got there before him because a clause in the original agreement made them owners of the building on Allen's land. In the lead-up to their stealthy dismantling of The Theatre on the icy morning of 28 December 1598, when Allen was away celebrating Christmas in the country, each side had been eyeing the valuable timber and wood.[1]

Its reuse was the lynchpin of a deal between the Burbages and five actor-sharers of the Chamberlain's Men, including Shakespeare, for building The Globe: the brothers offered to supply the main materials if the sharers contributed to the lesser expenses of construction and maintenance.[2] The Burbages had spent their savings on building an indoor theatre at Blackfriars two years before. Although it had begun to pay them rent, they could not afford to buy new materials because the price of wood and timber had risen 96 per cent over the quarter century since The Theatre had been built.[3] This inflation was the result of southern English woodlands being deforested.

Ancient English woodland and forests had been shrinking throughout the middle ages. By Henry VIII's time the pace began to accelerate. Worried about timber supplies for shipbuilding, the government took the first steps—largely ineffective—to manage depletions. Climactic and demographic pressures aggravated over-exploitation, and by the 1590s caused a fuel crisis in south-east England and the country's first major environmental controversy. Similar to the threat of warming global temperatures today, the stresses on southern English woodland—at that time the country's most essential but finite natural resource—reached an ecological turning point. A solution was in the offing, but it was a highly ambivalent one. Wood shortages and soaring prices led domestic consumers and industrial manufacturers to switch to coal—specifically, sea coal, which was mined near the surface in coastal areas of Newcastle and Scotland, and brought down England's eastern coast by barge.[4]

Shakespeare took notice of this momentous change in the rather unlikely figure of sometime bawd and inn-keeper Mistress Quickly. In *The Merry Wives of Windsor* she takes pride in her comfortably well-heated rooms when ordering her servant Rugby to prepare for the arrival of a new lodger, Dr Caius:

we'll have a posset for't soon at night, in faith, at the latter end of a sea-coal fire.
(1.4.7–8)

In *Henry IV Part Two*, Mistress Quickly accuses Falstaff of inveigling her into lending him money by promising to marry her. She proves the truthfulness of her charge by recalling the exact objects in the room where Falstaff committed himself:

Thou didst swear to me upon a parcel-gilt goblet, sitting in my Dolphin chamber, at the round table, by a sea-coal fire.   (2.1.85–87)

Aside from verifying her claim, Mistress Quickly's use of sea coal for heating displays her economizing modernity. Shakespeare likely appreciated the consumer choices involved in her decision because he was both a lodger in London and the owner of a large house with many fireplaces in Stratford-upon-Avon. For the same reason he understood the significance of the upwardly mobile Pages' more expensive fuel preference at the conclusion of *Merry Wives*. Neighbours and reconciled rivals gather at their house to celebrate Anne and Fenton's marriage around a wood-burning 'country fire' (5.5.235).

Shakespeare's distinction between traditional and modern types of heating reflects a national shift to sea coal, whose production through the early modern period rose 100 per cent every decade from the 1550s onward.[5] It had a much higher sulphur content than wood or pit coal (the latter was too expensive to transport from remoter areas of Scotland and Wales to southern English markets). Contemporaries recognized that the effects of burning sea coal in towns were choking smog and acid rain which destroyed local gardens and farmers' fields. By 1578 Queen Elizabeth avoided going into London at certain times because she was 'grieved and annoyed with the taste and smoke of sea coals'.[6] Michael Drayton idealized the 'sweet retired life' of a hermit living in Warwickshire's Forest of Arden away from 'the lothsome ayres of smoky citied Townes'.[7] The origins of human-generated climate change today lie partly in the shift to fossil fuel that began in Shakespeare's England.

Given their new experience of pollution from coal smoke, audiences would have heard in Mistress Quickly's fuel choice something more than a comic penchant for irrelevant detail. It would have resonated with Londoners weighing short-term costs and benefits against environmental damage, whose effects were suffered most by the least well off. The shift to coal signalled emerging trade-offs that have since become part of our global reality: private comfort versus public health; personal prosperity versus environmental degradation; social progress versus planetary risk.

Sea coal is one of the signs of modern environmental disturbance to be explored in this book, along with the social controversies these disturbances evoked, and the rapidly changing knowledge and uses of the natural world which framed them. Interweaving these signs into his dramatic narratives, Shakespeare's plays stage an early modern ecological consciousness. Contemporaries would not have called it that, of course, and the term 'ecology' does not appear in Shakespeare's writing. Historically it was the name Darwinian biologist Ernst Haeckel gave to the study of the *oikos*, or dwelling-place, of habitat and species relations. Nineteenth-century ecology's focus on organic interdependence within ecosystems dovetailed with Romantic protests against environmental destruction by factory methods of production and urban population growth.[8] Donald Worster has shown how evolutionary scientists such as Haeckel replaced the earlier cognate term 'economy' with 'ecology' to signal a shift in attitudes towards human relations with the natural world: from measuring social progress on the basis of maximizing resource extraction and production, to learning how to live within the natural limits of ecosystems shared with non-human life.[9] Ecology thereby added an ethical component of asking what nature ought to be, distinct from human interests, to the scientific goal of determining what nature is. From the early twentieth century, ecologists have pursued this joint mandate along two broad paths: disseminating knowledge that humans ought to have about their relationship with the natural world in an era of seriously degrading biodiversity and human-aggravated climate change (ecology as science); and advocating personal and public action to ensure sustainable use of the earth's resources in cooperation with its non-human life-forms (ecology as environmentalism).[10]

Shakespeare was able to imagine these double aims of ecology— epistemological and political—because the pressures of modernity just mentioned—more people, burgeoning towns, and capitalized production and consumption—emerged for the first time in sixteenth- and seventeenth-century England. Technological experimentation, state-sponsored development, and globalizing trade during England's 'first industrial revolution' gave instrumentalist outlooks towards nature cultural ascendancy.[11] Post-feudal attitudes towards the land as an exploitable commodity, as the commercial saw pit in Windsor Forest or Oliver's biodynamic farm illustrate in *The Merry Wives of Windsor* and *As You Like It* respectively, enabled these attitudes. Profitable production in an era of rising prices and colonial expansion made their prospects irresistible. And traditional assumptions about human dominion over the earth, authorized by classical and biblical mythologies, made these dreams socially acceptable. Western thought also tended to figure nature as hostile to human survival and social advancement, and therefore as something to be conquered. Early modern imperialism extended the environmental impacts of this subjugating mindset around the world.

As Mistress Quickly's domestic use of sea coal suggests, Shakespeare's contemporaries experienced these intensified but unsettling uses of the natural world mainly at household and community levels of shelter and subsistence. Their effects coincided with natural ecological pressures of severe weather and failed harvests. Both manmade and natural disturbances challenged traditional certainties about seasonal rhythms and the regenerative dependability of the natural world. As changing land-uses and growing consumption of resources threatened local environments, early modern men and women came to recognize that England's natural bounty of woodland, rivers, and arable soil, hitherto assumed to be unlimited, could no longer be taken for granted. This awareness prompted them to rethink human relationships with nature and take steps to protect it. Informed by new information about the natural world on global as well as local and regional levels, Shakespeare's work contributed to the formation of this new ecological worldview.

Global ecologies

The 'new philosophy calls all in doubt', observed John Donne in *The Second Anniversary* (1612). He was referring mainly to the new heliocentric system, which displaced the earth and humans from the centre of a finite Ptolemaic universe. Donne was also aware that the era's foundational instability was related to proliferating reports of newly discovered oceans, terrains, climates, peoples, animals, and plants. This initially mythical-sounding but increasingly verified information superseded the epistemological boundaries of the Mediterranean *oikos* and generated competing versions of nature's global origins and timelines.

If ecology in the broadest sense is the earth's story told from the perspective of its long-term geological and biological evolution, the early modern discovery of brave new worlds created a radically destabilized and open-ended ecological narrative. Donne and contemporaries like Shakespeare were discovering what modern research has confirmed to be the planet's normal condition: a world continually subject to geophysical ruptures, mutable climate patterns, and species change.[12] In our time this more authentically evolutionary paradigm has replaced theories of steady-state or homeostatic ecology, as well as earlier Romantic celebrations of nature as ideally balanced and unchanging, ostensibly represented by wilderness environments. Conservation biologists and ecologists now stress that human responses to environmental problems must be premised on anticipating continual fluctuations in local or global ecosystems that may be only partially predictable or manageable. More generally, humans must apply our efforts to repair the damage we have inflicted with greater realism and humility in the face of complex networks we may understand only imperfectly. The 2013 report of the Intergovernmental Panel on Climate Change, for example, acknowledges these realities while also demonstrating the absolute necessity of immediate multilateral action.[13]

The early modern discovery of nature's historicity anticipates the current rethinking of relations between humans and the environment in the light of non-equilibrium ecology, and it creates significant imaginative bridges between Shakespeare's environmental outlook and our own. Among educated people, early modernity's received ideas about nature derived partly from the accounts of natural historians such as Pliny and Aelian. (Natural history was the historical predecessor of ecology as science.) Shakespeare read them in school and recalled many of their animal and plant references in his writings. The existence of some creatures ('come, basilisk, / And kill the innocent gazer with thy sight' [*Henry VI Part Two*, 3.2.52–53]) had long been regarded as fanciful and/or in need of empirical confirmation. Implicitly they limited the credibility of the classical record. Shakespeare also referred to ideas of nature encoded in traditional organizing metaphors, such as the Aristotelian chain of being which modelled European social structures ('The heavens...the planets, and this centre / Observe degree, priority, and place' [*Troilus and Cressida*, 1.3.85–86]), and the Augustinian book of nature (*Romeo and Juliet*; see below in this overview). When these ideals were materially disrupted by the period's scientific discoveries and political upheavals, the unifying ethos of their figurative language was called into question.

Shakespeare's ideas about human interactions with nature also drew significantly on direct observation of the landscapes, flora, and fauna with which he had grown up in the rural Midlands, and later experienced living in London and journeying around England.[14] His unrivalled eye for such details led Romantic writers to elevate him as England's pre-eminent poet of nature, and his natural history became the object of 'green' studies. The latter evaluated the accuracy of Shakespeare's nature references in the light of early modern or the latest scientific information, usually with the aims of praising Shakespeare's keen-sightedness and reconfirming the sublime beauty that he was assumed to have admired in nature.[15] Still on a level of literal representation, Shakespeare's work also incorporates expanding empirical information disseminated by early modern maps, voyaging, travel literature, bestiaries and herbals, and by London's nascent scientific community.[16] Information from these sources, combined with personal observation, generated innovative metaphors of nature and a discursive layering of geophysical narratives. Together they reflected the openness of early modern biodiversity to physical expansion and cultural revision, thereby establishing epistemic continuity between Shakespeare's ecological knowledge and today's continually evolving scientific research and environmental criticism.

Another bridge between Shakespearian and present-day remodelling of human relations with the natural world are the crossovers between early modern and post-Cartesian ideas about human ontology. Inspired partly by modern research into the molecular ancestry of human physiology, and partly by arguments favouring the extension of universal rights to non-human animals, post-humanist and animal studies have reopened discussions about human nature and its inward connections with other life forms that writers such as Michel de Montaigne initially broached in the early modern period. Rational empiricists and Enlightenment philosophy subsequently rejected Montaigne's Humanist scepticism and re-essentialized humans as categorically separate from other creatures. Innogen's and Posthumus's immersion in the biodiversities of *Cymbeline*, however, or Hamlet's reflections on the symbiotic relations between humans and worms (Chapters 4 and 5, respectively), show Shakespeare joining Montaigne and anticipating Darwinian biology in presenting human and non-human life as enmeshed in nature's foodwebs and organic cycles of decay, regeneration, and adaptation.

Although the evolutionary theory underpinning ecology is hardly lacking in radical power or intellectual sophistication, environmental criticism is still sometimes discounted for lacking the kind of theoretical rigour that transformed literary studies during the last quarter of the previous century. One reply to this attitude is that both ecology as environmentalism and literary ecocriticism are strategically heterogeneous in concept and non-exclusionary in method. They have to be,

because confronting environmental problems typically involves negotiating complex geophysical interactions across multiple timelines, and
persuading assorted political and economic stakeholders to act beyond,
but not necessarily outside, their own interests. As a field of study,
ecology converges specialized knowledge from a range of scientific and
social domains to explain interdependent biological and environmental change, and to devise site-specific actions to avoid extinctions and
promote biodiversity. Biologist Edward O. Wilson calls this synthe-
sizing approach 'consilience', in which facts and concepts across dis-
ciplines are linked to create a common groundwork of explanation.[17]
Intellectually, ecocriticism similarly combines historical, post-structural,
ecofeminist, post-humanist, and other kinds of theoretical criticism
with scientific literacy and cultural analysis. This interdisciplinary
outlook seeks to unpack assumptions about nature reflected in Shakespeare's texts and their reception, and to reimagine both through the
lens of today's continually evolving relations with the natural world. In
both respects, the study of Shakespeare's ecologies seeks out historical
antecedents and conceptual templates for contemporary environmental knowledge and activism, whose current range of political commit-
ments range from: *reform environmentalism* (incremental and non-
radical change, now partly compromised by 'green marketing' and
corporatized goals of 'sustainability'[18]); to *biocentrism* (anti-hierarchical
attitudes towards nature that challenge anthropocentrism, or human-
centred interests); to *deep ecology* (species-levelling convictions, dedicated to radical political and institutional environmental change).[19]
Shakespeare, as I hope to show, analogizes all these positions (though
not of course all at once). His plays are well-positioned to communicate
ecological possibilities to modern audiences because, in performance,
his work is regularly staged in diverse indoor and outdoor venues and
locally adapted productions around the world. Shakespeare's signature
practice of drawing spectators' attention to the temporal and physical
actualities of stage performance also encourages them to reimagine
both natural and manmade environments not merely as the décor of
his dramatic narratives, but as dynamic contexts that materially shape
human and non-human relations and identities.

   In the remainder of this overview I shall briefly survey some major
environmental contexts which shaped the ecological awareness of
Shakespeare and his audiences while introducing the subjects of this

book's chapters. I'll begin with the period's natural disruptions of climate and population change, and continue with human pressures accelerating resource consumption which, for the first time, began to surpass England's natural limits and distort traditional relations with the natural world. Combining historical and present-day ecological perspectives, I'll then introduce three of early modern England's most serious environmental dangers represented by Shakespeare: deforestation in *The Merry Wives of Windsor* and *The Tempest* (Chapter 1); profit-driven agriculture in *As You Like It* (Chapter 2); and gunpowder's impairment of sustainable cultivation—the traditional remedy for wartime - destruction—in *Henry IV Parts One* and *Two*, *Henry V*, and *Macbeth* (Chapter 3). These discussions present a gradual shift in spatial relations associated with nested environments: from local landscapes and communities, to bioregional territories, to planetary ecosystems, or the biosphere. In Chapter 4 I examine how *Cymbeline* represents the scaled interdependency of all these networks. I conclude by exploring evolutionary micro-ecologies in *Hamlet* and *Antony and Cleopatra* in Chapter 5.

Environmental change and ecological consciousness: shifting climate patterns and extreme weather

'The seasons change their manners, as the year / Had found some months asleep and leaped over them', observes Gloucester in *Henry IV Part Two* (4.3.123–24).[20] Interpreting natural phenomena as signs of providential displeasure and/or impending political calamity was traditional to historical narratives, as Cassius demonstrates in *Julius Caesar* by reading the effects of a terrifying electrical storm as portents of a 'monstrous state' (1.3.57–71).[21] Gloucester similarly assumes the disordered seasons are metaphysical warnings of the upheavals that will follow King Henry's death.[22] But in 1596–97 his observations also had felt resonances for audiences watching the play in London's open-air theatres, since they were shivering through what climatologists today call the 'Little Ice Age'. Between 1300 and 1850 Northern Europe's average temperatures fell when the regular oscillation between low pressure over Iceland and high pressure over the Azores reversed.[23] Early modern winters were wet and icy, and normal seasonal cycles were disrupted. Similar long-term shifts again threaten Britain and other parts of the world today because of human-aggravated climate change.

Shakespeare alludes to Elizabethans' on-the-body experience of severe weather in many settings, from the 'rough winds' that 'shake the darling buds of May' in Sonnet 18, to the 'wind and the rain' of *Twelfth Night*, to the earth-battering storms of *King Lear*, *Macbeth*, and *The Winter's Tale*.[24] Having apparently brought England's Little Ice Age to Italy, Petruchio's servants grumble about the perishing cold (*The Taming of Shrew*, 4.1). London spectators could readily imagine the scenario of old Norway 'smot[ing] the sledded Pollacks on the ice' because the River Thames had recently been freezing over every winter (*Hamlet*, 1.1.63, 1.4.1–2). By contrast, the songs of winter and spring in *Love's Labour's Lost* (5.3) reminded audiences that seasonal patterns had become less stable and seemed subject to long-term change.

Frigid and flooded conditions of the 1590s devastated English regional landscapes and animal populations. Four failed harvests between 1593 and 1597 produced widespread famine and unemployment.[25] Experience of these real-life miseries intensified audiences' affective responses to Shakespeare's depictions of hunger and homelessness (e.g. Cade in *Henry VI Part Two*, Adam and Orlando in *As You Like It*, Poor Tom in *King Lear*, the people in *Coriolanus*, the citizens of Tarsus in *Pericles*). They also challenged contemporaries to make sense of their environmental causes. Shakespeare captures the difficulty humorously in attributing the period's devastating weather to the supernatural rows of fairies Oberon and Titania in *A Midsummer Night's Dream* (2.1.81–117). Human relationships to climate take a more serious turn when Shakespeare uses tropes of extreme weather to express personal tragedy. The increasingly powerless Richard II laments, 'We'll make foul weather with despisèd tears. / Our sighs and they shall lodge [i.e. flatten] the summer corn / And make a dearth in this revolting land' (*Richard II*, 3.3.160–62). Whereas Richard's devastating weather creates an ambiguous connection with the sympathy he is trying to stir, Scroop's comparison lends Bolingbroke's political ascendance a ring of authenticity:

> Like an unseasonable stormy day,
> Which makes the silver rivers drown their shores...
> So high above his limits swells the rage
> Of Bolingbroke.   (3.2.106–110)

The storm in *King Lear* materializes the king's catastrophic descent into madness punctuated by flashes of lucidity. Yet as Steve Mentz observes, Lear's insights fall short of reading any causal explanation into the play's extreme weather beyond his personal projections, like Richard's, of suffering and vengeance. The storm's random excesses overreach traditional theories about how nature is supposed to work—for example, in mirroring metaphysically ordered creation and human hierarchies, upon which Lear's whole worldview is based. The storm's oblique epistemology points to a less-than-fully-knowable relationship between humans and nature. In that way it is suggestive of both early modern and twenty-first-century conditions of living in meteorological and ecological uncertainty.[26]

Demographic pressures: 'The world must be peopled'

Benedict rationalizes overcoming his antipathy to marriage in *Much Ado About Nothing* by alluding to the biblical command to go forth and multiply (2.3.239). His linking of incongruous causes is characteristic of Shakespeare's humour and also typically veils a serious underlying issue: widespread concerns that late sixteenth-century England—in the Midlands and south-east—was becoming overcrowded. Historians estimate that the country's population grew from two to five million between 1500 and 1660, and from three to four million between 1559 and 1603.[27] These changes reversed the late-middle-ages decline caused by the Black Death and by the foreign and civil wars that Shakespeare dramatized in his English history plays. London in particular grew rapidly over Shakespeare's lifetime through migration from the provinces and immigration from abroad. Shakespeare's professional career and the French Huguenot family he lodged with for several years in London were representative of both these demographic trends.[28] In the Forest of Arden (near which Shakespeare grew up and set *As You Like It*), Victor Skipp has shown that England's rapidly expanding population created unprecedented imbalances in supply and demand for food, fuel, and the availability of shelter.[29] Shakespeare's Warwickshire contemporary Michael Drayton referred to the county's villages 'repleate with ragg'd and sweating Clownes [rural labourers]'.[30] In certain north Arden parishes, subsistence crises affected fertility and reproduction rates to the extent of creating what Skipp calls a 'Malthusian check' in the first decade of the seventeenth century (i.e. a reversal in population growth caused by resource shortfalls, a connection first theorized by late-eighteenth-century political economist Thomas Malthus).

Disturbances of climate and demography made early modern men and women more aware that a growing population's survival in either towns or the countryside depended on what modern ecologists call carrying capacity. This is the ability of a defined area to produce enough resources to sustain growth without causing long-term environmental degradation.[31] A related idea is ecological footprint: the total amount of land and water required in a given area 'to produce all the resources consumed, and to assimilate all the wastes produced' by that population.[32] When yields of crops, wood, and other commodities fell short of local carrying capacities, it became apparent that ecological footprints were difficult to shrink, and that demand and supply had to be managed for human and non-human benefit.

Shakespeare registers the period's recurring subsistence crises at both collective and individual levels of daily living. Food and employment are the focus of violent clashes between commoners and lords in *Henry VI Part Two* and *Coriolanus* that reflect early modern dearth, and ecological imbalances. Elsewhere Shakespeare alludes to these problems in the poetic textures of his dialogue. In *As You Like It*, Silvius equates the pain of his unrequited love for Phoebe with the desperate rural expedient of sifting agricultural stubble for scraps:

> ...I [am] in such as poverty of grace
> That I shall think it a most plenteous crop
> To glean the broken ears after the man
> That the main harvest reaps.   (*As You Like It*, 3.5.101–104)

Demographic pressures aggravated by severe weather caused the prices of food and other agricultural commodities to shoot up. When Lancelot jokes to Jessica about her conversion from Judaism that 'This making of Christians will raise the price of hogs' so that 'we shall not shortly have a rasher on the coals for money', his quip alludes to real economic conditions and not just Christian fantasy (*The Merchant of Venice*,

3.5.21–23). Price rises in all agricultural products and natural materials put certain kinds of food and fuel increasingly out of reach for commoners, whose wages had been falling or who were unemployed owing to labour surpluses.[33] They also had the wider effect of making mixed farming more profitable than traditional sheep-grazing. Farmers and landowners who practised or converted to agrarian and animal husbandry, like Justice Shallow in *Henry IV Part Two*, became richer than wool-producers. This situation seems to explain why the decaying sheep farm which Corin tends in *As You Like It* has been put up for sale. The absentee owner may be hoping to invest in land more suitable for the kind of high-efficiency and profitable farming practised by Oliver. The productive 'green cornfield[s]' and 'acres of the rye' celebrated in 'It was a Lover and his Lass' may represent Rosalind's economically/ecologically savvy ambitions after she initially purchases the farm to boost Corin's starvation wages (*As You Like It*, 2.4, 5.3.17–21). I'll say more about these contemporary agrarian contexts of *As You Like It* in Chapter 2 (also see below in this overview).

Widely held fears that growing numbers of people were overshooting the country's resource limits caused contemporaries to look beyond England. The Virginia Company's dreams of colonizing North America were based partly on hopes that the New World's seemingly empty spaces and limitless commodities would relieve population and carrying-capacity pressures at home. Shakespeare rewrote the Company's propaganda points into *The Tempest* with a wry twist, when Caliban threatens the island's European colonists with peopling 'their' island (1.2.349–50). He also represented English hopes of using foreign conquest to solve imbalances of production and consumption through historical but decidedly ambivalent examples. *Coriolanus* and *Antony and Cleopatra* stage the classical policy of relieving pressures on a region's carrying capacity by using war and territorial occupation to accommodate an expanding ecological footprint. Rome values Coriolanus's prodigious killing abilities to fulfil their goals of seizing their enemies' well-stocked flour mills and offsetting the patrician grain-hoarding which has caused a domestic dearth and street protests. Coriolanus turns enemy bloodshed into Roman nourishment (*Coriolanus*, 1.1.247, 1.2.10, 1.3.35–38, 2.1.31). Caesar's aggression towards Antony and Cleopatra is similarly related to Italy's later dependence on Egyptian corn to feed Rome's expanding population and legions (including the 'waste' with which Caesar rewards his soldiers after they capture Egyptian storehouses [4.1.15–16]). Antony's indulgence of Cleopatra's political ambitions threatens Roman food lines and makes Caesar's conquest as much a matter of ecological necessity as personal rivalry. Henry V's invasion of France is another instance. His campaign is motivated partly by the legacy of drawdowns and disease caused by his father's civil wars. Imperial conquest will create an expanded footprint to 'achieve' (if only temporarily) the resources of the 'world's best garden' (*Henry V*, Epilogue 7).

Exploitation, consumption, and ecological instability: deforestation

Elizabethans who benefitted financially from rising commodity prices, new industries, and globalizing trade bought more domestic and imported goods, and improved the material condition of their farms and households. Their expanding consumption put additional pressure on domestic supply and demand networks already stressed by population growth and climate disruptions. Shakespeare's family was possibly representative of this early modern class. His grandfather Richard had been a yeoman tenant farmer in the village of Snitterfield four and a half miles north-east of Stratford-upon-Avon. He would have ploughed *As You Like It*'s corn- and rye-fields. Perhaps because his grandfather had prospered from agrarian inflation, the playwright's father John was able to quit farming and set up as an initially successful glover in Stratford. After Shakespeare himself had become rich from his share in the Chamberlain's and later King's Men acting companies, he bought and refurbished New Place in Stratford.

One of the curious things about George Vertue's 1737 drawing of New Place—the only original image of the house to survive—is that it doesn't depict any chimneys, even though it was the second-largest house in Stratford (Figure I.1). With two-and-a-half stories, several wings, and multiple rooms, it in fact had at least ten fireplace chimneys.[34] By comparison, the smaller but still substantial Nash's House, where Shakespeare's wife Anne lived after his death, had three (Figure I.2). During the sixteenth-century building boom, chimneys gradually replaced central roof-openings which caused the smoky rooms Hotspur complains about (*Henry IV Part One*, 3.1.156). Besides being an index of the Shakespeares' taxable wealth,

Figure I.1. George Vertue's 1737 drawing of New Place, Stratford-upon-Avon. Reproduced by Permission of the British Library (BL Add 74038 f. detail).

Figure I.2. Nash's House, Stratford-upon-Avon. Reproduced by Permission of the Shakespeare Birthplace Trust.

chimneys were a display of comfortable modernity, as Mistress Quickly's pride in her sea coal-heated rooms suggests. A warming fire was a tangible reminder of the period's unpredictable climate and its relation to wider environmental disturbances. Grumio's or Lavatch's appreciation for a fire would have resonated feelingly with early modern audiences enduring the period's great frosts. Discomfort escalated to a survival issue in many homes when the weather became extreme. The First Carrier in *1 Henry IV* laments how the doubling 'in the price of oats' killed 'Robin ostler' and his inn-keeping business. In the same moment he glances wistfully at a nearby 'new chimney', presumably built from profits of the same inflation. This working chimney stands in contrast to the one in the impoverished carriers' own house, whose cold fireplace lacks for wood and is useful only for urinating in (2.1.2–19).

Like sea coal, chimneys are another sign of essential and discretionary consumption in an era of ecological instability. Their presence reveals Shakespeare's ecocritical eye for contemporary built and natural environments as evidence of new links between economic growth and ecological stress. Multiple fireplaces in rebuilt and expanded houses used greater quantities of wood than regions in southern England could regenerate by traditional methods such as coppicing. The wood shortages underlying Mistress Quickly's domestic switch to sea coal were aggravated by new manufacturing industries such as glass- and iron-making. Overconsumption on both levels created early modern England's most urgent environmental problem: deforestation. In Chapter 1 I focus on Shakespeare's representation of its Elizabethan controversies in the Windsor Forest action of *The Merry Wives of Windsor*. Shakespeare's most contemporary play reflects the era's growing conservationist awareness by juxtaposing two emblematic sites: a commercial in-forest saw pit and a nearby mature tree, Herne's Oak. The former represents the increasing commodification of royal forests by Tudor monarchs and governments who allowed forests to be carelessly exploited by nascent consumer and export industries such as glassmaking, which operated local saw pits of the kind represented in *Merry Wives*.

Anxieties over deforestation generated a rearguard attempt by writers such as forest-keeper John Manwood to revive the conservationist mandate of long-compromised English forest laws. The visible degradation of southern English woodland also prompted attempts to export fuel-supply problems overseas. In this regard, I briefly detour in Chapter 1 to *The Tempest*'s allusions to England's glassmaking in Virginia and consider their relationship to present-day debates over sustainability, before returning to Windsor and Herne's Oak.

Shakespeare's staging of an increasingly rare oversized oak tree at the heart of his romantic comedy suggests two routes into environmental activism: giving mature trees names to endow them with protective rights; and using 'ecological optics' to discern symbiotic relations with local woodlands.[35] 'Ecological optics' is James J. Gibson's term for the way human and non-human animals perceive and react to the affordances, or situational promptings, of their material environments and living inhabitants. Over evolutionary time, physically and kinetically afforded signs have shaped adapted behaviours, such as the Windsorites' unconscious physical interactions with a large oak tree. Recognizing such phenomenological impacts in *Merry Wives* fosters an ecological literacy that challenges the later Enlightenment separation of human mind and physical matter. Moreover, because local environments are continually affected by natural and human-generated changes which both constitute and disrupt affordances, their consequences are unpredictable and invite improvisation. The ecological realism rather than idealism suggested by this complexity finally characterizes the eco-poetics of deforestation encoded by the stand-off between Windsor Forest's saw pit and Herne's Oak.

Exploiting and conserving husbandry

Ovidian literary traditions and the Romantic pictorial imagination have made woodland scenes in *The Merry Wives*, *Titus Andronicus*, *A Midsummer Night's Dream*, and other Shakespeare plays known visually as somewhat fearful places of dense trees inhabited by wild animals. By contrast, parks such as the King of Navarre's in *Love Labour's Lost* conjure up images of more varied landscapes associated with royal or gentry estates: grassland, fields, individual trees, and woods. In fact this natural and manmade diversity was typical of both early modern forests and parks. Shakespeare accordingly dramatized his Forest of Arden in *As You Like It* as a mixture of landscape patches, or ecosystems, within the Midlands bioregion: the wood in which Duke Senior and his court live in exile; the pasture where Corin grazes his sheep; cultivated corn and rye; streams and rivers which outline and interconnect these natural and manmade habitats; and adjoining human domains such as Oliver's farm. Together these heterogeneous elements form a mosaic: a cluster of patch ecosystems and water and land corridors in a regional area.

Human impacts over hundreds of years had transformed English woodland into patchy mosaics. The effects of these changes were more visible in Shakespeare's Forest of Arden than elsewhere because it was a former royal forest that had lost its conservationist mandate. It had suffered more intensive deforestation and conversion to arable and other land-uses. These impacts accelerated in the sixteenth century in attempts to remedy widespread food and fuel shortages caused by the period's poor harvests and population growth. New ideologies of the land as a for-profit resource also gave social licence to more aggressive exploitation. In both respects ecological disturbance increased beyond 'background' levels of traditional sustainability, as early modern writers of England's landscapes such as Michael Drayton and William Harrison recognized. Memories of what Arden's woodlands used to look like compared to its present shrinking, degraded, or simply changed conditions gave rise to ecocritical perspectives. Shakespeare and his family had rites of memory in the Forest of Arden as well as profitable interests in its modern land-uses. The playwright deployed knowledge of its environmental historicity in adapting Thomas Lodge's popular prose-romance *Rosalynde* into the forest comedy *As You Like It*, whose topical contexts of agrarian and ecological controversy I explore in Chapter 2.

Orlando's opening complaints against his brother introduce agricultural enclosure as one of the play's two leading tropes of environmental change. From its late-medieval origins in the conversion of common land to more profitable private sheep-grazing, enclosure had been the object of frequent and often violent rural protests. Shakespeare reflects this popular tradition not only in *As You Like It* but also in the rebellions of Jack Cade and his followers in *Henry VI Part Two* and the starving citizens in *Coriolanus*.

From the second half of the sixteenth century, however, the motives for enclosure began to diversify. These shifts have been less well recognized by modern critics, but the changes Shakespeare makes to

Lodge's *Rosalynde* reflect their contemporary realities. Common land was increasingly enclosed not for pastoral sheep-farming but for producing food to feed the period's growing numbers of people and domestic animals. In that sense, enclosure-related husbandry responded to both natural and manmade disturbance for what was arguably the community's welfare. But mixed-farming enclosers like Oliver also looked greedy in seeking to maximize the productivity of their estates. Many also profited from the commodification of land introduced by the new Tudor property market; they adopted innovations in agricultural and animal husbandry aimed at boosting local and national self-sufficiency; and they benefited from rising prices for all agricultural products in the period. While these practices made landowners like Oliver (and Shakespeare) upwardly mobile, they also aggravated unemployment in an era of surplus labour, and imposed pitiful wages on rural journeyman. Corin is Shakespeare's dignified representative of this whole underclass. He suffers directly from his own landlord's strategic neglect of his sheep farm, and more contextually from the displacements of enclosure underwritten by emerging ideologies of maximal growth, and worsened by transnational flows of capital and trade.

Not all disruptions related to agrarian enclosure and improvements were negative, however. In the late-sixteenth-century Forest of Arden, as Victor Skipp has shown, overexploitation of common land by growing numbers of people caused soils to become eroded, thereby reducing the biodiversity and ecological resilience of local communities. In the face of this original 'tragedy of the commons',[36] enclosure and agrarian innovations such as convertible husbandry—the play's second major environmental trope—represented shifts to long-term structural conservation. An early form of traditional ley farming (alternating sown and fallow ground) and crop rotation, convertible husbandry gave landlords the right to enclose exhausted common land to give it an opportunity to regain 'heart', which we would today define as nutrient and microbiological vitality.

Early modern biodynamic cultivation recognized the need to preserve the physical health of local environments and reaffirmed ancient principles of shared human and non-human dwelling in the world. These attitudes anticipate the bioregionalism of twentieth-century conservation biologist Aldo Leopold and his successors. In Chapter 2 I argue that Rosalind can be seen to reflect both early modern and contemporary bioregional activism in the way she practises two kinds of convertible husbandry: environmental, on the degraded sheep farm she buys from Corin's master; and romantic, on Orlando's culturally eroded Petrarchanism. Her ecological vision animates the natural cycles of fertility, reproduction, and decay of Hymen's masque and its symbolic mosaic of marital fortunes.

The twilight of swords into ploughshares

Bioregionalism is a stance of practical and ideological resistance to the diffused agencies of modernization and globalization. Its twentieth-century focus was agrarian and watershed land-use. Kirkpatrick Sale and other American activists challenged industrial models of farming which replaced biologically diverse ecosystems with technically efficient monocultures.[37] Bioregionalism's legacy today is the huge array of often consumerized modes of localism, including a return to organic methods of farming and viticulture. These were the same practices that early modern husbandry writers advocated to sustain food and fuel supplies and to cultivate bio-integrity amid the ecological stresses of the period. In both cases, early modern and twentieth-century bioregionalists have been inspired by the ethics and practical advice of classical georgic, epitomized by Virgil's *Georgics* (29 BC, trans. 1589, and known to Shakespeare). Whereas other ancient husbandry writers concentrated exclusively on farming practices, Virgil situated his practical advice in the context of recent Roman civil wars (the historical events of Shakespeare's *Julius Caesar* and *Antony and Cleopatra*). These had severely disrupted Italian agriculture by forcing local farmers to abandon their fields and orchards to become soldiers. Virgil's *Georgics* implicitly presents a dialogue between positive and negative forms of human labour and production. It celebrates peacetime agriculture as an ethically and ecologically superior state to war, whose social and environmental damage will be regenerated by cultivation. Virgil's trope for this process is the image of beating swords into ploughshares. Shakespeare adapts it at various points in his histories and tragedies along with the companion image of olive branches, signifying peacetime prosperity ('And peace proclaims olives of endless age', Sonnet 107.8).

War's actual or systemic dangers are a topical context that connect (neo-)Virgilian georgic, twentieth-century bioregionalists, and Shakespeare. Renaissance and modern agrarianism are linked even more closely by threats from mechanized warfare supported by military-industrial levels of resource consumption. In our time, comparable dangers arise from the globalized trade in chemical, biological, and nuclear weapons. Ordinary citizens have little control over these corporate transactions, even though they have substantial, if often covert, impacts on day-to-day life. Shakespeare recognized earlier versions of such threats in gunpowder warfare. Staging their direct and contextual disruptions created further imaginative paths into ecological knowledge and activism for contemporary spectators.

The events portrayed in Shakespeare's English history plays took place when new catastrophically destructive cannons, mines, and firearms were replacing older rams, catapults, longbows and pikes in European warfare, as the artillery in *Henry V* depicts with forward-looking accuracy. The English transition to mechanized warfare was slower at home than on the Continent, however, so signs of its development in Shakespeare's *Henry IV* and *Henry VI* plays are anachronistic. They nonetheless present what seem to be a recurring focus. One indication of this is the major presence of cannons in pre-gunpowder *King John* (thirteenth century). Significantly, artillery is completely absent in the closely related *Troublesome Reign of King John* (1591). Shakespeare's tragedies and comedies also often refer to gunpowder weapons even when armed conflict is not a main concern. Venetian Othello, for example, is personally invested in the new military-industrial culture, and it may be a sign of his Muslim roots, since European knowledge of gunpowder came from China through Islamic culture. At the tipping point of his destructive jealousy, Othello compares the loss of his martial 'occupation' to the annihilating force of 'mortal engines, whose rude throats / Th'immortal Jove's dread clamours counterfeit' (3.3.357–58; similarly, Henry V's 'ordnance', Chorus 3.26).

Producing iron for cannons and saltpetre for gunpowder were the twinned ambitions of Tudor armament manufacturing. Henry VIII established a foundry in Sussex devoted to making Europe's first cast-iron cannons—the kind the unnamed Man in Shakespeare's *Henry VIII* facetiously imagines would disperse the multitudes who have crashed the palace to celebrate Princess Elizabeth's christening (5.3.12–13). By the end of her reign, national furnaces were producing 1000 tons of ordnance annually at £10 a ton. At five times the price of bar iron, ordnance became a hugely profitable export. It is tempting to connect Philip the Bastard's allusions to cannons' thundering destruction in *King John* and his cynical embrace of 'commodity' with England's transformation into Europe's leading manufacturer of cast-iron artillery, and a global exporter of its human and environmental devastation, since national navies were the main purchasers of English cannons.

Ordnance manufacturing consumed vast amounts of wood in its furnaces, and generated what may have been the first recorded environmental enquiry. Deforestation by the iron industry in the south-east was never officially reined in, however, because national militarization took priority over the needs of other manufacturing and local communities. The same interests governed the English production of saltpetre (gunpowder's main ingredient), which unintentionally generated a guns-versus-butter controversy as well as mass environmental protests. In Percy's accurate but caricatured derision of an effete lord in *Henry IV Part One*, Shakespeare reflects public anger towards government-commissioned saltpetremen, who forcibly confiscated fields fertilized with animal and human manure from which saltpetre was produced. Unsurprisingly, the lord's complaints are dismissed by 'gunpowder Percy'. The saltpetre industry nonetheless severely disrupted farmers' efforts to feed growing numbers of people during years of chronic dearth. Although rural protests had little long-term effect on England's advancing militarization and global arms trade, they were another indication of ecologically attuned awareness and resistance to industrial warfare's dislocations.

In Chapter 3 I discuss these controversies in the course of focusing on four Shakespearian aspects of gunpowder's remaking of modern world ecologies: cannon warfare and manufacturing; military technology's blurring of human and mechanical reflexes; gunpowder's contribution to the late sixteenth and early seventeenth-century deforestation crisis; and national protests against the ransacking of local farms by saltpetre producers. I then examine in closer detail Falstaff's corrupt recruiting practices in *Henry IV Part Two* as a dramatic emblem of these networked disturbances. Like the presence of cannons and firearms in the play, national conscription reflects Elizabethan rather than fifteenth-century military conditions. Shakespeare also has Falstaff impress the men destined to become 'food for [gun]powder' not in London but in rural Gloucestershire. This allows him to juxtapose gunpowder's dislocations with Justice Shallow's thriving georgic community, and thus to test the modern viability of the Virgilian pattern of alternating war and husbandry. The ambivalent results call into question the classical theory of bioregional redemption in the face of the emerging military-industrial complex. They also point to a new ecological reality of unavoidable risk, or 'reflexive modernization', conceptualized by sociologist Ulrich Beck, and troped by gunpowder more generally in Shakespeare. Beck demonstrates how modern systems of resource consumption and wealth-generation produce environmental boomerang effects. This is because growth-oriented economies are willing to tolerate degrees of pollution and overexploitation, while their societies consent to being exposed to 'containable' health hazards for the sake of employment and the availability of consumer goods. Beck provides a framework for the familiar trade-off between short-term economic gain and long-term environmental deterioration which goes to the heart of present-day smog alerts, oil spills, and radiation blooms. *Henry IV Part Two* anticipates Beck's insight that environmental dangers are fundamentally cultural problems of addiction to excessive growth and consumption.

I conclude Chapter 3 by tracing the breakdown of the Virgilian paradigm of swords into ploughshares to *Macbeth*, where Shakespeare imagines militarization reaching global levels of ecocidal risk and biospheric push-back. The harbingers of these thresholds are the Weird Sisters. They clamour on behalf of the earth's filthy air, incarnadined waters, and mutilated creatures. All are victims of Scotland's possibly unredeemed culture of war, of which the Macbeths are the latest avatars. Whether the victorious Malcolm will correct the hostility towards nature responsible for the country's environmental disasters depends on how we interpret his equivocal use of Birnam Wood. I shall consider a range of possible readings.

Preserving biodiversity in a multipolar world

Staging a retreat from the dangers of environmental catastrophe depends on recognizing nature as a more-than-human, long-term entity; that is, as biodiversity.[38] Its pre-modern model was the 'book of nature', which Friar Lawrence 'reads' while gathering medicinal herbs and minerals:

> The earth that's nature's mother is her tomb;
> What is her burying grave, that is her womb…
> O mickle is the powerful grace that lies
> In plants, herbs, stones, and their true qualities;
> For naught so vile that on the earth doth live,
> But to the earth some special good doth give….
>
> (*Romeo and Juliet* 2.2.9–10, 15–18)

Like Duke Senior in Arden, Friar Lawrence seeks to find spiritual revelations in the myriad uses of nature's bounty.[39] And like modern scientists, he sees biodiversity not just as a collection of individual elements and life forms, but as an integrated process working on seen and unseen levels. As an early modern physician, moreover, he perceives, like his secular counterpart Cerimon in *Pericles*, that it is the synergies of plants and minerals as well as their discrete chemical properties that produce the medical and other benefits of traditional (or modern herbal) medicine (*Pericles*, 12.28–35).

While the traditional book of nature continued to be valued during the early modern period, it also began to be recognized as an incomplete record of the earth's biodiversity. The arrival of non-native species from the New World exposed gaps in the book's classical European foundations (e.g. glow-worms [i.e. fireflies] and potatoes from America [*A Midsummer Night's Dream*, 3.1.161, *The Merry Wives of Windsor*, 5.5.19], nutmegs from the Moluccas [*Henry V*, 3.7.18], and new species from further abroad in the known world, such as monkeys and Barbary cock-pigeons from North Africa [*The Merchant of Venice*, 3.1.111–16; *As You Like It*, 4.1.137, 139]).[40] Unheard-of species produced competing empirical and imaginative versions of a newly global book of nature. And they re-stimulated curiosity about still-unanswered questions of natural history: 'FOOL: Canst tell how an oyster makes his shell? / LEAR: No. / FOOL: Nor I neither' (*King Lear*, 5.24–26).

The unifying ethos of Friar Lawrence's book also found it increasingly difficult to account for cosmopolitan levels of cross-breeding and hybridization enabled by overseas travel and trade. These transactions confused national and 'natural' taxonomies and created anxieties about native species being denatured. In his survey of the state of Elizabethan gardens and orchards, William Harrison simultaneously expressed pride and distress at the hundreds of 'strange' (foreign) plants, fruits, nuts, and flowers that had recently become naturalized in England.[41] Harrison's mixed feelings point to wider ideological tensions in the proprietary relationship between biodiversity and cultivation. Friar Lawrence exemplifies the Humanist ideal of working within the renewing energies of providential creation. Its practical spirituality seeks to arrest postlapsarian decay, whose instabilities many people in Shakespeare's day believed were getting worse on the evidence of the period's religious upheavals and demographic changes:

> POET   ... How goes the world?
> PAINTER   It wears, sir, as it grows.
> (*Timon of Athens*, 1.2–3)

Yet Humanist goals of reforming nature and trying to recapture golden or Edenic worlds were blurring into more aggressive ambitions of perfecting it through empirical innovation. Francis Bacon argued that direct observation and experiment would uncover nature's secrets and fulfil providentially ordained dominion over nature ('Of Riches'). In a more utilitarian spirit, manuals on gardening and viticulture advocated unfettered trial and error while updating classical and medieval knowledge with regional facts about English climates, soils, and plants. Like the overlapping advice of husbandry manuals, print culture disseminated these improving techniques to a new generation of yeoman and gentry farmers, such as Shakespeare's Iden, Shallow, and Oliver.

Besides husbandry metaphors, Shakespeare's leading trope for debates over instrumental versus conservationist attitudes to biodiversity was grafting. The range and precision of his allusions hint at personal experience, possibly augmented by books such as Leonard Mascall's popular and finely illustrated *A booke of the arte and manner how to plant and graffe all sorts of trees how to sette stones and sow pepins, to make wild trees to graffe on, as also remedies & medicines* (1572). Shakespeare's most famous discussion of grafting is Polixenes and Perdita's debate about hybridization in *The Winter's Tale*. Unconscious of the ironies of his position, the disguised Polixenes argues on the side of improvers such as Mascall and Bacon by asserting that when 'we marry / A gentler scion to the wildest stock', the effect is to 'make conceive a bark of baser kind / By bud of nobler race' (4.4.92–95). In *Variation Under Domestication* (1868), the book that followed *On the Origin of Species* (1859), Charles Darwin demonstrated the biological continuities between artificial and natural selection by documenting historical practices of cross-breeding domestic plants and animals with wild or non-native species to revitalize them.[42] This prevented domestic varieties from being gradually weakened by overlong preservation of visible varietal, or phenotypical, traits deemed to be attractive or useful. The underlying problem is the gradual loss of genetic variability and vigour, which is restored by cross-breeding. Since Darwin was not aware of the genetic processes underlying natural selection discovered by his near-contemporary Georg Mendel, he based his arguments about natural selection on zoological and botanical observation and metaphorical analogies. Shakespeare used similar reasoning in his dramatic dialogues about natural history, and so was able in certain ways to anticipate Darwin without a theory of evolution. Polixenes looks forward to Darwin by implying that techniques of artificial selection mimic natural processes of adaptation in speeded-up ways; *viz.* grafting 'is an art / Which does mend nature—change it rather— but / The art itself is nature'. Perdita concedes this is true: 'So it is' (4.4.95–97).

But like many contemporaries then and now, Perdita does not feel convinced by such arguments.[43] She believes hybridization transgresses the spirit of naturally evolving biodiversity, or 'great creating nature'. She too reasons analogously by invoking the morally contentious art of cosmetics:

> I'll not put / The dibble in the earth to set one slip of [gillyvors],
> No more than, were I painted [i.e. wearing make-up] I would wish
> This youth [Florizel, disguised as Doricles] should say 'twere
>   well, and only therefore
> Desire to breed by me. (4.4.99–103).

Perdita thinks the 'piedness' or streaked colours of gillyvors (dianthus) are the product of artificial cultivation, even though some contemporaries, such as widely read herbalist and physician John Gerard,

understood that they were natural hybrids.[44] Echoing today's arguments about genetically modified plants, fish, and animals, Perdita
believes hybridization arrogantly disrupts nature by rushing the
slower-paced change of natural systems. She questions whether
humans can safely manipulate species within the manifold interdependencies of biodiversity, whose barriers to complete understanding modern scientists acknowledge.[45] The errors of Leontes and
Polixenes represent an arrogant refusal to respect such limits, while
the oracle's corrections support Perdita in suggesting that human
knowledge will never reach the god-like level of 'great creating nature'.
The earth is a matrix of 'germens', or cellular seeds, with an infinite
capacity for random variation, but not all that potential is, or should
be, realized at once (*King Lear*, 9.8, *The Winter's Tale* 4.4.475–76).

On the other hand, Perdita's decision to keep her garden free of
artificially bred gillyvors does not mean that she avoids disturbing
nature. By cultivating flowers that only appear to be non-hybrids,
Perdita is unwittingly selecting to preserve varietal traits that would
otherwise evolve, and will evolve, though not in ways she can predict.
Her cultivation unavoidably intervenes in nature and will in the long-
term be overtaken by its adaptations and extinctions. In this regard, it
may be telling that Perdita's mother, Hermione, implicitly approves of
selective breeding in animal husbandry when she playfully invites
Leontes to 'cram's with praise, and make's / As fat as tame things'
(1.2.90–91).

Perdita's and Friar Lawrence's real epistemological adversary is the
Queen in *Cymbeline*. She is both the proverbial wicked stepmother and
a vicious example of the age's new 'empiric', ruthlessly exploiting
animals, vegetables, and minerals as tools of personal dominance.
Her animal-testing of poisons violates biodiversity's core ethic: the
intrinsic value of all life forms. In Chapter 4 I discuss *Cymbeline* as a
romance of nested planetary ecologies in which potential extinctions
posed by nascent utilitarian thinking like the Queen's are averted by
the forces of ecological altruism. The Queen's malevolent empiricism
corresponds with Cymbeline's shortsighted devaluing of social and
natural diversity. His court has abandoned its former georgic policy
of regenerating Britain after its wars with Rome. It has also turned its
back on relations with the Continent, whose more cosmopolitan
values define regional boundaries as portals of cultural exchange.

(For the negative ecologies of Roman imperialism, see the next section and Chapter 5). Cymbeline's embrace of parochial monoculture has made Britain vulnerable to internal and external shocks. But like the public resistance precipitated by early modern deforestation and salt-petre controversies, the court's policies generate conservationist responses from Britain's non-elite citizens in London and Wales. Joined by the banished outlaw Posthumus, Belarius, Guiderius, and Arviragus defend Britain from the tribute-denied Romans by applying their local experience of resilience-enhancing bioregionalism. It regen-erates Britain's cultural and environmental heritage, personally embodied by the adaptive survivor, Innogen. She is reclaimed by Lucius and finally Posthumus, who re-integrate her and Britain into worldwide environmental citizenship.

Evolutionary transience and transcendence

The middle acts of *Cymbeline* depict Belarius, Arviragus, and Guide-rius surviving in the Welsh mountains by reciprocating the instinctive (that is, evolutionary) behaviours of its wild animals. Their environ-mental mutualism resembles that of Caliban and his island's fauna before he is enslaved by Prospero (*The Tempest*). Both scenarios present what Giorgio Agamben calls a 'zone of indeterminacy' between human and animal life. 'Civilized' invaders such as Cloten and Prospero project essential differences onto the natives' animal-human condition to assert their superiority over nature.[46] Although they fail, Prospero comes to recognize that these distinctions are as factitious as his magic. The savage profile he stamps on Caliban ultimately serves to reveal the lack of any fundamental separation between them ('this thing of darkness I / Acknowledge mine', 5.1.275–76). The fluid boundaries between interdependent life forms in *Cymbeline* and *The Tempest* touch on wider early modern debates about what really divides humans from other species.

The self-conferred supremacy of European humans was called into question partly by the irrational violence and cruelty of early modern wars, and partly by the Humanist rediscovery of materialist philo-sophers such as Lucretius and Plutarch, who were sceptical of any absolute distinction between humans and animals.[47] From a Western perspective, their arguments were part of a minority pre-Aristotelian

and last chapter I examine such transformations by focusing on Hamlet's attention to worms and their foodwebs. They lead him to recognize tensions in conventional ideas of worldly transience, such as when human souls are separated from mortal bodies, and life forms pass into non-transcendent plenitude. I also compare Hamlet's observations with the worms of Nilus in *Antony and Cleopatra*. As the Queen's passport to an afterlife in Egypt's fertile ecosystems, they represent a value-system beyond cultural binaries and paradoxes, which in her suicide Cleopatra pursues in addition to two redemptive goals: political revenge against Caesar's plans to wipe out her family dynasty, and reunion in the afterlife with her poetically transfigured lover. She stages this triple desire in an Isis-like ritual for Caesar and Western posterity. Her journeys into metaphysical and metabiotic consummation clarify Hamlet's less clearly resolved options of heroic revenge violence, which in theory will restore the imbalances in providential creation caused by his father's murder, and of worm-oriented redemption through metabiosis.

Localism, Deforestation, and Environmental Activism in The Merry Wives of Windsor

Poisoned towns and rivers, species extinctions, and now climate change have confirmed many times over how modern dreams of limitless growth combined with relentless technological exploitation have compromised planetary life at every level. In response to such degradation, the integrity of local place has been a major orientation for environmental ethics and criticism.[1] The origins of localism are conventionally traced to late-eighteenth- and nineteenth-century critiques of urban industrialization, and Romanticism's corresponding veneration for rural authenticity and wilderness spaces. Mid-twentieth-century environmentalism revived this 'ethic of proximity' in denouncing the release of pollutants and carcinogens into local soils, waters, and atmospheres by civil offshoots of military manufacturing and industrial agriculture.[2] Those releases did not stay local, but soon penetrated regional water systems and wind patterns to become worldwide problems. Such networks of devastation continue to grow, especially in developing countries eager to mimic the worst aspects of Western consumer culture.

In response to these developments, ecotheorists have partially revised locally focused models of environmental protection. Planetary threats such as rising global temperatures, melting polar ice sheets, and more intense storms have made it imperative to update the famous

Sierra Club slogan and to act globally as well as locally. Localism has also been reshaped by conservation biology's new recognition that geophysical disturbances and organic change are structural features of all healthy ecosystems. Within these more complicated ecological paradigms, the cultivation of relatively balanced and genuinely sustainable local relationships nonetheless remains an important conservationist worldview. In early modern England it was the leading life experience out of which responses to new environmental dangers were conceived.

In this chapter I shall discuss Shakespeare's representations of one of the three most significant of these threats—deforestation—in *The Merry Wives of Windsor*. (The other two, exploitative land-uses and gunpowder militarization, will be the subjects of Chapters 2 and 3 respectively). Early modern English writers and governments treated deforestation as a national problem, even though its impacts were concentrated mainly in the Midlands and the south-east. Ordinary people extrapolated wider impacts from their personal interactions with local forest landscapes and consumption of woodland products. This is how Shakespeare imagines the contemporary degradation of English forests in *Merry Wives*, his most locally detailed play. Set in a small town next to a royal castle and surrounding fields and forest in eastern Berkshire, its fine-grained mosaic of natural and human ecosystems (woods, parks, chases, fields, heath, mead, urban and rural buildings) is meshed by distinct corridors (the River Thames, a ditch, footpaths, roads, streets). These features direct much of the toing and froing of the play's domestic intrigue. Shakespeare's knowledge of Windsor place names and topography might have come from the new generation of maps and chorographies, or place-writings, that represented English town and county history. The spatial accuracy of Shakespeare's references, however, suggests that he also visited the area, possibly when the patron of his acting company, Lord Hunsdon, was installed as a knight of the Garter at Windsor in 1597. Mistress Quickly (playing the Queen of Fairies) alludes somewhat extraneously to its ceremonies in the final scene.[3] Whether Shakespeare's local knowledge of Windsor was direct, received, or a bit of both, *Merry Wives* represents the ecology of Windsor Forest and the town within its boundaries as more than local colour for the play's plot-driven comedy of romantic elopement and social correction. I'll begin this chapter by relating the implications of Shakespeare's possibly direct knowledge of Windsor's urban and woodland landscapes to his life-experiences of local ecologies, and I'll return to this biographical perspective briefly at the beginning of the next chapter on the more personally invested *As You Like It*.

Like other ecologically minded writers such as William Wordsworth or Henry D. Thoreau, Shakespeare's environmental imagination was shaped by contrasting place-attachments. Life-long connections with Stratford-upon-Avon in Warwickshire oscillated with his experiences of urban and increasingly cosmopolitan London.[4] Shakespeare's rural and regional identities set him apart from other London playwrights such as Marlowe, Middleton, Jonson (in his drama), and Dekker, all of whom were city-born (Marlowe excepted) and metropolitan in outlook.[5] Their relative lack of imaginative engagement with what Jonathan Bate calls 'deep England' is apparent in their tendency to stage country people as the gulls of court sophisticates and city schemers. Seeking to thrive in the London theatrical marketplace, Shakespeare played this game too, in the urbanely condescending wit of Touchstone in *As You Like It* or Autolycus in *The Winter's Tale*. But when he was seeking a foothold in London's commercial theatres, Shakespeare was tactically self-depreciating. The Induction of *The Taming of The Shrew* makes fun of Shakespeare's Warwickshire provincialism in the figure of Christopher Sly, a drunken tinker who is tricked by a county lord into thinking he is the victim of a fifteen-year lunacy and has now woken up to his true identity as a nobleman. Sly proves hilariously incapable of shifting his language or behaviour beyond his native village horizons. His earthy parochialism illustrates the process by which 'thin' abstract space becomes associatively 'thick' place by accumulating emotionally charged physical and social attachments to local communities.[6] These links transform the neutral playing-space of the Elizabethan theatre and the generic profile of the folklore jest into a richly localized dialogue. Similar personal signatures of Shakespeare's rural identity recur throughout his plays. They identify part of the experiential basis for his perceptions of ecological relations in wider regional and national contexts.

Sly's incorrigible rootedness also defines Shakespeare's evolved experience of place through physical and imaginative migration to urban London. His journey mirrored that of thousands of country people seeking employment in Elizabethan towns and cities. Their feelings of deracination possibly intensified their former sense of local belonging. Yet like Shakespeare, in London they also encountered people and material objects associated with overseas place-identities. These connections provided tangible evidence of the period's imaginative shift from finite European *oikos*, or local dwelling, to worldwide space.[7] *The Taming of the Shrew* captures these overlapping place-relations by juxtaposing the Induction's Warwickshire allusions with the city-space of Padua in the main play. The latter is marked less by its built environment and more by its globally traded commodities, familiar to London consumers. Sly's localism reappears later in the guise of Petruchio's bustling country-house scenes. Their rural isolation enables his abuse of the urban Katherine. This environmental cause-and-effect suggests Shakespeare's dramatic interest in how shifts in, or detachments from, place could remould personal subjectivity, for better or worse.

Shakespeare presents another ecologically revealing contrast between rural and urban place-identities in *Henry IV Part Two*, where the comments of the quintessentially urban Falstaff position us to laugh at Justice Shallow and his bumptious Gloucestershire servants:

> It is a wonderful thing to see the semblable coherence of [Justice Shallow's] men's spirits and his.... Their spirits are so married in conjunction, with the participation of society, that they flock together in consent like so many wild geese. (5.1.56–63)

In these and other moments in his plays, Shakespeare's humour is distinctive because it layers comic provincialism over local relationships of irreducible integrity. To Falstaff, the herd instincts of Shallow and his farm hands absurdly blur the lines between humans and animals. Their kinship nonetheless represents an organic bond that eludes all the political elite—King Henry, his sons, and the rebels. To Falstaff's amazement, moreover, Shallow's community is wonderfully self-sufficient, easily able to ride out wartime scarcities characterized by diseased horses, rotten fodder, and starved turkeys in the London suburbs of *Henry IV Part One*. Shallow's bioregional ethos and his estate's sustainable agrarian practices challenge Falstaff's glib worldliness, doomed by attitudes of reckless consumption (among other things). I'll leave Shallow's Gloucestershire for now, but return there in Chapter 3.

After becoming rich from his share in the Chamberlain's Men, Shakespeare became somewhat Falstavian himself when he exploited the disparity between scarce local supplies and high prices of barley, used for malting, for personal gain. Whatever the ethics of his actions, they revealed a pragmatic education in the changing Elizabethan ecologies of rural production, consumption, and profit.[8] His grandfather Richard had been a yeoman tenant farmer in the village of Snitterfield four-and-a-half miles northeast of Stratford-upon-Avon. He would have ploughed the 'green cornfield[s]' and 'acres of the rye' celebrated in 'It was a Lover and his Lass' (*As You Like It*, 5.3.17, 21). Shakespeare knew that the soil beneath these fields consisted of a rich reddish clay called marl, much valued by farmers and soil theorists.[9] In *Much Ado About Nothing*, Beatrice sarcastically compares prototypical husbands to marl, precisely localizing her accompanying allusion to the 'dust' of the earth which forms men in Genesis (2.1.60–61).

The land Richard Shakespeare worked was owned by Shakespeare's maternal grandfather, Robert Arden of Wilmcote, about three miles northwest of Stratford. The Ardens were part of an old and extensive county family. Traditionally they had been woodland people, owners of parks in the nearby Forest of Arden at the level of noble branches of the family, and managerial keepers of parks and chases at the gentry level.[10] Parks (enclosed areas of woodland and pasture) and chases (unfenced areas of the same) were used for multiple purposes: raising deer for hunting, domestic animals for food, and livestock for market; growing timber (large mature trees, usually oak, used to make beams and long planks for the frames of ships and buildings, such as The Globe theatre); and cultivating underwood (smaller trees and shoots used for building materials, furniture, and fuel [e.g. for malting barley]).

After Shakespeare's father John left farming to become a glover in Stratford, he and his family forged new ties to the Warwickshire leather and tanning industry through John's friend Henry Field, whose son Richard went to school with Shakespeare and later became a bookseller who published his highly successful non-dramatic poems *Venus and Adonis* and *The Rape of Lucrece*.

Shakespeare therefore accumulated personal knowledge of virtually all of Warwickshire's environmentally related economies: woodmanship, hunting, and agricultural cultivation; artisanal trades such as leather-tanning linked to animal and woodland husbandry;[11] and craft industries.[12] Like many characters in his plays (Baptista, Capulet, Leonato, King John, Justice Shallow, Brutus, Oliver, Northumberland) he owned an orchard where he and his gardeners cross-bred fruit trees and plants to produce new, or preserve desired, varietal characteristics. These experiences interwove with the urban and globalizing economies of London, including those being developed by immigrant communities of French, Italian, and Dutch artisans (e.g. glassmakers, see below in this chapter). Together they constituted Shakespeare's extensive knowledge of dynamic interactions among environments, animals, and people.

Like many early modern men and women whose ties to or memories of the land were closer than those of present-day urban spectators and critics, Shakespeare's ecological knowledge was shaped by relationships with a physical world that was understood to be alive and phenomenologically determining rather than inert and mechanistic. Contacts with both rural and urban environments were far less distanced by modern technologies than they are today. Above all, what made Shakespeare stand out amongst his London colleagues was his readiness to use his knowledge of human and non-human place-identities to shape the poetic textures of his dialogue, and to integrate them into the social and political narratives of his plays. In both respects his work suggests that human survival or extinction—ways of life encoded by dramatic comedy and tragedy—are complexly linked to subjective attitudes and material relations with more-than-human environments and species. The proliferation of Shakespeare's work in global contemporary productions and adaptations means that his ecological insights carry the potential to address today's environmental questions around the world.

Deforestation: through a glass darkly

Writers in Shakespeare's time observed that mature trees were becoming scarcer in the English countryside and that woodland in general was being rapidly encroached and depleted.[13] The pressure on supplies of timber and wood was generated partly by the unprecedented demands of what modern historians call 'the Great Rebuilding' of early modern England.[14] Although its origins were partly demographic (*viz.* new

Figure 1.1. Hardwick Hall, Derbyshire. <http://en.wikipedia.org/wiki/Hardwick_Hall#mediaviewer/File:Hardwick_Hall_in_Doe_Lea_-_Derbyshire.jpg>.

housing for growing numbers of people), older buildings were also enlarged and refurnished thanks to price rises in agricultural products that benefited tenant farmers such as Shakespeare's grandfather, and landowners like Charles and William in *As You Like It* and Ford and Page in *The Merry Wives of Windsor*. Richer gentry showed off their wealth by building Renaissance show houses featuring one of early modernity's technological fashions: glazed windows. Perhaps the most famous example of this ecologically destabilizing trend is the flamboyant Hardwick Hall ('more glass than wall'), which Elizabeth Talbot (Bess of Hardwick), Countess of Shrewsbury, built over seven years by sacrificing her own woodlands (Figure 1.1).[15]

As a sign of both personal consumption and an expanding environmental footprint, windows are prominently visible in George Vertue's drawing of Shakespeare's New Place (whose undepicted but numerous chimneys I discussed in the introductory overview, pp. 14–16). Vertue shows New Place's windows occupying a major proportion of the building's 60-foot frontage. They indicate that Shakespeare's house would have been bright compared to older neighbouring buildings. In that respect it mirrored the general improvement of interior light in Elizabethan houses owing to the availability of bigger glass windows. Shakespeare imagines contemporary architecture looking this way when Bottom resourcefully but somewhat redundantly notices that a casement of the 'great chamber window' can be opened to let the moon shine on the 'tedious brief scene of young Pyramus / And his love Thisbe' (*A Midsummer Night's Dream*, 3.1.57–58). Pandarus tries to stir Cressida's competitive desire for Troilus by reporting that Helen met with him in the exposed intimacy of a 'compassed window' (i.e. projecting bow [semi-]circular window; *Troilus and Cressida*, 1.2.106). Bay windows, historically recessed from the wall line to capture more light, rectangular in shape, and grouped in panels of two or three, became a display-feature of grander Renaissance houses like Hardwick Hall. Feste's taunt to the imprisoned Malvolio about his dark room's imaginary 'bay windows' adds a barb at his social pretensions to the jest's cruelty (*Twelfth Night*, 4.2.37–38).

The Elizabethan glassmaking industry fed desires for light-enhancing windows as well as newly fashionable drinking glasses, and artisans were encouraged by Tudor governments to achieve national self-sufficiency and build up an export economy. Victorian keeper William Menzies documented early evidence of these commercializing trends in Windsor Forest.[16] In 1568 William Cecil, Lord Burghley, Elizabeth's most powerful minister, licensed two French glassmakers to cut wood for their furnaces in Windsor Great Park. The wood was processed by in-forest saw pits like the one Shakespeare represents in *The Merry Wives of Windsor* and juxtaposes spatially against the large mature tree, Herne's Oak (4.4.51, 5.4.2).[17] The quantities of wood required by glassmakers were huge. When a fire destroyed Jacob Verzelini's crystal glassworks in London in 1575, Holinshed reported that

The fourth of September . . . a certain glasshouse which sometime had been in the crossed friars hall neere to the Tower of London burst out in a terrible fire. . . . [T]he same house a small time before had consumed great quantitie of wood by making of fine drinking glasses; now itself having within it neere fortie thousand billets of wood was all consumed to the stone walls. . . .[18]

Eleanor S. Godfrey puts the wood consumed by Verzelini's fire into wider perspective by calculating that in 1575 he was using 500,000 billets a year at a price of 12s per thousand billets.[19] His fuel costs were therefore about £300 annually. By 1608 the price had risen to 18s 8d per thousand billets and his fuel costs were £466. During this time Verzelini was purchasing woodland to mitigate the price rises that had a proportionate effect on the cost of glass, which became a status symbol. Falstaff urges Mistress Quickly to pawn her silver goblets and replace them with glasses ('the only drinking' [*Henry IV Part Two*, 2.1.140]) to pay his debts. Falstaff does not specify the kind of glass. But since he is looking to maximize his credit, he probably does not have in mind crystal but the other kind of glass produced at the time, forest or 'green' glass. It was also considered elegant for drinking vessels—and therefore flattering to Mistress Quickly's susceptibility to modern consumption trends—but was cheaper than crystal as a substitute for plate or pewter.

Unlike crystal glassmaking, which was monopolized and effectively restricted to operating near London, green glassmakers such as the ones operating in Windsor Forest were unregulated. They solved their fuel-supply problems by constantly shifting woodlands and saw pits when the local wood had been exhausted, since the cost of moving glasshouses was minimal, and county landlords or the Crown were willing to grant them short-term contracts for cutting.[20] By the 1590s, there were at least fourteen to fifteen forest glasshouses operating in England. Each produced 3000–4000 cases of window glass annually, which brought imports from the Continent to an end. The increased demand for wood fuel was met partly by landlords deforesting their properties to cash in on rising prices to feed their growing spending and consumption habits. Henry Percy, ninth earl of Northumberland, confessed to his son that he put the 'axe . . . to the trees' to supply the glasshouse on his Petworth estates and generate income to pay for his 'hawks, hounds, horses, dice, cards, apparel and mistresses.' (He later did ecological penance by sowing acorns to replant his woodland.)[21]

The profligacy of landowners like Percy and Elizabeth Talbot, abetted by well-off consumers such as the upwardly mobile Ford, Page, and Shakespeare households, contributed substantially to late-Elizabethan deforestation. Ultimately King James and his council solved the problem by ordering the glass industry to stop burning wood and to switch to coal in 1608.[22] Like chimneys, the presence in Shakespeare of green glass and related production sites such as the

Windsor Forest saw pit are signs of England's nascent consumer capitalism beginning to exceed its ecological carrying capacity. They also indicate that the boundaries between urban and national economies and local forest ecologies were becoming porous.

Before the government forced glassmakers to switch to coal, both Parliament and the Council recognized that local supplies were being used up faster than traditional woodland practices of coppicing could renew the resource. (Coppicing consists of selectively cutting down mature hardwood trees in order to rejuvenate shoots from the stump for use as fuel, furniture, and tools.[23]) The fuel crisis in London and the south-east prompted parliamentary bills in 1589–90 and 1593 proposing to monopolize the industry and export its carrying-capacity problems to Ireland. The bills were defeated, however, by landowning MPs unwilling to outsource glassmaking when profits were still to be made from exploiting their remaining woodlands.

Brave new worlds and sustainability

The idea of exporting England's wood-shortage problem was too tempting to disappear, however, and was revived to justify New World colonization by the Virginia Company. *The Tempest* alludes to this momentous ecological shift by staging displays of wood to encode New World abundance (e.g. 1.2.312 14, 3.1). Topically they represent the material contribution of the 'still vex'd Bermudas' to Sir John Gates's rebuilding of his supply ships after they were wrecked off its coast on their way to Virginia in 1609. Bermudan wood allowed Gates to continue sailing to Jamestown and then return 'miraculously' to England.

The Tempest also stages contemporary speculations about New World solutions to English carrying-capacity problems. At the time the play was first performed, Rooke Church had been surveying James I's forests and reporting the 'exceeding abuses' to which they and private woodland throughout the country had been subjected, as well as their 'lamentable scarcity' of coppices and wood.[24] Prospero's tasking of Ferdinand with piling logs (probably represented by sawn billets on the Jacobean stage) shows off a future imperial commodity which had become more realistically coveted than the fabled El Dorado that Walter Raleigh had failed to discover in Guiana. During Raleigh's

attempt to colonize Virginia in the 1580s, Thomas Hariot had depre-
cated finding gold in his widely read *A brief and true report of Virginia*
(1588) in favour of exploiting far more dazzling New World commodities. America's true riches, Hariot argued, were its plentiful
resources and temperate climate which could supply the needs of a
burgeoning English population.

The *Tempest* stages a dialogue with Hariot's optimistic views.
Caliban's intimate knowledge of his island's ecosystems echoes
Hariot's admiring descriptions of Virginian environments and native
Algonkians' social and spiritual symbiosis with them. These associations also reminded potential Virginia or East India Company invest-
ors of the native skills and hospitality on which overconfident and
underequipped Europeans depended for survival, but which Prospero
tries to turn into disciplinary tools ('thy food shall be / The fresh-brook
mussels, withered roots, and husks' [1.2.462–63]).

On the other hand *The Tempest* suggests that exporting the problem
of English wood shortages will create unpredictable ecological and
social consequences, the effects of which were being reported in
contemporary news pamphlets. Caliban's contested weirs (2.2.175)
seem to allude to the betrayal of sustainable Algonkian fishing techniques and, from a present-day perspective, the collapse of North
Atlantic cod and other marine stocks caused by industrial overfishing
(represented symbolically in Rupert Goold's 2006 Royal Shakespeare
Company production of *The Tempest* by Ariel rising as a harpy out
of the belly of a dead whale; see Epilogue, pp. 169–70). *The Tempest*
may also be looking back comically on the Virginia Company's rueful
decision to establish a glasshouse in Jamestown. It was the first factory
industry in England's American colonies, and one of the earliest
cautionary environmental tales from the New World. The Company
hired eight Polish and German glassmakers to be sent along with
Captain Newport's Second Supply mission in autumn 1608. Their
glasshouse, measuring 37 by 50 feet, produced green glass for more
than a year. Production was ended by the Europeans' lack of prepared-
ness during the 'Starving Time' winter of 1609–10. It was also
allegedly disrupted by violent mutinies among the Germans who
expressed their hostility towards their co-workers and English masters
by dressing and behaving like 'salvages' while using the glasshouse as
their base camp. Nonetheless, enough glass was produced to send

samples, including bottles, back to London for display.[25] Their well-publicized arrival possibly created associations in the minds of London spectators with the prominent bottle of sack that Stephano brandishes and Caliban drinks from, inciting his 'monstrous' revolt against Prospero (2.2).[26] Caliban expresses his defiance by refusing to fetch any more wood for Prospero's 'firing', a word that recalls the furnaces used to make New World glass (2.2.176–77; *OED* Firing n. 7).

English failures to relocate the glassmaking industry to Ireland or America, or to relieve the home-grown fuel shortage, coincided with technical advances in furnace construction that allowed the Council to compel the substitution of coal for wood. During the public and parliamentary debates which accompanied this contested decision, preservation of the country's woodland was the chief reason given in favour of the change. Chief Justice of the Common Pleas Sir Edward Coke specifically argued that 'the expending of wood' by glassmakers was 'injurious' to the health of both people and woodland. Shakespeare's patron King James backed the Council's prohibition of 1608 with a royal proclamation two years later. Even though his rationale contradicted Falstaff's self-interested advice to Mistress Quickly, it mirrored the opinion of some people that drinking glasses were an unnecessary luxury.[27] Within a few years the shift to non-renewable fossil-fuel by the glassmaking industry was complete, and iron-making followed later in the century.

Environmental disputes related to colonial and domestic resource exploitation anticipate present-day debates over globalization and sustainability in several respects. In 1987 the influential Brundtland Commission defined 'sustainable development' as that 'which meets the needs of the current generations without compromising the ability of future generations to meet their own needs.'[28] In this spirit, the Jacobean suppression of wood fuel for glassmaking was a significant acknowledgement that English woodland had natural limits as a shared public resource. It prioritized long-term integrity by looking to the needs of future generations of both human and non-human life. It seems to have been the only area in which James acted on the advice of contemporary advisors to protect crown forests as woodland and animal sanctuaries.

In hindsight we know that the move to coal shifted the essential problem of excessive consumption to exploitation of higher polluting fuel on regional and global levels. Contemporaries became immediately aware of the negative effects of coal-derived air pollution and acid rain (although they did not name them that). In *A new, cheape and delicate Fire of Cole-balles* (1603), for instance, Hugh Plat argued that the 'smootie substance & subtile *atomies*' (fine residue) of coal smoke destroyed city and suburban gardens, soiled indoor furniture, wall hangings, and clothes, and created health risks for local residents (B4r-v) (Figure 1.2). He proposed substituting artificially made coal-balls (i.e. a mixture of pulverized coal and organic matter) to reduce the 'offensive . . . smel' and 'soile' (i.e. ash) of 'ordinary seacole fires' like the one Mistress Quickly burns in *Merry Wives*. Elsewhere contemporaries recognized the environmental dangers of burning coal but accepted them as the cost of commercial expansion (or, like Plat, saw profitable opportunities to 'green' such hazards). From our perspective, the turn to fossil-fuel use, instead of moderating production and consumption, ramped up ambitions for economic and social progress in a finite world. Pioneering conservation biologist Aldo Leopold conceptualized these contradictory tendencies as a capitalist 'growth ethic' and an ecocentric 'land ethic', with the latter reprioritizing the more-than-human value of local ecosystems. As I shall discuss further in Chapter 2, Leopold proposed active stewardship of bioregions as an alternative model of ecological dwelling in which humans occupy just one of many interdependent niches.[29]

Although the Brundtland Formula may have aspired to the spirit of Leopoldian biocentrism, international cooperation has not followed from it. Even worse, 'sustainability' has been co-opted by corporate and technocratic 'green' agendas which tend to hide rather than quantify real environmental costs. In reality, ecological solutions depend on humans reimagining themselves as sharers in the planet's well-being with non-human stakeholders. Stacey Alaimo notes that achieving this shift in thinking requires social and cultural re-modelling as well as scientific knowledge.[30] Leopold recognized this when he argued that environmentally progressive policies would be adopted only by changing subjective convictions towards the natural world.[31] This is where environmentally oriented criticism and performances of plays like *The Merry Wives of Windsor* have a role to play. They invite audiences 'to stop dreaming green dreams'—meaning, hanging on to Romantic notions of separating nature from abusive culture—and to envisage

A new, cheape and

delicate Fire of Cole-balles, wherein
Seacole is by the mixture of other com-
bustible bodies, both sweetened
and multiplied.

Also a speedie way for the winning of any Breach:
with some other new and seruiceable In-
uentions answerable to
the time.

Regium est cum feceris bene, audire male.
S. Ha.

Imprinted at London by P E T E R S H O R T dwelling
at the signe of the Starre on Bredstreet-hill.
1 6 0 3.

Figure 1.2. Hugh Plat, *A new, cheape and delicate Fire of Cole-balles* (1603), title
page illustration. STC 1328: 11. Reproduced by Permission of the Henry
E. Huntington Library and Art Gallery.

new ways of living in a post-sustainable world, including rethinking the Western and now globalized fantasy of relentless economic growth.[32]

Environmental history: first steps in conservation and reforestation

The political origins of the environmental face-off between Shakespeare's Windsor Forest saw pits and Herne's Oak go back to the reign of Henry VIII. His government began to worry about the threat to supplies of timber for the expanding English navy caused by private encroachments on crown woodland and the rapid growth of the iron industry (initiated, in fact, by Henry's government. I'll discuss the iron industry's contribution to deforestation in Chapter 3).[33] In 1526 Parliament introduced regulations to preserve timber in royal forests by requiring at least twelve 'standils or storers' (i.e. mature standard trees) to remain for every acre of wood that was cut. After this and further measures failed, Parliament tried a more targeted policy in 1581 by forbidding trees more than 'One Foot Square at the Stubbe' (or base) from being cut in any area within fourteen miles of the sea or navigable rivers. And in 1585 it cancelled the previous exemption granted to cutting wood or timber in the Weald, the ancient forest located in Kent, Surrey, and East Sussex, where the English glassmaking and iron industries were concentrated.[34] These were preludes to the prohibition on glassmakers in 1608.

Heightened anxiety about the state of her forests prompted Elizabeth to take the first documented steps towards actively regenerating crown woodland. In 1580 she ordered a thirteen-acre plantation of acorns (and a little beech mast) in Cranbourne Walk, and an eighteen-acre plantation in Ice House Field, both in Windsor Great Park. By 1625 the first of these plantations was reported to have grown into 'a wood of some thousands of tall young oaks bearing acorns, and giving shelter to cattle'. By 1862 William Menzies reported that the surviving trees had reached a circumference of thirteen feet at the five-foot level.[35]

Elizabeth's replanting of Windsor Forest was an enlightened yet token gesture in the context of the Crown's long-standing degradation of royal forests. Oliver Rackham has shown that medieval monarchs exploited forests for timber, wood, and game, and to forge patronage networks. There was no concern for long-term integrity. By the early modern period, the importance of venison as social capital had declined, even though deer continued to have important status value and gratified Elizabeth's and James's personal love of hunting. In *The Merry Wives of Windsor*, Justice Shallow mimics the traditional use of royal forests as instruments for patronage by 'gifting' Page with venison from his private chase or park, possibly created from licensed or disafforested crown woodland, exempted from the conservationist protections of forest laws (1.1.72–76). Shallow's gift simultaneously binds and distances Page in a residual feudal relationship that points to conflicting and ultimately unresolved attitudes of woodland nostalgia and modern consumption in the play.

Crown forests, in any event, had long since become mainly important for profit. Rackham confirms the empirical assessment of early modern observers such as Standish and Church that woodland was being degraded because cash-strapped Tudor monarchs increasingly leased out portions to private and industrial users to generate income.[36] Shakespeare captures the contemporary range of such compromises by opening the play with Justice Shallow raging against Falstaff's apparently wanton raid on his hunting lodge. The implication is that Shallow's private lodge and its surrounding chase or park have been profitably leased from the Crown in Windsor or some other royal forest (e.g. Dean or Cirencester in Gloucestershire). This also explains why Shallow vows to charge Falstaff with a riot in the court of Star Chamber, rather than having him prosecuted under forest laws (of which more below; *Merry Wives*, 1.1.1–110). Framing the forest intrigue of *Merry Wives* at the other end of the play, Shakespeare has Anne and William Page, Evans, and his fairy-charges hide in a saw pit (probably represented by the trapdoor and space beneath the stage) near Herne's Oak while waiting to take their revenge on the predatory Falstaff.[37] The forest saw pit suggests a symbolic punishment for his woodland violence against Shallow. But paradoxically, it also extends and environmentalizes his outlaw behaviour by introducing notes of entrepreneurial exploitation into the play's folkloric ritual and romantic conclusion. Moreover, its spatial proximity to a mature named tree threatens the conservation principles that ostensibly justified the royal privileges of forests and parks such as Windsor. As Elizabethan lawyer and royal forester John Manwood explained in *A Brefe Collection of the*

Lawes of the Forest (1592),[38] crown forests were intended to create sanctuaries for trees, plants, and animals, collectively referred to as 'vert [i.e. woodland] and venison'. This included protection from local poaching and encroachment when unprotected common land became overexploited in an era of population growth and resource scarcity.[39]

Elizabethans such as Manwood would have recognized the saw pit in *Merry Wives* as a telling sign of confused attitudes towards royal forests. Manwood was another contemporary writer who lamented the 'decayed and spoiled' condition of late-sixteenth-century woodland. In law, as he explained, forest ecosystems and non-human inhabitants were protected by an ancient but increasingly abused system of prerogative laws and courts. These placed forest habitats beyond common-law jurisdiction and the expanding sphere of private property rights.[40] In practice, however, crown forests such as Windsor had long suffered from policies of disafforestation and enclosure by English governments, who increasingly treated them as regulated common land. This allowed them to generate revenue from privately licensed hunters (like Shallow, perhaps, or Ford when he goes 'a-birding' within the surrounding Windsor Forest as a feint to entrap Falstaff in his second assignation with Mistress Ford [3.5.42–53]), and from farm-rents, timber-cutting, underwood production, and industrial manufacturing such as glass- and iron-making.[41] From the late middle ages English monarchs and their governments had in practice been converting forests into a multi-commodified resource. The saw pit in *Merry Wives* can thus be seen as a dark reflection of the Crown's commercialized violence against its own woodland resources and conservationist principles.

The contradictory attitudes to forests in *Merry Wives* are illuminated by the rebels' decision in *Henry IV Part Two* to confront the king's forces in the Forest of Galtres, where they are tricked by Prince John. If *Merry Wives* was written just before *Henry IV Part Two*, as many scholars now believe, it would have provided dramatic background to the confrontation in Galtres. On the other hand, if *Merry Wives* was performed after, *Part Two* would have clarified the forest politics framing its comic action. Galtres was an ancient forest north-west of York. Like most royal domains, including Windsor, it was not continuous woodland but more like a park, a mixture of wooded and pasture areas. Under the Romans, all game in Galtres had been in common, but the Normans imposed forest laws to reserve the land and its animals exclusively for the Crown's use. Their successors gradually deforested Galtres and exterminated its indigenous deer, wolves, brown bears, and most of its badgers. By the mid-fourteenth century large timber trees were gone, and much of the area had been leased to private coppices and parks. James I finally sold off the entire forest.[42]

Forest laws, which operate in the legal realms of equity and the royal prerogative separate from the common law, implicitly govern the different expectations of the rebels and the king's forces in ways that reflect the political and ecological contradictions of Windsor Forest in *Merry Wives*. The Archbishop of York and his allies come to Galtres because forests were legal and environmental refuges. They are the woodland equivalent of the church sanctuaries which York and his dramatic colleagues, such as the bishops in *Richard III* and the Abbess in *The Comedy of Errors*, preside over. York thus regards Galtres as a safe haven where settlement of the rebels' grievances will get a fair hearing. But as Robert Pogue Harrison explains, forests have been immemorial sites for struggles between political authorities. Medieval monarchs aggregated the human conquest of woodland wilderness to sovereign power, expressed ritually in the exclusive privileges and human–animal imbalances of the royal hunt.[43] Within the king's forest, York and the rebels are therefore intruders subject to Henry's absolute prerogative violence. Although both sides gather in Galtres ostensibly to negotiate a peace, the rebels' outlaw status excuses Prince John from any obligation to treat them according to legal norms of accountable language or due criminal process ('I pawned thee none'). Like the conservationist intentions which ostensibly justified Galtres's or Windsor's special standing outside the common law, the rebels' complaints are put off by John's ambiguous, 'after-times' pledges ('these griefs shall be with speed redressed'). The rebels unsuspectingly lower their defences, mistakenly believing their grievances will be resolved under the peace agreement, and are mercilessly hunted down by John's still-mobilized soldiers. Coleville of the Dale's abject surrender in the next scene (4.2), after he wanders into Falstaff's mighty aura, parodies monarchical authority within Galtres.

One suspects John Manwood would have applauded Prince John's ruthlessness, however. According to *A Brefe Collection of the Lawes of the Forest*, the degradation and encroachment of crown woodland were caused largely by lax enforcement. Yet, seeking government patronage through his publication, Manwood avoided accusing the Crown directly of neglecting its forests. Instead he offered readers a proto-Romantic narrative of the spoil of the once-Edenic English woodland by greedy private interests. He also exhorted Elizabeth's ministers to defend the country's most important resource by restraining 'euery man from cutting downe of his owne woods within the freedom of the forest;' in other words, government officials should curtail owners of alienated crown woodland from unrestricted personal uses. But Manwood knew that such proposals touched on bitterly contested prerogative and property rights. Leasing, licensing, and disafforestation created legal grey zones between forest and common-law jurisdictions called 'purlieus'. Shakespeare's allusion to them in *As You Like It* recognizes their clashing conservationist and pragmatic outlooks (see Chapter 2, pp. 70–71).[44] Manwood spends considerable time trying to clarify these ambiguous but potentially profitable sites. Purlieus nonetheless remained vexed public spaces in the same way that today's commercial and tourist expansion in Banff National Park in Alberta or Bunya Mountains in Queensland arouses passionate opposition from deep ecologists, but not necessarily from reform environmentalists satisfied about their 'sustainability'.

Environmental activism in Windsor Forest

If Shakespeare visited Windsor Great Park, he might have spotted Elizabeth's dedicated young grove of 'maiden trees' representing a new practice of environmental stewardship. It was a modest gesture that more radical advocates of English woodland plantations—what we would call reforestation—argued should become domestic and colonial policy.[45] The opposing saw pit and Herne's Oak in *The Merry Wives of Windsor* suggest several possibilities of local ecological rebalancing in the context of early modern debates about the condition of England's forests and woodland.

London audiences familiar with shortages and high prices were aware that outsized timber, especially oak, was difficult to conserve or renew.[46] One means of saving prominent local trees was to name and attribute to them folk-histories to confer quasi-human protection and informal rights, as earlier residents of Windsor did for Herne's

Oak.[47] Since the eighteenth century, scholars have tried to discover a historical source for the legendary tree prior to *Merry Wives* and/or to identify it with a particular oak in Windsor Great Park. None of these efforts has been conclusive, and it is now accepted that the tree is fictional and Shakespeare invented the Herne myth.[48] By staging a large oak in a crown forest with a name and memorable story bestowed by environmentally minded residents, Shakespeare stages the ability of citizens to impose community limits on public resource-use, even at short-term economic cost to themselves. In these ways *Merry Wives* imagines a new model of environmental sustainability which lays the cultural groundwork for systematic programmes of reforestation being proposed at the time by writers such as Church and Standish.

Merry Wives also encourages a shift in spectators' environmental convictions by suggesting the physical power of Herne's Oak to shape human perceptions of the natural world. Its subjective agency over the play's characters is clarified by James J. Gibson's idea of environmental affordance. Gibson argues that both natural and built environments 'afford', or physically invite and enable, specific instincts, behaviours, and identities among human and non-human inhabitants who use or pass through them.[49] This happens because animals interact with their environments not as abstract 'empty' space filled with inert objects (the classical model of Cartesian and Newtonian physics), but as places thick with fluid mediums (e.g. air, water) and changing material surfaces (plains, rocks, trees, mountains). Their potential meaning continually alters with the perceivers' positioning, paths of movement, and interactions. Gibson calls these negotiations 'ecological optics'. Local places thus provide discoverable opportunities for environmentally oriented behaviours in humans and non-humans alike. In open-air theatre performances this includes physical affordances beyond human control, such as winter and summer light, wind and rain, overhead birds and aeroplanes.

The ecological optics represented in live stagings of Herne's Oak expands audiences' notions of a big local tree on which residents have projected a quaint folk-legend. Bodily memories of instinctive physical safety, shelter, and awe associated with Herne's, recalled by spectators' experiences of comparable trees, are partly what prompt Mistress Page to the idea of a midnight meeting there, notwithstanding her dismissal of its legend as a product of the 'superstitious idle-headed eld' (4.4.33). In its natural habitat, moreover, the oak's physical presence simultaneously affirms and subverts human assumptions. Both its Ovidian associations with the Acteon legend and its massive verticality heighten Falstaff's phallic desires (e.g. as Geraint Wyn Davies implied by subtle interactions with a huge stage oak in the 2010 Stratford Festival production of *Merry Wives*). Falstaff's sense of Herne's woodland dominance also flatters his (ultimately overconfident) sense of mastery over Mistress Page and Mistress Ford. Once that superiority is dashed, the tree's shadowy surfaces confuse his ability to sort out the human and nonhuman realities of his deception (4.4.25ff; 5.5.121–27). The tree's phenomenological shaping of Falstaff's refracted vision underscores the ecological lesson of Shakespeare's Windsor Forest that humans cannot control nature or determine its destinies absolutely. Environments and their affordances modify human will, disrupt ambitions, and propel impacts in unforeseen directions. Although Herne's Oak spatially anchors the Fairies' torment of Falstaff, this physical cooperation also creates a distraction which allows Fenton to escape with Anne Page, and Caius and Slender to 'elope' with their boy-fairies. Both Falstaff and the Wives also seem to be unconsciously influenced by the tree as a morally neutral object. Feeling dejected rather than guilty after his punishment by the citizens, Falstaff goes as far as to confess himself being made an ass but not to surrender to shame or repentance (5.5.160–62). Resonances of the oak's natural charisma also point to the core of biological otherness that Mistress Ford and Mistress Page seek to appropriate (with ambivalent results) in their Artemisian revenge against the attempts of Acteon-antlered Falstaff to violate their chastity.

The theatrical ability of Herne's Oak to shape 'ecological optics' holds true whether it was represented mimetically by a stage prop, or figuratively by the wooden columns and structures of an Elizabethan playhouse. Philip Henslowe's Rose Theatre owned several stage trees, so it seems likely that The Theatre, where the Chamberlain's Men originally staged *Merry Wives*, would have used them in performances. Alternatively, the exposed timber beams and wooden furnishings of London's public theatres provided metadramatic signs of the woodland origins of Herne's Oak. And they reminded spectators of the timber shortage affecting contemporary building construction and heating costs. As Vin Nardizzi observes, they allowed spectators to visualize the trees of Windsor Forest throughout the scene of Falstaff's midnight assignation and public 'felling'.[50] Such ecological associations are now again recaptured by modern reconstructions such as Shakespeare's Globe in London or by outdoor productions in local parks.

Shakespeare responds to his age's unprecedented deforestation crisis not as a proto-Romantic nature lover but as an early modern playwright aware of increasingly entangled social and environmental interests. Windsor's current citizens, it must be admitted, seem quite comfortable hiding in the Great Park's saw pit. Do they condone industrial activity in Windsor Forest? Are their priorities local employment, economic growth, and unchecked consumption over preserving woodland biodiversity or sustainability? Mistress Page's ridicule of the Herne folk-legend indicates she may be oblivious to either its afforded or biocentric values. In his analysis of conflicting new historical and environmentalist criticism of *Merry Wives*, Nardizzi argues that the citizens' use of the saw pit as a cover for punishing Falstaff for his sexual stalking represents an allegorical poaching of crown timber by private citizens. By violating forest laws, royal jurisdiction, and the social and economic privileges of gentry patrons such as Shallow and Slender, the citizens' actions constitute the liberal individualism of an emerging urban middle-class. Yet since the mandate of forests was conservation of 'vert and venison', to approve the citizens' felling of Falstaff as a surrogate for royal timber, as recent cultural materialist critics have suggested, is to condone a symbolic act of 'environmental destruction on crown land'.[51] To this ideological friction one can add the contradictions of the Pages' higher priced fuel for their wood-burning 'country fire'. While it may affirm their bourgeois triumph over decaying gentry like Slender, Caius, and Falstaff, it also flaunts their inflationary consumption of increasingly scarce woodland resources, and it flies in the face of the community action towards long-term sustainability implied by the naming-preservation of Herne's Oak. So does the Pages' ownership of a chimney big enough for Falstaff to consider 'creep[ing] up into' (4.2.43). Shakespeare's contextual associations with the threatened state of the nation's woodlands subject the play's final alluring image of merrymaking around a blazing woodfire to eco-critique.

The Merry Wives of Windsor mobilizes the power of dramatic fictions to stage contemporary forest controversies and clarify an emerging ecological ethics. It thereby encourages the kind of change in environmental imagination that Peggy L. Fiedler, Peter S. White, and Robert A. Leidy call for in their discussion of modern ecology's shift from a steady-state to a non-equilibrium model of nature, in which non-catastrophic disturbance and adaptation are the normal conditions of evolutionary life on earth. The scientific evidence for this paradigm shift is not in question. What Fiedler, White, and Leidy are calling for is an eloquent representative who will: (1) communicate this more complicated model to a public still largely wedded to Romantic ideals of unchanging nature; (2) prevent conservation efforts from being undermined by wariness of a messier environmental order. 'Where', they ask, 'are the ecologists who will speak eloquently to the lay public about natural disturbance and patch dynamics [i.e. interactive nested ecosystems]...as central features of conservation in theory and practice?' Their prescription for creating ecologically literate citizens in the midst of today's complex natural and manmade instability is cultural transformation though art: 'if the shift in ecological paradigms is to ring true, if it is to shake empires...then we must have, in addition to the clarity of thought of a trained scientist, the clairvoyance of a poet'. 'Clairvoyance' is rather mystical, and Shakespeare was not a scientist. But dramatic narratives like *The Merry Wives of Windsor*, which represent ecological problems and remedies in affective images and symbolic action, answer their call for an eco-poetic shake-up.[52]

The implications of Shakespeare's environmental activism in *Merry Wives* also return us to Aldo Leopold's remarks about creating an ecological consciousness that will motivate changes in personal behaviour and public policy. Leopold argued that ecological change does not happen simply through scientific education or improved conservation technologies, important as they may be. He cites the instance of Wisconsin farmers in the 1930s who knew the local topsoil was being eroded by over-intensive cultivation—a latter-day tragedy of the commons—and were empowered by the state to propose remedies. The farmers adopted only those changes which were profitable, and the region continued to be degraded. What was lacking, according to Leopold, was a shift in human feelings and attitudes towards nature that would coalesce into progressive environmental action: 'No important change in ethics was ever accomplished without an internal change in our intellectual emphasis, loyalties, affections, and convictions'.[53] *The Merry Wives* exemplifies the power of Shakespeare's locally attentive and afforded performance to encourage such imaginative and emotional breakthroughs in on- and off-stage spectators. Leopold invokes Hamlet's metaphor when he calls for 'a change in the mental eye' to create active ecological convictions.[54] Bioregionalism—an expanded vision of eco-localism—was the conceptual framework though which Leopold and his mid-twentieth-century successors hoped to shape modern environmental ethics and action. In Chapter 2 I shall examine Shakespeare experimenting with equivalent Elizabethan perspectives in *As You Like It* to call into question new exploitative practices of agricultural cultivation.

Land-Uses and Convertible Husbandry in As You Like It

Thinking like a forest

Having made jibes at Orlando's love-verses and drawn defensive reactions from Rosalind, Touchstone gently reproves her by appealing to nature as a third party: 'You have said; but whether wisely or no, let the forest judge' (3.2.117–18[1]). Thinking ecocritically, we might hear in his advice an anticipation of Aldo Leopold's landmark book, *A Sand County Almanac* (1949). Leopold redefined ecological ethics by reading his local Wisconsin landscape for signs of its biodiversity, whose value he asserted independent of its economic and social utility. He also encouraged readers to think about reciprocity and fairness in their dealings with the environments and resources they share with non-human life. Jaques's viewpoint in *As You Like It* is hardly as self-disinterested as that of a forest. Yet he captures the essence of Leopold's biocentric principles by reminding Oliver that the trees into which he has thoughtlessly, if romantically, carved his verses are entitled to their own physical integrity (3.2.251–52). Leopold's outlook inspired the later movement, bioregionalism, which looks to identification with a landscape's terrain, climate, and biota, or collective plant and animal life, as the basis for resistance to environmental damage caused by distant political authorities and transnational economies. In conceiving environments as 'life-territories' with natural rights that extend beyond those of human culture, Leopold invited people to imagine cooperative attachments to regional modes of subsistence and dwelling.[2]

Arden and surrounding Warwickshire were the life-territory where Shakespeare learned to think bioregionally. Whereas his knowledge of Windsor in *Merry Wives* came from passing acquaintance, his sensitivity to Arden's place-attachments was both deeply personal and critically detached, and he integrated both perspectives into *As You Like It.* Topographic and social contouring of Warwickshire's historically changing terrains dramatically heightens the visibility of Arden's early modern bio-relations. I'll begin exploring these by considering how Shakespeare gave his dramatic adaptation of Thomas Lodge's prose romance *Rosalynde* (1590) a distinctive environmental profile. In doing so, Shakespeare created an ecological meta-commentary on Lodge's popular forest romance.

Forest space in history and theory

Michael Drayton's *Poly-Olbion* (1612) suggests that early modern audiences would have been receptive to Shakespeare's bioregional transformation of Lodge. Drayton was Shakespeare's fellow countryman and poet, and the Warwickshire section of his national epic of local place-writing, or chorography, shares affinities with particular plot elements and topographic themes of *As You Like It*. Prominent among these is the physical deterioration of the 'old forrest of Arden':

> When Britaine first her fields with Villages had fild,
> Her people wexing still, and wanting where to build,
> They oft dislodg'd the Hart, and set their houses, where
> He in the Broome and Brakes had long time made his leyre.
> (Song 13, 25–28)[3]

Woodland biologist Oliver Rackham confirms Drayton's view that Arden had been under environmental pressure from population growth for a long time. In prehistoric Britain the Forest of Arden covered most of Warwickshire.[4] By Anglo-Saxon times the area below the central River Avon began to be deforested and turned into arable fields. Sometime after the twelfth-century Arden also lost its status as a royal forest. This meant that, unlike Windsor Forest, its ecosystems and animals were no longer protected by forest laws from encroachments or privatization. So, for hundreds of years before the sixteenth century, the woodlands of Arden had been gradually converted, especially south of the Avon, into tillage and grazing lands. By Shakespeare's and Drayton's time the appearance and ecology of this mixed landscape of forest and felden, or open cultivated fields, was clearly marked off from the remaining unofficial Forest of Arden—what Drayton's map in *Poly-Olbion* pointedly referred to as 'Now the Woodland of Warwick Shyre'—north of Stratford and the River Avon.[5] Drayton didn't need the information supplied by his main source, William Camden's *Britannia* (1589, trans. 1610) for this section of *Poly-Olbion*, but it confirmed what he and Shakespeare already knew:

> The Feldon lieth on this side Avon southward, a plain champagne country, and being rich in corn and green grass yieldeth a right goodly and pleasant prospect.... [T]he woodland which above the River Avon spreadeth itself northward is much larger in compass than the Feldon, and so is for the most part thick set with woods, yet not without pastures, cornfields, and sundry mines of iron.[6]

Both Camden and Drayton make it clear that Arden itself was not a uniform landscape of uninterrupted woods, but a mosaic of ecosystem patches ('But of our Forrests kind the quality to tell, / We equally partake of with Wood-land as with Plaine' [34–35]).

Shakespeare captures this geographic diversity precisely in *As You Like It*. He maps Warwickshire's forest and felden divide, and Arden's finer-grained asymmetry between woodland and open pasture, on to the historically real but fictionalized Ardenne Forest in *Rosalynde*.[7] A. Stuart Daley has shown that although *As You Like It* has traditionally been staged as a forest play in the modern sense, in fact it contains only four woodland scenes (2.1, 2.5, 2.7, and 4.2). Twelve others are set in pastureland, which reflected the landscape mosaic of early modern Warwickshire and Arden. The play begins on Oliver's farm in what appears to be the felden, the area 'inland' from the forest where Orlando says he was bred (2.7.96). This stands in contrast to Arden's mixture of wooded and grassy areas to which disguised Rosalind, Celia, and Touchstone flee from Duke Frederick's court. During these scenes they meet the shepherd Corin and buy the farm he tends. It remains their home for the rest of the play, and is where the Duke and his exiled court arrive from the woods in the play's finale. Shakespeare also keeps a cave from *Rosalynde* (a spiritual refuge) and non-English trees and animals that function as generic markers of literary pastoral (e.g. olive trees, lions). But *As You Like It*'s flora also signal an English Midlands place-identity. Brambles, hawthorns, oak trees, osiers (willows) and 'palm trees' (a Warwickshire dialect name for the goat-willow) reflect a botanical cross-section of contemporary Arden.[8] Landscape patches such as woods and fields are separated and connected by a river-corridor (a prominent focus in Drayton's *Poly-Olbion*). It begins in the woods as a 'swift brook' (2.1.42) along which Orlando and Jacques walk to arrive at Rosalind's sheep farm (3.2.245ff). By then it has slowed to a 'murmuring stream' banked by osiers (4.3.80) to which Shakespeare ascribes additional regional associations (see below in this chapter). When rewriting Lodge, Shakespeare imagined precisely what his English Arden would look and sound like.

Michael Drayton also noted Arden's topographic variations. He lamented the demographic pressures that had shrunk its ancient woodlands, and he decried their destruction by rapacious deforestation and enclosure:

> For, when the world found but the fitnesse of my soyle,
> The gripple wretch began immediatly to spoyle
> My tall and goodly woods, and did my grounds inclose:
> By which, in little time my [natural] hounds I came to lose.[9]

In other words, deforestation and land-exclusions by privatizing enclosure accelerated the destabilization of Arden as a shared human and natural environment. In the context of postcolonial anthropology, Gilles Deleuze and Félix Guattari used the term 'deterritorialization' to refer to conquered indigenous spaces being stripped of their natural resources and traditional modes of governance by imperial regimes.[10] Ursula K. Heise has adapted Deleuze and Guattari's concept to identify environmental ruptures by capitalist modes of technology and globalization.[11] Sixteenth-century enclosure, like deforestation, qualifies as an early example of deterritorialization because it was a locally diversified movement motivated in part by national land-market fluctuations and European trade competition. In objecting to the deterritorialization of Arden's woodland landscape, Drayton presents the landscape biology of Warwickshire as neither stable nor timeless, but changing under modern pressures of growth-driven exploitation.

Drayton's poem does not go into details about enclosure's degradation of Arden's woodland, but *As You Like It* does.[12] Through
allusions to its controversies embedded in the romantic comedy's
personal encounters, the play invites audiences to consider Arden's
contested land-identities and -relationships. In his influential study,
'The Land Speaks: Cartography, Chorography, and Subversion in
Renaissance England' (1986), Richard Helgerson traced England's
emergence as an imagined nation-state to the shift from chronicle
history's focus on dynastic monarchy to the new geography's emphasis
on surveyable landscapes by common-law-oriented landowners, as
well as by chorographic writers like Drayton.[13] Shakespeare gives his
dramatic place-writing a distinct ecological orientation by staging
Arden as a landscape mosaic reflecting diversely integrated levels of
human and more-than-human life. His biocentric, or more-than-
human-focused, framework positions Arden to speak as a 'geographical terrain and a terrain of consciousness ... about how to live in that
place'.[14]

From this original definition by American ecologists Peter Berg and
Raymond Dasmann, the bioregional movement's bottom-up and back-
to-the land stances of resistance towards environmental degradation
have become both more flexible and radically focused. Kirkpatrick
Sale's classic manifesto, *Dwellers in the Land: The Bioregional Vision*,
was written in the wake of the energy crisis of the 1970s. Its context
of new global threats is analogous to the regional crises of deforestation and enclosure emerging in Shakespeare's time. Sale voiced
growing alarm at irreversible resource depletions and habitat
destruction.[15] His remedy was to rediscover symbiotic attachments
to pre-industrial communities and pre-Cartesian attitudes towards
nature—both of which were traditional paradigms in early modern
England. 'Dwelling', for Sale, means re-identifying mutualistically
with a regional landscape and its life forms, and refusing to subor-
dinate them to mechanistic Western attitudes towards the natural
world.[16]

Sale's place-sensibility is dominantly agrarian and American, and
more recent post-equilibrium and post-human perspectives have
updated his Romantic tendencies towards 'hard-shell localism' on
the one hand and 'fancying [that] one is in tune with ... "Gaia"' on
the other.[17] Landscape ecologists, for example, now apply one of

bioregionalism's guiding principles of long-term structural conservation to vulnerable urban as well as rural terrains.[18] Mike Carr has
recast bioregionalism as a scalable concept of 'globalization from
below' which reflects critical practices of social ecology, deep ecology,
ecofeminism, and other 'dark green' movements.[19] Understanding *As
You Like It* and other Shakespeare plays as bioregional drama suggests
it can be analysed from multiple positions on this ecocritical spectrum.

Forest mosaics also raise theoretical questions about how the natural
world is to be valued apart from human interests. Concepts of space
developed by sociologists Michel de Certeau and Henri Lefebvre in
the 1980s and 90s asserted that identities of built and natural environments are constructed by social uses, such as when the mechanicals
in *A Midsummer Night's Dream* turn their green clearing into a stage
(3.1.2–5).[20] Ecocritics today would point out the tendency to exclude
non-human life and values in such projections, whether their impacts
are benign, as in the case of the mechanicals, or destructive, such as
when Henry V's wars reduce the fertile French countryside to sub-
human 'savagery' (*Henry V*, 5.2.37–62; *Henry VI Part One*, 3.3.44–55).
The presence of real non-human animals such as Crab in *The Two
Gentlemen of Verona*, represented ones in virtually all of Shakespeare's
plays (most notably the bear in *The Winter's Tale*), or hybrid creatures
like Bottom in *A Midsummer Night's Dream* or Caliban in *The Tempest*, also unsettle ideas about nature as stable or neutral ground on
which cultural meaning can be complacently imprinted. Ecofeminists
have drawn attention to the masculine power structures that have
licensed these inscriptions, and to the alliances between women and
the natural world that resist them. Mariah Gale's performance of
Ophelia in Gregory Doran's 2008 Royal Shakespeare Company production of *Hamlet*, for example, suggested the ability of herbs and
flowers to 'talk back' to Claudius's patriarchal authority.[21] Woodland
spaces likewise have self-determining biorhythms and timescales, as
Roger Deakin and Richard Mabey have shown, and which Jaques
partially recognizes in *As You Like It*. Their energies do not require our
control to give them value or to help them survive unmolested. Forest
mosaics need our protection only because human survival depends on
shielding them from our own abuses.[22] Even the environmental identity of a quintessential cultural space such as The Globe theatre, as
Gabriel Egan and Vin Nardizzi have argued, is represented as much by

the life cycles of trees visible in its timber construction as by the commercial and social relations of its stage performances.[23]

John Pogue Harrison combines aspects of both constructionist and biocentric approaches to physical space in his masterly cultural history of forests. He shows how Western societies have built their material and social identities in opposition to the ancient woodlands that once covered all of Europe (he refers to forests generically, although he also discusses them in the English legal sense, which I examined in relation to *The Merry Wives of Windsor* in Chapter 1). On the one hand, Western civilization cleared physical and symbolic light from the threatening woodland darkness. Immemorial fears of forests as places that confound species distinctions are audible in Shakespearian characters describing them as 'desert', anti-social, or shape-shifting spaces. They also serve as the symbolic Otherness against which human identity must be defined, as when Richard of Gloucester imagines axing his way out of a choking wood to assert his politically ambitious individualism (*Henry VI Part Three*, 3.2.172–81). On the other hand, the untamable vitality and existential apartness of forests has inspired mythologies of freedom and non-conformism embodied by the romanticized Outlaws in *The Two Gentlemen of Verona*, or by Duke Senior's fantasy of pastoral exile in *As You Like It*'s Forest of Arden. (The similar physical and symbolic qualities of oceans are associated with pirates such as Walter Whitmore in *Henry VI Part Two* and (possibly) Antonio in *Twelfth Night*.) Romantic critics admired Shakespeare for apparently juxtaposing the liberating wildness of old-growth forests against instrumentalist assumptions that their conquest would affirm human ingenuity and social progress.

Pogue Harrison's study also suggests that changing ideas of landscape ecology can open up new critical approaches to Shakespeare's forest mosaics. The Romantic idealization of wilderness inherited by twentieth-century first-wave environmentalists was supported scientifically by the now outdated theory of succession dynamics. It posited that ecosystems reach self-perpetuating stability after passing through a series of ecological shifts. Ancient woodlands were treated as iconic examples of this paradigm because they appear to be Edenic spaces unaltered by human or natural disturbances. As I mentioned at the end of the Chapter 1, however, over the past half-century biologists have dismantled the succession model in favour of a new non-homeostatic paradigm. It insists that all natural environments are subject to continual human, non-human, and geophysical changes on interconnected levels. Such disturbances are in fact one of the drivers of evolutionary adaptation.

Landscape and conservation ecology have grown out of non-equilibrium models of biology which embrace change as intrinsic to planetary life (while opposing human destruction of its habitats and species). In theoretical terms, they avoid dividing nature and culture, instead seeing them as inseparable factors in the recent evolution of the earth's environments ("recent" meaning the last 20,000 years or so). The historically legible changes in English forests such as Arden illustrated this kind of ecological dynamism.

Shakespeare introduces this perspective in *As You Like It* by updating the place-identities of *Rosalynde's* three brothers, and 'environmentalizing' the opening quarrel between Oliver and Orlando. Changing the family name Bordeaux to de Boys (an anglicized form of French *bois*) suggests that the brothers, evidently no longer of the woods, are territorially displaced—perhaps distantly like Shakespeare's mother's family the Ardens. In both Lodge and Shakespeare the middle brother is exiled to school or university. Like *Rosalynde's* Rosader, Orlando's journey into the Forest of Arden represents a return to a foundational identity. In this he resembles his famous namesake, Orlando Furioso, who in the middle of Ludivico Ariosto's epic must re-enter and conquer the forest to rediscover the symbolic source of his inner strength.[24] Instead of having his Orlando furiously topple trees, however, Shakespeare maps his psychodrama onto a literary form of deterritorialization—his Petrarchan views of women—from whose estranging artifice he must be liberated by Rosalind.

Meanwhile the name de Boys ironically sharpens Oliver's deracinated identity in terms of an emblematic shift of affinity from forest to feldon, and woodwardship to mixed cultivation. In *Rosalynde*, Saladyne, the equivalent character to Oliver, is bequeathed 'fourteen ploughlands', the manor houses, and plate of his father John de Bourdeaux. The middle son, Ferdinand, inherits twelve ploughlands, but the youngest, Rosader, equivalent to Orlando, receives sixteen in addition to his father's horse, armour, and lance. The revelation that Rosader 'was his Father's darling', which accounts for the disparity in inherited wealth, rankles Saladyne. He takes revenge by amassing wealth in order to 'purchase lands' and surpass his father's social rank. He starts by confiscating his younger brothers' fortunes, which he still controls as their guardian, and raises Rosader as a peasant. Until one day, 'walking in the garden', Rosader rebels and demands his proper inheritance and education as a gentleman.[25]

Improvement and thrift

What has Oliver done with Orlando's thousand-crown inheritance? Capitalized his farm, which is now geared towards profitable 'growth', a word repeated several times in their opening dialogue with shifting implications. Orlando measures his brother's prosperity against the lowliness of his upbringing:

> ...call you that keeping for a gentleman of my birth, that differs not from the stalling of an ox? His horses are bred better, for besides that they are fair with their feeding, they are taught their manège, and to that end riders dearly hired. But I, his brother, gain nothing under him but growth, for the which his animals on his dunghills are as much bound to him as I.   (1.1.8–15)

While Oliver shares Saladyne's social ambitions, Orlando's references to agrarian and animal husbandry invoke controversies over early modern agricultural practices. Oliver's mixed husbandry makes him representative of a new class of upwardly mobile farmers bent on improving their land's efficiency and increasing its profitability. During the Middle Ages, 'profit' meant being rewarded with the fruits of the land as part of a spiritual and occupational contract with providence. As Andrew McRae has shown, land was understood to be a common resource, or 'treasury', from which landlords, farmers, and labourers benefited collectively and to which they claimed customary rights.[26] Corin has these benign meanings of profit in mind when he invites Rosalind, disguised as Ganymede, to consider buying the neglected sheep farm of Corin's master: 'Go with me. If you like upon report / The soil, the profit, and this kind of life, / I will your very faithful feeder be, / And buy it with your gold right suddenly' (*As You Like It*, 2.4.96–99).

The ideology of profit shifted, however, in the new sixteenth-century land-market. Henry VIII had created this market—Europe's first—when he dissolved the monasteries and sold off vast tracts of church property. Land became a commodity which individuals sought to exploit for maximum growth and wealth. The improver justified his material ambitions according to the virtues of thrift.[27] Its values also changed in the sixteenth century under the influence of Calvinist antipathies towards poverty, idleness, and neglect of employment (later theorized by sociologist Max Weber's Protestant ethic, in which work and wealth generation become signs of moral superiority). Oliver signals his approval of thrift using a traditional frame of reference, the prodigal son story. Shakespeare here takes up a hint in Lodge and builds on Orlando's earlier references to pigs and husks: 'And what wilt thou do [Orlando, if I give you your inheritance]—beg when that is spent?' (1.1.71). Oliver projects onto his brother the character of a wastrel who will squander his money in the manner of Shakespeare's Bassanio rather than make it breed as a sign of his godly observance like Shylock. Anticipating the logic of modern agronomics, Oliver decides Orlando's weedy kind of growth must be eradicated rather than accommodated within traditional practices of social reciprocity and biodiversity ('I will physic your rankness' [1.1.81–82]). Since Old Adam is also slow in profit, he too can be ditched: 'Get you with him, you old dog' (1.1.77).

Oliver's kind of thrifty individualism created tensions with community-oriented practices of georgic cultivation. Renaissance husbandry writers had rediscovered these practices from classical treatises such as Virgil's *Georgics* (translated 1589) and Hesiod's *Works and Days* (translated 1615). Georgic celebrates human labour, the change and qualities of the seasons, and reciprocity of human and non-human life and the land. As a literary mode, Alastair Fowler observes, georgic tends to express a writer's place-attachments, in contrast to pastoral's idealization of supposedly universal values which elide social relations and evolutionary principles.[28] When Shakespeare invests Lodge's romance with detailed signs of contemporary georgic based on personal knowledge of Midlands ecologies and economies, he challenges the pastoral ideals of rural detachment and aristocratic leisure conceited in the images of courtly shepherds living in Arcadia. Duke Senior aspires to this dream by imagining his exile as form of sylvan retirement, 'fleet[ing] the time carelessly, as they did in the golden world' (1.1.113–13). His fantasy is undercut, however, by modern northern realities such as winter's 'icy fang' and stags shot and left suffering to die. Jaques exploits these gaps between pastoral make-believe and late-Elizabethan adversity with a dissenting biocentric perspective that reflects the real Arden's environmentally contested worldviews.

Shakespeare thus bioregionalizes *Rosalynde* by writing into its narrative natural and anthropogenic changes to Warwickshire land-uses and production values. The interplay between georgic realism, pastoral idealism, and ecological disturbance represents another instance of Shakespeare refashioning the stories his drama tells us about human relationships with the natural world in ways that may orient spectators towards realistically progressive ecologies.[29] *As You Like It*'s engagement with late-sixteenth-century land-uses overwrites *Rosalynde*'s romance narrative with the comedic desires of an emerging environmental ethics.

Affording conversion

Paradoxically, these hopeful orientations begin with Oliver, again because of his contemporary agrarian profile. Although he starts as the proverbially oppressive older brother of the story, to some members of Shakespeare's audience living in an era of chronic dearth and dislocation, his dedication to agrarian and animal husbandry might have seemed admirable. *As You Like It* introduces this possibility by alluding to the acute rural famines of the 1590s when Rosalind begs Corin for food and shelter to help the failing Celia, but he has nothing to offer them (2.4.70–85). By the time Adam arrives in Arden he is starving, leading Orlando to burst in on Duke Senior and his court-in-exile and demand that everyone should stop eating till 'necessity be served'. He returns bearing the failing Adam on his back or in his arms (2.6.1, 16SDD). Although Adam is temporarily relieved, he disappears from the play thereafter.

The late-sixteenth-century context of recurring dearth also complicates Orlando's denunciation of Oliver's agricultural 'growth'. Some spectators could have heard echoes of contemporary complaints against agrarian hoarding.[30] Yet Orlando's inventories also tacitly reveal signs of biodynamic techniques which English husbandry writers rediscovered in Virgil and naturalized in practical manuals designed to remedy early modern food shortages and promote regional and national self-sufficiency.[31] Oliver's farm evinces well-cared-for domestic animals to work the fields, crop rotation and ley farming, and manuring. Integrated seasons and methods feed the farm's animal and human community, including the hogs Orlando later rants against. There is biocentric irony in his resentment, since Oliver's fraternal malice yet modern husbandry leads Orlando to disparage the oxen, horses, and pigs that affront his gentle status and human superiority on the traditional chain of being.

In his outstanding ecological study of the resource and subsistence crises in the late-sixteenth and early seventeenth-century Forest of Arden, Victor Skipp has shown that diversified husbandry practices like Oliver's eventually contributed to establishing greater ecological resilience and agricultural sustainability in the face of demographic pressures.[32] The main agrarian adaptation introduced during the time of *As You Like It*'s first performances was a legal change in primary land-use called convertible, or 'up and down', husbandry.[33] It increased the community's arable acreage and food production by allowing private farmers to plough up common pasture or waste (i.e. uncultivated or unwooded) land in order to sow crops for several years before the land reverted to common pasture. The downside came during the 'up' period, when landless commoners and small-scale tenant farmers lost their customary land for subsistence grazing. During the extreme weather and severe famines of the 1590s and early 1600s this became a life-and-death issue for many and provoked violent rural protests.

The 1597 act permitting convertible husbandry coincided with the even more embattled practice of enclosure, in which common fields were bounded by hedgerows or fences and turned into more profitable private farms. Enclosure was traditionally associated with the conversion of open grazing land into sheep pasture. Because wool was more profitable than corn up to the first half of the sixteenth century, this kind of enclosure gave landlords an opportunity to reverse falling incomes caused by inflation eating away at fixed rents. But as wool exports declined in the second half of the century and population growth raised incomes from land used for food production, the motives for enclosure shifted in ways that addressed new ecological problems.[34] *Henry VI Part Two* dramatizes the earlier context when the Second Petitioner presents a complaint signed by 'the whole township' against 'the Duke of Suffolk, for enclosing the commons of [Long] Melford', implicitly for sheep-grazing. Unfortunately he mistakenly hands the petition to the haughty Duke himself (1.3.22–26).

William C. Carroll has shown how the original early and later texts of this play track the period's changing contexts of enclosure by revising the presentation of Kentish landowner Alexander Iden. In the earlier *First Part of the Contention* (1594) his accusations of trespassing against the famished Jack Cade mark him as an encloser: 'Thou hast broke my hedges, / And enterd into my ground without the leave of me the owner' (G4ʳ). But in the revised Folio text (1623) the details of enclosure are replaced by Iden inheriting the property from his father as a 'fee-simple', or freehold property, which includes the legal right to seize any stray animal which enters its grounds (thereby symbolically reducing Cade to the status of a wild unprotected beast).[35] Iden's brick-walled garden in the Folio text becomes a georgic space of sustainable hospitality to the local poor (his pastoral smugness aside), whereas the hedged enclosure in *The Contention* is an aggressively privatized domain.

Pressures to enclose land were felt most acutely in the intensively cultivated counties of the Midlands, including Shakespeare's native Warwickshire, where a weak system of manorial oversight accelerated land-conversions. *Oliver* further reflects contested discourses about them. Like Shakespeare, he is generationally divided between a woodland past and an agrarian present. Oliver's profit-oriented modernity is evident in Orlando's complaint that he '[bars] me the place of a brother' (1.1.18), 'bar' conveying the efficiency of exclusion. Orlando's resentful self-comparison to Oliver's farm animals likewise suggests they have all been exploited as utilitarian resources for his hyperproductive estate. Duke Fredrick's treatment of his brother Senior and his niece Rosalind parallels Oliver's usurpation of his brother's rights through mental and material enclosure. Frederick stakes out Rosalind's new boundaries with the precision of enclosure's complementary new technology of land surveyance: 'Within these ten days if that thou beest found / So near our public court as twenty miles, / Thou diest for it' (1.3.41–43).

Richard Wilson observes that these topical details 'plunge the [play's] action into the bitter contradictions of England's agricultural revolution' centred on disputed land ideologies. For Wilson, Oliver represents 'the Elizabethan success-story of the rise of the gentry by engrossing and enclosure at the expense of evicted relatives and tenants'.[36] Corin is representative of this displaced class, and Shakespeare emphasizes his vulnerability by making him a landless wage earner who must earn money to buy food or else starve. This contrasts with Corin's background in *Rosalynde*, where he is a better-off tenant farmer whose landlord suddenly ends his leasehold (implicitly reflecting the different legal and environmental contexts of the original medieval French story).

Whither nature?

One of Corin's traditional but illicit subsistence options, as Shakespeare knew (and legend associated him with), was poaching game. The RSC's controversial 'dead rabbit' production of *As You Like It* (2009) interpolated this scenario to draw audiences' attention to the poverty, hunger, and marginalization suffered by early modern rural communities. During the interval with the house lights on, the actor playing Corin, Geoffrey Freshwater, came on stage carrying a real (dead) rabbit. Working impassively at centre stage, he proceeded to skin the animal and then casually carry it off stage (to his pot in the story; to the bin, presumably, in real life). Many spectators were outraged by this apparent display of cruelty. Animal rights discourse quickly displaced director Michael Boyd's historically contexualizing intentions. The RSC cut the scene when the show transferred to New York City.

   Andrew McCrae argues that fewer people in Corin's situation suffered under the older feudal system of 'juridical-conditional' relations between English peasants and landlords. From the sixteenth century onwards, however, partly as a consequence of the widening gap between falling wages and rising prices and partly owing to the new capitalist land market which swept away customary land rights and obligations, Corin's class emerged as a highly visible and volatile demographic. The Elizabethan government, always anxious about threats to property, stigmatized them as vagrants and thieves in the way Iden denigrates Cade.[37] Agricultural historian Joan Thirsk reminds us of what this situation looked like to Corin and others displaced by agrarian improvements in these conditions:

The Midland peasant lived in the midst of events and saw only one widespread movement to enclose and convert the land to pasture. He saw more cattle and more sheep in the closes. He saw rich farmers taking up more and more land but giving less employment than ever before to the labourer.... It was difficult to keep a balanced outlook when one's own livelihood was at stake.[38]

Shakespeare, however, presents Corin not as vengeful threat but as an example of agrarian equanimity:

Sir, I am a true labourer. I earn that I eat, get that I wear; owe no man hate, envy no man's happiness; glad of other men's good, content with my harm; and the greatest of my pride is to see my ewes graze and my lambs suck.

(3.2.69–73)

Perhaps too ideally, Corin's biocentric relations with his sheep and local community express the bioregional resilience of both classical and Elizabethan georgic. Though Touchstone mocks this 'natural philosophy' as naïve in the same way that he mocks Orlando's poetry (showing that he too is capable of not seeing the forest for the trees), he fails to falsify Corin's personal integrity, which later mentors Rosalind's convertible husbandry (of which more below).

Corin's master is a more realistic figure, an absentee landlord who gives back nothing to his farm, starves Corin, and renders him incapable of offering charitable relief to the famished Celia, Rosalind, and Touchstone:

> [I] wish, for her sake more than my own,
> My fortunes were more able to relieve [Celia];
> But I am shepherd to another man,
> And do not shear the fleeces that I graze.
> My master is of a churlish disposition,
> And little recks to find the way to heaven
> By doing deeds of hospitality.   (2.4.75–81)

Like Oliver, 'Old Carlot', as he is later named, is a believer in Calvinist thrift. He conveniently belittles hospitality as a form of discredited Catholic works in order to impose his selfish agenda on the land and its dwellers. Shakespeare does not reveal Carlot's motive for putting the farm up for sale, but we can infer he hopes to make a better investment elsewhere—such as the profitable 'green cornfields' mentioned later. His farm's location also hints at why he cannot covert the pasture into arable land in accordance with the 1597 statute. It stands in the 'purlieus' or 'skirts' of the forest. As I mentioned in Chapter 1, these spaces refer to recently disafforested crown land that had not been fully privatized and was still subject to certain protective rights and restrictions that were disputed by purchasers or leaseholders (4.3.77, 3.2.323, *OED*; purlieus have the same ambiguous royal status as King Lear after devolving power to Goneril and Regan). Carlot may have initially bought the disafforested land and farm as an engrosser, but then decided to sell them to turn a quick profit after inflation had raised their value.

Engrossing was the practice of buying and gathering parcels of land to enclose them for private use or to turn their mixed uses into monocultures.[39] In contrast to the practices of enclosure, whose ecological effects could be positive or negative depending on local negotiations, engrossing was less socially and ecologically equivocal as an agrarian practice. It aggressively asserted individual property rights within the scope of the common law's growing hegemony. Joan Thirsk confirms the harsh reality of Shakespeare's brief sketch of Old Carlot's farm: 'when two or more farms were thrown together, the superfluous farmhouses were either reduced to the status of cottages or left to decay'.[40]

Carlot's potential buyer is Silvius, whose name (derived from *silva* [Latin], woods) suggests another deracinated figure like the de Boys brothers. Like Orlando, his social ambitions are encoded in contemporary land-uses overlain with sentimental expressions of romantic desire. But Silvius evidently has enough capital (from his sold-off woodland?) to buy Carlot's farm and acquire the gentle status associated with pastoral sheep farming. This plan is diverted, however, by his erotic enslavement to Phoebe, which he expresses in hyperbolic images of rural poverty:

> So holy and perfect is my love,
> And I in such a poverty of grace,
> That I shall think it a most plenteous crop
> To glean the broken ears after the man
> That the main harvest reaps.   (3.5.100–104)[41]

Silvius's romantic displacement of historical miseries points to deeper tensions in *As You Like It*'s cultural representations of nature that are the focus of a searching discussion by Robert N. Watson.[42] He is sceptical about deriving any workable environmental ethics from the play because he sees Shakespeare insisting that human desires to return to nature are incapable of escaping the anthropocentrism that everyone in Arden indulges in. As Michael Boyd's stage production inadvertently revealed by trying to rebalance competing demands of romance and material history, *As You Like It* suggests that when we get closer to nature, we see only versions of our own alienating self-consciousness. For Watson, Corin's on-the-body experiences, for example ('the property of rain is to wet, and fire to burn; that good pasture makes fat sheep; and that a great cause of the night is lack of the sun...' [3.2.25–27]), epitomize the 'entire subject-object problem' that bedevils 'the difficulty of knowing nature objectively', owing to the self-referential nature of human language. Corin's philosophy is only rhetorically different from the more 'sophisticated, interventionist way[s] of understanding and loving nature' expressed by the urban exiles in Arden. Their comically framed dialogues tend to mask human impulses to dominate, which Shakespeare conveys in hunting and Petrarchan languages of 'stalking' nature (e.g. Silvius and Orlando).[43]

If one takes Watson's epistemological point that human experiences of nature are always filtered by language, does this exclude relating to it knowledgably through other pathways? Does culture prevent people from thinking like a forest—to recall the challenge of Aldo Leopold's land ethic?

Possibly not if we question the exclusion of biophysical ways of knowing from the categorical essentialism that has traditionally defined human nature, including the supposedly unique human capacity for speech.[44] The significance of Corin's empirical philosophy may lie less in its homely wisdom or entrapment in human discourse, and more in the relational dynamics constituted by Arden's physically afforded behaviours (to return to James Gibson's idea of 'ecological optics' introduced in Chapter 1, p. 51). Corin perceives the biotic and non-organic worlds not as radically separate from human existence, but as elementally related (we might now say, as physiologically and genetically enmeshed). Macro- and microphysical networks shape his instinctive actions and rational choices as a human animal. These include a shared capacity for affective empathy, which Boyd's production again revealed inadvertently by provoking spectators' disgust at the sight of a real animal, killed for the gift of theatrical presentation, being skinned by an actor who was not starving (and however much audience responses were simultaneously mediated by present-day attitudes towards animals). Instead of believing, like Oliver, Frederick, or Old Carlot, in his superiority to the bio-community, Corin's interactions with the forest generate a subjective conviction to become what Leopold calls 'a plain member and citizen of it' (*A Sand County Almanac*, 204). Although the signals of Boyd's production were mixed, they demonstrated that physically embodied performance is capable of generating viscerally empathetic, evolutionarily derived, connections to non-human nature.

No end of conversion

Corin's bioregional identity also invites us to reconsider early modern rationales of enclosure and improvement other than growth and thrift. To some extent they were shaped by new perceptions of the land's value and needs beyond exclusively human uses and profit. Although economic historians (and literary critics following them) tend to regard early modern enclosure as a wholly negative imposition by belligerent landlords like Suffolk in *Henry VI Part Two*, it was beginning to be motivated by ecological priorities as well. The 1597 act permitting convertible husbandry was aimed not only at increasing food production to relieve famine but also at sustaining local soil, which had become degraded by unmanaged overgrazing of common land. Ecologist Garrett Hardin referred to this situation as 'the tragedy of the commons' and used it to expose the environmental silences in Adam Smith's laissez-faire economics.[45] The Midlands were the most populous areas of ancient settlement and intensive cultivation in England, where incentives to preserve the land's biological health by rotating tillage and pasture became an ecological necessity in the last half of the sixteenth century.

One particular area of focus in early modern husbandry manuals was regenerating and maintaining soil fertility. Joan Thirsk notes that many of the complaints made in Star Chamber to the government commission investigating the causes of the 1607 Midland Revolts (alluded to in *Coriolanus*) related to overexploited plough land. Commissioners recommended that exhausted common pasture could be revitalized by being manured, sown for grassland, and ploughed under to 'regain heart'.[46]

Orlando alludes to the first of these practices—composting and manuring—in his outrage at being treated no better than Oliver's dung heaps. Identical to the biodynamic aims of organic farming today, revitalizing fields and orchards with composted vegetable and animal waste returned nutrients to the soil to increase productivity and sustain resilience. Hugh Plat explained these virtues while offering readers a taxonomy of composts and manures for regional English soils in Part Two of his *Jewell House of Art and Nature* (1594), 'Diuerse new sorts of Soyle . . . for manuring both of pasture and arable ground' (A1r-H4v). Shakespeare recognized the deep-green cycles beneath such mucky practices when Timon of Athens calls the earth (in his characteristically bitter way) 'a thief / That feeds and breeds on composture stol'n / From general excrement' (14.440–42). Hamlet's obsession with his mother's sexuality turns manuring into an image of unproductive growth (from an exclusively human viewpoint) when he admonishes Gertrude not to 'spread the compost o'er the weeds / To make them ranker' (3.4.147–48). He characterizes her affections towards Claudius as misdirected from the natural object of sustaining her first husband's memory. In the English history plays, war's devastations likewise twist positive associations of manuring into images of human blood drenching the soil and denaturing national husbandry (e.g. *Richard II*, 4.1.138–39; see Chapter 3).

Popular husbandry writer Thomas Tusser argued that nurturing the biodiversity of local environments through local enclosure and management of overexploited common land was essential for meeting a region's subsistence needs and preserving long-term ecological resilience:

> More plentie of mutton and beefe,
>   corne, butter, and cheese of the best,
> More wealth any where (to be breefe)
>   more people more handsome and prest,
> Where find ye? (go search any coast:)
>   than there, where enclosure is most?[47]

John Fitzherbert had likewise argued that enclosure for mixed farming created local employment when many people were looking for work (Oliver's numerous farmhands seem to confirm this claim). It allowed both human and non-human forest-dwellers to share its resources more equitably.[48] The practical advice of Fitzherbert, Tusser, and later husbandry writers Hugh Plat and Gervase Markham gave shape to the emerging bioregional principle that 'the land must speak to us; we must stand in *relation* to it; it must define us', rather than we exclusively determining it.[49] By the end of the sixteenth century, English communities were recognizing the logic of multi-scaled land-use and conservation and often arranged to enclose common ground through mutual agreements.[50] *As You Like It* reflects human and environmental values interacting in both structurally destructive and conserving ways, much like the personal desires of its characters.

It is true that writers such as Fitzherbert and Tusser were arguing from a landowners' perspective (similar to barley hoarder(?) and prospective encloser William Shakespeare[51] and his ironically laconic stand-in, the 'so-so' rich William in *As You Like It* [5.1.25]). Nonetheless, their ecologically informed programmes of husbandry attempted to remodel the adversarial dialectic of enclosure as a shared relationship of human and more-than-human interests.[52] Timothy Morton theorizes this paradigm from a post-humanist perspective in *Ecology Without Nature* (2007). He argues that dividing the natural world according to human interactions perpetuates the Romantic and first-wave environmentalist dreams of returning to or restoring an Edenic nature virtually untouched by human use. The rural–metropolitan Shakespeare uses the urban–woodland Jaques to satirize such utopian aspirations, encoded by Duke Senior's pastoral make-believe. Jaques also catches glimpses of a more radical ecology in his species-leveling empathy with animals callously mistreated by 'outlandish' citizens. Having intuited but not fully articulated this forest experience, Jaques withdraws to Duke Senior's abandoned cave—a bit like Henry Thoreau's pondside cabin—to think it through.

For his part, Corin's rejection of Touchstone's nature–culture binaries demonstrates through lived practice that while human uses of nature are inevitable, their good uses are not. These become the proper object of environmental responsibility working through place-afforded perceptions and relations on multiple levels. *As You Like It* suggests that Rosalind is inspired by Corin to fulfil the desires of convertible husbandry in both ecological and romantic modes. Like Oliver she becomes a private landlord when she buys old Carlot's farm and employs Corin as her shepherd. But unlike Oliver, her improving attitudes do not divide agronomic and bio-responsive impulses, but reflect empirical negotiations of Arden's demographic and subsistence crises of the kind documented by Victor Skipp. Rosalind also learns to think like a forest by practising a symbolic version of 'up and down' husbandry on Orlando, whose language and outlook on women she redeems from the minor tragedies of sentimental versifying. Shakespeare associates Rosalind's linking of the two modes with the landscape corridor he lays out between her reclaimed sheep farm and the revitalized fields of 'It was a lover and his lass'. Celia's reference to the 'rank of osiers by the murmuring stream' (the same that will bring the newly converted Oliver to Rosalind's sheepcote) indicates that Rosalind has turned Carlot's moribund sheep pasture into a community-building farm like Oliver's but without the hyperactive growth. Osiers or willow trees supply material to make baskets and other farm utensils. They are a bioregional marker of a thriving Forest of Arden cottage industry which created valuable employment for displaced labourers and provided a supplemental income to the farmer.[53] Meanwhile Oliver's place-related clash of improving and ecological agrarian identities (entirely absent in Lodge's *Rosalynde*) leaves him subjectively open to the conversion he acts out in the rarer actions of rescuing Orlando from a 'sucked and hungry lioness' (4.3.99ff) and ploughing under a windfall revenge. Duke Frederick's peevish humours parallel Oliver's fluid subjectivity by registering the psychosomatic effects of Arden's environmental imbalances. He is converted tongue-in-cheek by the romance cliché of a 'religious old man' who steers him towards restoring Duke Senior's lands.

Rosalind's staging of Hymen's blessing on the concluding marriages at her farm further indicates she has benefited from Corin's georgic insights into a more-than-human ecology: 'Then there is mirth in heaven / When earthly things made even / Atone together' (5.4.103–105; ritually enacted by Rosalind's playfully ambiguous manner of surrendering to, and seizing possession of, Orlando [5.4.111–12]). During Hymen's stage-epiphany, Arden's topographic mosaics serve not merely as pretty backdrops but also channel the reproductive desires and energies of forest ecosystems. Because these are active cyclical agencies, they shadow the human festivity with future intimations of metabiotic decay, decomposition, and regeneration (about which more in Chapters 4 and 5). Like Corin's bioregional consciousness, Rosalind's perceptions of phenomenological connectivity and wider ecological time frames reach beyond the attempts of growth-defined production and consumption to transcend nature by ignoring its limits.[54]

Rosalind, we may imagine, invests her income from Carlot's reclaimed farm in the neighbouring fields of 'It was a lover and his lass' which she cultivates biodynamically. 'Between the acres of the rye' indicates she has allowed furlongs or strips of land to lie fallow while adjacent acres are under cultivation. When the crop is harvested, both the grassland and the stubbled fields will be thrown open to grazing animals as well as local wildlife not under human control.[55] Rosalind's rotating crops also supply food year-round, if 'rye' stands in early modern English for grains in general rather than the barley specifically. Tracing the play's wider seasonal arc from winter to 'the prime', the lovers 'pass over' the 'green cornfield' to hide between the rye-acres, because by spring they would have been much taller. Winter ryes or wheat are planted in the autumn and mature by spring, reaching three or four feet by June. Whereas the 'green cornfield' refers to spring-planted wheat, which in May is still young.

Shakespeare does not hint at the fate of Rosalind's bioregionally sustainable farms beyond the final marriages. Legally, they will pass into the control of Orlando under the marital laws of coverture. Does Rosalind's convertible husbandry extend to Orlando's agrarian education as well as his Petrarchan rehabilitation? Will he honour the georgic husbandry he once despised? Or is he merely the lucky recipient of Fortune's gift, surpassing Oliver's ambitions of social advancement through agronomics by gaining control of both his brother's and his wife's estate (5.2.10–11)? If so, the question becomes, will he be co-opted by the aristocratic-pastoral ideal of living off the land and the labour of others while attending Duke Senior in the 'pompous' (i.e. ambitiously consuming) court? *As You Like It*'s contentious and transitioning land ideologies stimulate these speculations while encouraging audiences to think beyond pastoral romance to what constitutes sustainability in a modern era of natural and human-made environmental pressures. In Chapter 3 I want to examine early modern cultivation and bioregional ethics coming under greater threat from the global gunpowder economy.

3

Gunpowder, Militarization, and Threshold Ecologies in Henry IV Part Two *and* Macbeth

The disputed land-uses and cultivation practices represented in *As You Like It* responded to unprecedented changes in Elizabethan climate, population, and economic relations. Traditional modes of rural dwelling were no longer protected by virtue of their rural isolation or autonomy, but were becoming inescapably tied to national and global orders of competitive growth and resource exploitation. Perhaps the most disruptive of these modernizing turns was the development of gunpowder technologies and the armament industry.

As in other western European countries, military culture became ubiquitous in England by the late sixteenth century as a result of innovations in gunpowder weapons and the formation of national armies.[1] During the Middle Ages, low-tech weaponry and feudal mobilization had limited the social and environmental impacts of war. This situation began to change from the fifteenth century onwards with the development of far more deadly cannons, mines, and firearms. Influenced partly by the Erasmian ethics of his Humanist education (like Queen Elizabeth and King James in their attitudes to war), Shakespeare drew attention to gunpowder's devastating effects on human and non-human animals and their environments in virtually all his history plays and several of his tragedies, even though most of these references were anachronistic.[2] By layering historical and contemporary viewpoints he registered changing material realities and cultural assumptions about the ecology of war: from self-regulating cycles of martial destruction and agrarian regeneration, to incremental technological mastery reliant on ever-increasing resource consumption.

Traditional ideas about redeeming war through cultivation are captured by the Virgilian image of beating swords into ploughshares. It suggests that peacetime cultivation will heal wartime damage, and that periods of war and peace routinely alternate. The swords-into-ploughshares trope also encodes temporal assumptions that the arc of catastrophe, in its political, ecological, and dramatic senses, is limited in scope and ultimately reversible. In this chapter I want to examine the emerging gunpowder regime putting pressure on this paradigm, and replacing it with modern structures of recoiling environmental risk and planetary push-back, represented in *Henry IV Part Two* and *Macbeth* respectively. I shall begin by surveying four aspects of early modern militarization that compromised the swords-into-ploughshares ethos: cannons, cyborgs, deforestation, and saltpetre. I'll then look more closely at how the Gloucestershire scenes in *Henry IV Part Two* dramatize the faltering hopes of agrarian renewal by representing both the remedial power and social vulnerability of traditional English bioregionalism. Gunpowder's attenuation of agricultural redemption looks forward to *Macbeth*. Despite being set in pre-gunpowder Europe, the play relates the hyperbolic energies of early mechanized war to Scotland's deep-rooted culture of competitive violence, epitomized by the Macbeths' self-destructive ambitions. Whereas *Henry IV Part One* and *Two* and *Henry V* stage regional impacts of gunpowder displacements, *Macbeth* shows these disturbances reaching a threshold of global disaster, equivalent to today's dangers of climate change and species extinctions. The Weird Sisters are the earth's harbingers of this environmental nemesis. Their shows display the modern scales of global degradation that gunpowder militarization in Shakespeare's time began to set in motion.

Before I discuss cannons, etc, a note about the ecocritical uses of anachronism. Shakespeare heightens the visibility of modern warfare's environmental devastation through his conscious allusions to gunpowder weaponry that belonged properly to Tudor armies and manufacturing. The two tetralogies begin chronologically with Richard II's reign, not long after artillery was introduced into European warfare from the Islamic world in the 1320s.[3] Henry V's French campaign accurately represents the fifteenth-century transition to cannon-and-siege warfare on the Continent to the point of failing to mention the famous English longbow men at Agincourt. During the later Wars of the Roses, however, English combat remained largely wedded to traditional field battles with limited use of (still unreliable) gunpowder weapons. Yet throughout both historical tetralogies, Shakespeare's characters refer routinely to artillery, calivers, pistols, and arquebusses, with their accompanying bullets and firepower (e.g. Montague's cannon-like death-rattle, 'Gunpowder Percy', Pistol himself). These weapons only completely displaced lances and pikes as standard-issue weapons in the late sixteenth century when Shakespeare was writing his plays for technically knowledgeable London audiences.[4] Yet their presence in pre-gunpowder settings was ecocritically productive. The juxtaposition of temporal perspectives invited early modern spectators to consider the behavioural changes and long-term environmental damage being wrought by gunpowder technologies. Temporally layered history was, and remains today, a matrix of ecological understanding in Shakespeare. The eclectic postmodern weaponry of the English Shakespeare Company's *Wars of the Roses* (1987), Julie Taymor's feature film *Titus* (1999), or Ralph Fiennes's *Coriolanus* (2011), represents recent instances of directors contemporizing Shakespeare's multi-temporal vision of war. Their adaptations clarify the modern domination of local and regional environments by globalized war-technologies. Implicitly they invite audiences to translate their recognition into contemporary political choices.[5]

O you mortal engines, whose rude throats / Th'immortal Jove's dread clamours counterfeit... (*Othello*, 3.3.357–58)

In addition to the magnetic compass and the printing press, the European 'invention' of gunpowder and its role in subduing New Worlds became a defining commonplace of early modern progress.[6] Francis Bacon declared that all three inventions had 'changed the appearance and state of the whole world'.[7] But whereas navigation and printing were seen as unequivocally positive for civilization, gunpowder was not. Apologists such as Richard Eden enthused that gunpowder technology had suche marueylous force, that mountaynes of moste harde rockes and stones, are not able to resyst their violence, but are by them broken in peeces, and throwen into the ayre with suche violence, that neyther the spirite of *Demogorgon*, or the thunderbolts of infernal *Pluto* can doo the lyke.[8]

Anticipating Henry V's threats to turn the Dauphin's tennis balls into gunstones (i.e. cannonballs) which will smash France to pieces (*Henry V*, 1.2.282, 225), Eden unwittingly attests to gunpowder's catastrophic powers of devastation, comparable to today's heightened dangers of nuclear, chemical, and biological warfare. When Fortinbras arrives to find the Danish court heaped in dead bodies, he can make sense of the slaughter only by relating it to his experience of death by artillery: 'so many princes at a shot / So bloodily... struck' (*Hamlet*, 5.2.319–20). Iago dissembles his trust in Othello's self-control to Desdemona by alleging his refusal to become angry even when cannon 'hath blown his ranks into the air / And, like the devil, from his very arm / Puffed his own brother' (*Othello*, 3.4.131–33). By contrast, from the complacency of his civilian upbringing, Petruchio burlesques such dangers in his unlikely boasts of 'hear[ing] great ordnance in the field, / And heaven's artillery thunder in the skies' (*The Taming of the Shrew*, 1.2.198–99). Also in a comic frame, Ford feels as certain about Falstaff's page Robin serving as a go-between for Mistress Page's affairs, as a 'cannon [that] will shoot point-blank twelve score' (*The Merry Wives of Windsor*, 3.2.29). Jaques, on the other hand, derides the illusory heroism of fighting under such conditions as 'Seeking the bubble reputation / Even in the cannon's mouth' (*As You Like It*, 2.7.152–53). Gunpowder's annihilating reality similarly colours Henry's double-handed threats of violence and mercy towards Harfleur:

> If I begin the batt'ry again
> I will not leave the half-achievèd Harfleur
> 'Till in her ashes she lie burièd.   (*Henry V*, 3.3.87–89)

An earlier description in *Henry V* by the Chorus implies that cannon-assaults have changed the limits of medieval warfare by making human environments as well as combatants the total object of mechanized destruction:

> Behold the ordnance on their carriages,
> With fatal mouth gaping on girded Harfleur...
> ...the nimble gunner

> With linstock now the devilish cannon touches,
>> *Alarum, chambers go off*
> And down goes all before them.   (*Henry V*, 3.0.26–34)

This disproportionate level of destruction spurs Joan la Pucelle to try to persuade Burgundy to desert the English by appealing to his sense of outrage and compassion (echoed earlier by Talbot at the cannon-fire that instantly kills Thomas Gargrave and grotesquely disfigures Salisbury):

> Look on thy country, look on fertile France ...
> And see the cities and the towns defaced
> By wasting ruin of the cruel foe.
> See, see the pining malady of France.
>> (*Henry VI Part One*, 3.3.44, 47–49)

Her speech anticipates the lament of Burgundy's namesake for Henry V's devastation of the French countryside and its agrarian economy (*Henry V*, 5.2.24–62, discussed below).

Shakespeare's recurring links between guns and environmental as well as human destruction reflect a modern awareness of what Michel Serres calls war's 'objective violence', which reduces the natural world's physical realities to a stage backdrop, or 'theatre of hostilities', to act out myopic struggles for conquest.[9] When Henry V claims that the invading Scots '[galled] the gleanèd land with hot assays', he implies that the land's produce had already been *harvested* and the stubble traditionally *gleaned* by the local poor. But the Scots were trying to wipe out its life biologically by conducting a scorched-earth policy (*Henry V*, 1.2.151). *King John* has struck many modern directors and critics as staging the same kind of blinkered aggression. It creates this impression partly by referring more often to cannons than any other Shakespeare play, even though its events take place a century before the revolutionary transformation of warfare by gunpowder:

> The cannons have their bowels full of wrath,
> And ready mounted are they to spit forth
> Their iron indignation 'gainst your walls
> ... And but for our approach, those sleeping stones ...
> By the compulsion of their ordnance
> By this time from their fixèd beds of lime
> Had been dishabited ....   (2.1.210–20)[10]

John terrorizes the citizens of Angers with the same physically indiscriminate destruction as Henry does at Harfleur, as Shakespeare summons up the modern reality of gunpowder's fearfully inescapable damage to human and non-human life. This new reality stands in contrast to Shakespeare's source-play, George Peele's *The Troublesome Reign of King John* (pr. 1591), which refers only to bows and archers. Overall, *King John* goes so far as to suggest that the deadly effects of firepower and cannon bullets have compromised earthly climates, with cosmic order seeming to reassert itself in *King John*'s revelatory terminal events.[11]

'Turning Tech'[12]

Like other mechanical inventions, artillery and firearms created anxieties about humans taking on and/or involuntarily mimicking the non-human 'behaviour' of machines.[13] Shakespeare's characters reflect such transformations when their bodily functions are described in terms of guns or gunpowder. When Lucy comes to claim Talbot's body and Joan reduces his lofty praise to the maggoty corpse at her feet, he fantasizes merging his frustration with firepower's overwhelming force: 'O, were mine eye-balls into bullets turned, / That I in rage might shoot them at your faces!' (*Henry VI Part One*, 4.7.79–80). *Henry V* exhorts his soldiers to embrace this cyborgian metamorphosis as well: 'lend the eye a terrible aspect, / Let it pry through the portage of the head / Like the brass cannon' (3.1.9–11). But in Fluellen's case Henry is aware that being as 'hot as gunpowder' carries the risk of backfiring like real early modern guns; so he sends the more reliable Gower to shadow Fluellen when he meets Williams's challenge on Henry's behalf (*Henry V*, 4.7.173). In *King John* the Bastard delights in mocking the kinaesthetic transformations of gunpowder weapons: 'He speaks plain cannon – fire, smoke, and bounce' (2.1.463). As I shall suggest later in this chapter, human subjectivities are distorted more tragically when Macbeth and Banquo slaughter their enemies 'As cannons overcharged with double cracks' (*Macbeth*, 1.2.37).

George Basalla connects early modern fears that new technologies such as firearms were deranging human nature to wider cultural shifts in the period. He points out that until the sixteenth century, organic and mechanical states were treated separately. But as early modern technology drew on new principles of mathematics to invent devices that could outdo nature, the physical world became re-theorized as a mechanical entity. Attributes of the 'artificial' and the 'natural' began to blur as culture absorbed the mental and physical conditioning of technological innovations.[14] Industrialized mechanization in particular created categorical confusions between organic and manufactured properties. Gunpowder-enhanced militarization, enabled by inflows of state and transnational capital, deterritorialized, or structurally displaced, community-oriented modes of production and subsistence.[15] Its distortions of daily life in *Hamlet* lead Horatio and the watch initially to suppose that it is connected to the Ghost's first appearances. Marcellus wonders at the 24/7 'cast of brazen cannon' and frenzied shipbuilding that have replaced natural cycles of work and rest with a techno-rhythm of 'sweaty haste' (1.1.70–79). Horatio and Claudius explain independently that Fortinbras is trying to rival Denmark's 'warlike state' of production by 'shark[ing] up' Norway's citizens and resources into a totalized national polity: 'the levies, / The lists, and full proportions are made / Out of his subject' (1.2.31–33). Norway's and Denmark's post-chivalric aggression resituates soldiers, sailors, and non-combatants as the objects of environmentally parasitic regimes.

Not surprisingly, Claudius's preferred way of displaying his modern rule is cannon-fire (1.2.126, 5.2.217). In performance, its presence reflects the Elizabethan theatre's commercially profitable embrace of gunpowder risks, evident from '*Ordnance [going] off*' in *The First Part of The Contention* in 1590 (Shakespeare's earlier version of *Henry VI Part Two*) to the burning of The Globe during a performance of *Henry VIII* in 1613, when a faultily discharged backstage cannon set the thatched roof on fire. Not even Claudius's tragic antagonist is immune from gunpowder's mentally reshaping effects. Hamlet compares the Ghost's rumblings in the cellarage to a fast-working 'pioneer', or military miner, who blows up enemy fortifications (1.5.171). He later apologizes for the lameness of his love-verses to Ophelia by implying that their banality is owing to his subjective enthrallment to Denmark's mechanized culture: 'Thine evermore, most dear lady, whilst this machine is to him, Hamlet' (2.2.122–23).

Falstaff cynically exploits this dehumanizing turn when he dismisses the local recruits too poor to bribe their way out of impressment as 'good enough to toss; food for power, food for powder'. Afterwards he breezily writes off 147 of his 150 'peppered' ragamuffins (*Henry IV Part One*, 4.2.62–63, 5.3.35–38). Experimenting with the new metaphor of cannon fodder (which he possibly invented[16]), Shakespeare layers the catastrophic killing-power of artillery over late-medieval battles in which firearms played a limited role—and no part at all in the fighting of the play's chivalric class. As Falstaff assimilates common soldiers to the physical 'life' of guns, organic life becomes virtual in a terrifyingly destructive feedback loop.[17]

Deforestation militant

The inherent tendencies to competitive escalation in the use and manufacture of gunpowder weaponry pushed Henry VIII into establishing a national iron foundry at Newbridge, Sussex devoted to making cast-iron cannons. His supervisor, William Nevett, brought over skilled French workers to join Kentish craftsmen, and together between 1545 and 1547 they produced 120 cast-iron cannon using county ore and nearby timber from Ashdown Forest. These were the first cannon manufactured successfully from cast iron. They were so cheap compared to bronze artillery that nine more furnaces were built in the Weald by 1573, producing 500–600 tons of iron ordnance per year. Arming for war with Spain, the Elizabethan government expanded the number of furnaces countrywide, and by the turn of the century, forty or more were producing 1000 tons of ordnance at £10 per ton, in contrast to the price of bar iron at £2 a ton. This expansion transformed England into Europe's leading exporter of cast-iron cannon, and thus of human and environmental devastation to Ireland, the Netherlands, France, and around the world, since the leading buyers of iron artillery were national navies.[18]

An unintended consequence of this rapid progress was the iron industry's inordinate consumption of local wood. The depletion of trees and loss of primary habitat caused by the Sussex ironworks generated local complaints which forced the government to call the first environmental inquiry in England.[19] Heralding the future effectiveness of such bodies, no conservation measures were forthcoming. Resource exploitation by national iron and gunpowder manufacturing was privileged over the concerns of county residents. Local deforestation by iron manufacturing coincided with the equally voracious demands for wood and timber by glass and other new industries to produce a fuel crisis in south-east England in the last quarter of the sixteenth century.[20] As I mentioned in my introduction, owing to steeply rising wood prices, people such as Mistress Quickly turned to cheaper but highly toxic sea coal (i.e. fossil fuel) to heat newly chimneyed and enlarged Elizabethan houses (see pp. 2–3). In the race for wood amid public anxieties over deforestation, armament interests eventually took priority over glass-makers, who were forced by the government to abandon wood and switch to coal in 1608.[21] The iron industry, on the other hand, was allowed to change over more slowly during the seventeenth century. Industrial consumption of wood and timber fell temporarily when peace with Spain in 1603 reduced production levels of cast-iron ordnance and gunpowder. But exports to Protestant allies kept demand at profitable levels until the threat of war in the 1620s started increasing them again.[22]

The decision to privilege guns over other forms of manufacturing represents an early sign of reflexive environmental risk-taking linked to modern production. According to sociologist Ulrich Beck, such risks have a boomerang effect. Societies which tolerate environmental deg-radation for the sake of generating wealth and employment (e.g. clear-cutting, overfishing, strip-mining, pollution) also collectively expose their populations to unforeseen negative consequences, like the defor-estation that is currently causing renewed outbreaks of the Ebola virus in Africa.[23] Macbeth captures the idea of this hazardous dynamic in his awareness that choosing murder over loyalty to Duncan will 'teach / Bloody instructions, which being taught, return / To plague th'inventor' (1.7.8–10). His handling of the assassination's aftermath also illus-trates the way modern societies seek to manage rather than reverse dangerous risks by selectively dividing their negative impacts among competing corporate and public stakeholders, who become preoccu-pied with calibrating variables of safety and danger. Risk societies thereby avoid addressing ecological dangers directly, or outside the framework of human interests.[24] Historically, the ethos of good or profitable risk is traceable to the development of early modern com-mercial voyaging and insurance, and thus to Shakespeare's large class of venturing and commodity metaphors, from Grumio and Tranio's competition in galleys and galliasses for Bianca in *The Taming of the*

Shrew (2.1.367–73), to Posthumus and Giacomo's aggressive gamble over Innogen's chastity in *Cymbeline* (1.3). Modern wagers between addictive growth and self-inflicted damage are now shifting in scale and volatility. Rising sea levels, species extinctions, and other globalized dangers are challenging modern risk calculations by introducing planetary thresholds of natural disaster and catastrophic inversions of human dominance.[25] *Macbeth*, I will suggest later, prefigures these environmental tipping points.

'Villainous saltpetre'

A second major sign of early modern England's transition to an environmental risk society was the production of saltpetre. Hotspur refers to this primary ingredient of gunpowder in his satirical description of an effete lord on the battlefield:

> Came there a certain lord, neat and trimly dressed...
> [Who talked] so like a waiting-gentlewoman
> Of guns and drums and wounds—God save the mark!—
> And telling me...
> ...it was great pity, so it was,
> This villainous saltpetre should be digged
> Out of the bowels of the harmless earth,
> Which many a good tall fellow had destroyed
> So cowardly, and but for these vile guns
> He would himself had been a soldier.   (*1 Henry IV*, 1.3.33–64)

While it is couched in a humorous anecdote, Shakespeare's topical satire of saltpetre's contentious production is historically accurate and purposeful: it frames the canonical story of Prince Hal's rise to power with a parallel narrative of modern ecological destruction. Rising European demand for potassium nitrate (KNO_3) was met first by domestic manufacturing and later by growing imports from India in the seventeenth century. Bert S. Hall argues that the late-medieval success of Continental production created an economy of cheap saltpetre that drove the rapid specialization of artillery, firearms, and gunpowder from the fifteenth century onwards. They reached a technological standard by the late 1500s that allowed Europe's bigger and more reliable guns to conquer the world.[26] In England, saltpetre production lagged behind the Continent until the Elizabethan government organized a national programme. Like the Tudor cannon foundries, it caused unprecedented environmental upheavals.

Saltpetre was produced from earth composted with human and animal wastes that farmers used to fertilize their fields.[27] Creating an early guns-versus-butter conflict, the government commissioned saltpetremen to set up nitre beds and boiling factories near plentiful wood and water supplies. They then searched local farms systematically to dig up waste-drenched earth or compost to a depth of six to eight feet.[28] The saltpetremen were supposed to fill in holes they made and repair the buildings they damaged, but evidently they often failed to do so. They also did not pay for what they took since farmers were supposed to be contributing a strategic resource to national security. Disturbances to birds and cattle did not matter. The petremen loaded up the black earth in barrels and hired local carters to transport it to county works. But the wage of 4*d* a mile was niggardly and damage to carts uncompensated. If farmers or carters refused, the petremen impressed them by force on the authority of their royal commissions. Like the glassmakers who set up their works sporadically in woods across England, once the locality's resource had been exhausted, the saltpetremen moved on.

These abuses aroused fierce complaints to government officers and MPs. As David Cressy observes, dissenting voices emerged 'from all points of the ideological spectrum, from champions of parliament . . . to arch-royalists.'[29] Evasion through bribes, in the manner of nationally impressed conscripts Mouldly and Bullcalf, was common (*Henry IV Part Two*, 3.2[30]). Saltpetre's conflicts were temporarily mitigated by the shift to a peacetime economy in 1603. But this contraction was also kick-started by mass regional protests. Local farmers took advantage of the queen's death in that year to claim defiantly that the saltpetremen's patents had lapsed. The patent holders petitioned the Council that their activities were 'a matter of Royall prerogative inseperablie [*sic*] belonging to the imperial crowne'.[31] For a while the peacetime fall in demand for saltpetre undermined their efforts. But by the 1620s the build-up to war again overrode farmers' complaints.

The georgic contract and its limits

Gunpowder's literal disembedding of community ecologies effectively detached England's militarism from its territorial carrying capacities.[32] Today, however, climate and other geo-physical crises are striking back at the hubris which gunpowder materially puffed up. To avoid crossing catastrophic thresholds and to re-adapt to nature's boundaries, Michel Serres proposes replacing the environmental parasitism of competing nation-states with a deep-ecological contract, in which the human world gives the earth rights of its own.[33]

One model for cultivating this reciprocity, as Rosalind's convertible husbandry in *As You Like It* suggests, is the environmentalism of classical georgic. James C. Bulman has shown that the dialectic of spilling blood and tilling the soil which Virgil set out in the recently translated *Georgics* (1589) gave Shakespeare a framework for interpreting patterns of political change across the English history plays.[34] I suggest it also provided him with an environmental grid for mapping the effects of industrial militarization. In the Gloucestershire scenes of *Henry IV Part Two* and other material details of his English histories, Shakespeare tested Virgil's cyclical pattern in relation to the resilience and vulnerability of traditional English bioregionalism to the emerging gunpowder episteme.

War's traditional peace dividend was the restoration of productive farming. In *Richard III*, Richmond invokes its promises to frame the approaching battle at Bosworth as a definitive end to the Wars of the Roses and the beginning of a redemptive upturn:

> ... cheerly on ...
> To reap the harvest of perpetual peace
> By this one bloody trial of sharp war.   (5.2.14–16)[35]

Georgic's core idea—that peacetime cultivation will compensate for wartime damage—goes back to classical and biblical texts.[36] Shakespeare introduced it early in the First Tetralogy when the Duke of York anticipates returning to England from Ireland to 'reap the harvest' which his subversive agent Jack Cade has 'sowed' against Henry VI (*Henry VI Part Two*, 3.1.380–81).[37] As the *Henry IV* plays and Burgundy's complaint of peace in *Henry V* demonstrate, the Second Tetralogy continues to invoke the classical theory of armed conflict alternating with regenerative husbandry. In the tragedies it underlies Malcolm's victorious promise of peace being 'planted newly' at the end of *Macbeth*, and the imagery of 'sustaining corn' associated with Cordelia in *King Lear*. In his 1991 Royal Shakespeare Company production, Nicholas Hytner represented Cordelia's symbolic relationship to agrarian renewal by decorating the scenes of her return to England with sheaves of wheat and other harvest colourings (*Macbeth*, 5.7.95; *King Lear*, 18.6).

War and husbandry were also connected because farmers were thought to make good soldiers. In both cases closeness to the soil and medical theories that individual bodies absorbed the humoral environment of their birthplace made husbandmen ideal defenders of their country.[38] Henry V has these relationships in mind when, in another variation on the swords-into-ploughshares trope, he rallies his army's yeoman, 'Whose limbs were made in England[;], show us here / The mettle of your pasture; let us swear / That you are worth your breeding' (3.1.25–28). New policies of national impressment to replenish armies decimated by gunpowder weapons destabilized these assumptions, however, by replacing more limited feudal models of recruitment. The Son who has killed his Father in *Henry VI Part Three* distinguishes between past and present conscription practices to explain how a parent and child could end up fighting each other on opposing sides: 'From London by the King was I pressed forth. / My father, being the Earl of Warwick's man, / Came on the part of York' (*Henry VI Part Three*, 2.5.64–66). Richmond recalls the Son's dilemma to announce the soldier-husbandman's freedom to return to productive cultivation after Bosworth: 'The son, *compelled*, [has] been butcher to the sire' (*Richard III*, 5.7.26, my italics). In *Henry IV Part Two*, Falstaff's trawl for recruits through Gloucestershire dramatizes the Son's backstory by satirizing the corruption of Elizabethan impressment (topically coded by the handling of pistols as a means of testing ability[39]). Mouldy argues that being forced to become a soldier will mean abandoning his pre-harvest crops and impoverishing his wife: 'My old dame will be undone now for one to do her husbandry and her drudgery ... she is old and cannot help herself' (3.2.110–11, 222–23).

Burgundy expands on this protest in his moving lament for war-devastated France during the peace negotiations which follow Henry V's victory at Agincourt (*Henry V*, 5.2.23–67). There is a note of Edenic pastoral in the image of France as the 'best garden of the world' (echoed in the play's heroically deflating Epilogue). But Burgundy's emphasis on agricultural tools and work, seasonal rhythms, and named plants define his rhetorical mode as georgic realism.[40] Although his point-of-view is not strictly biocentric, since it does not value nature apart from human uses, it nonetheless critiques war's anthropomorphic equation of the war-torn environment with the wildness and 'savagery' of husbandmen who 'nothing do but meditate on blood' after being mobilized (5.2.60). Speaking diplomatically, Burgundy avoids mentioning Henry's imperial war as the cause of these derangements, instead emphasizing peacetime hopes of agricultural and social reconstruction. He conceives of this process ecologically as a making 'even', or restoration of long-term mutualism between human and organic rhythms of nature. His approach recalls the Gardener's horticultural principles in *Richard II*, whose political allegory of balance and moderation is rejected by Richard's eavesdropping Queen (3.4.36).

The Gloucestershire scenes of *Henry IV Part Two* substantiate Shakespeare's georgic framework by presenting an unexpectedly detailed picture of Elizabethan husbandry. Acting within a culture of grass-roots resistance like that mounted by early modern farmers against saltpetre confiscation, Shallow's agrarianism in *Henry IV Part Two* stages a bioregional alternative to Henry IV's wartime displacements, contextually related, as we have seen, to Elizabethan England's burgeoning trade in gunpowder armaments. Shallow's homely discussion with Davy about ploughing, sowing, dining, and paying off farm debts represents georgic discourse on the edge of self-parody, and tests Falstaff's patience (5.1). Their conversation is usually understood as rural grist for the performance of Shallow's dotty provincialism, which we laugh at from Falstaff's urbane perspective. But Falstaff is also amazed at Shallow's growth from the 'very genius of famine' into squiredom: 'Fore God, you have here a goodly dwelling, and a rich' (3.2.299, 5.3.5–6). Like Mistress Quickly's offhand remarks about sea coal, Shallow's seemingly irrelevant details contextualize and demystify this social transformation. They confirm Shallow's empirical understanding of a two-way relationship between the land's carrying capacity and his farm's ecological footprint. Representative of the period's profitable shift from grazing sheep to mixed farming,[41] and metadramatically enlivened by signature place-names,[42] his dialogue makes sustainable relationships between production and consumption materially visible. Their presence not only suggests a remedy for wartime dearth and disease, but also advertises the community's ecological resilience to the severe weather alluded to throughout both parts of *Henry IV*.[43] Asked, for example, about using the hade (Quarto text) or head (Folio text) land, Shallow tells Davy to sow it with 'red wheat'. The Quarto reading refers more precisely to strips of unploughed land between fields. Red or winter wheat was sown in late summer, whereas white or spring wheat is already growing in the fields.[44] Elizabethan audiences who experienced the climatically aggravated subsistence crisis of 1596–97 and the war-scares of the following year (*Henry IV Part Two*, Ind. 12) would have appreciated the implication of no ground being wasted and being put to seasonally productive use.

If the hade has been lying fallow, the discussion of plough-irons also indicates that Shallow has been practising crop rotation. As I discussed in Chapter 2, the georgic principle of conserving biological integrity by allowing the soil to regain 'heart' after intensive cultivation was rediscovered by English husbandry writers such as Hugh Plat and Gervase Markham. Shallow echoes their techniques for boosting farmers' yields and profits in an era of subsistence shortfalls. Yet the husbandry writers' biodynamic advice about local composting and manuring (burlesqued by Falstaff in his paean to sherry [4.3.113–15]) was thwarted by the visitations of saltpetremen serving the interests of national manufacturers and exporters. The official privileging of the gunpowder economy also raised prices for related commodities such as soap ash, which was traditionally used to lime fields and wash clothes but was now in demand to refine raw saltpetre.[45] (The fact that the Fords can afford it for their buckwashing [i.e. bleaching] instead of having to make do with cheaper kinds of soap ash is a further sign of their rising status, and of Shakespeare's eye for the environmental consequences of modern consumption habits in *The Merry Wives of Windsor*.) Iron for cannons also competed with husbandry because arable land was expanded by cutting down woods, and these areas were already being lost at a visibly unsustainable rate (see Chapters 1 and 2). Moreover, centralized agencies such as the Ordnance Office catered to Continental clients by using the power of prerogative patents and Council regulations to contract out military production to a growing network of artisans and merchants. Their transnational interests were at odds with community priorities of feeding residents and surviving severe weather.

In 5.3 a post-prandial Shallow ushers Falstaff and others into his orchard to eat a banquet of local sweetmeats (caraways) and apples (pippins, leathercoats) which he has cultivated himself. This abundance stands in contrast to the barrenness of Shrewsbury's bloody fields (Ind. 24) and Northumberland's orchard (1.1), a space of contrived and actual disease. The only biological activity going on there is the burial of Northumberland's 'hold of ragged stone' by earthworms. Their fertilizing labours are slowly regenerating an ecologically exhausted landscape and converting a stagey theatre-of-war into Gloucestershire's reconstituting bioregionalism, in which the soil and its biota claim a stake with their human co-inhabitants.[46]

Shallow's pride in growing his own food reflects the new wave of gentry interest in national husbandry that was replacing nostalgia for martial chivalry. Leonard Mascall's *A booke of the arte and manner how to plant and graffe all sortes of trees how to sette stones and sow pepins, to make wild trees to graffe on, as also remedies & medicines* (1572)[47] instructed farmers in how to increase varietal resilience by experimenting with hybridization techniques. In *All's Well That Ends Well*, the Countess of Roussillon echoes Mascall's main theme in the course of easing Helen into acknowledging her socially ambitious love for Bertram. She encourages Helen by explaining how grafting improves native plants through the absorption of resilience-enhancing differences:

> 'Tis often seen
> Adoption strives with nature, and choice breeds
> A native slip to us from foreign seeds.   (1.3.144–46)

Touchstone is predictably more ambivalent. He mocks Corin's 'damnable' lack of courtly sophistication by insinuating an argument from grafting in his sardonic cant: 'God help thee, shallow man. God make incision in thee, thou art raw' (*As You Like It*, 3.2.67–68). Shakespeare normally uses 'incision' to signify the surgical mingling of bloods. But here Touchstone imagines Corin as a weak plant which needs to be rejuvenated with a robust cultivar. Rosalind turns grafting against Touchstone when he criticizes Orlando for 'infecting' local trees with his banal verses: 'I'll graft it with you, and then I shall graft it with a meddler' (*As You Like It*, 3.2.113–14, punning on yew/you, and medlar [a type of pear]/meddler). In *Henry IV Part Two*, by contrast, Justice Shallow takes pride in showing off his orchard, 'where, in an arbour, we will eat a last year's pippin of mine own grafting' (5.3.2–3)— that is, when these popularly cultivated apples were healthiest, according to writers such as Thomas Cogan in his widely read *Haven of Health* (1584).[48]

Urban prosperity was also whetting appetites for more varied and better diets. Shallow's locavore menu of chickens, pigeons, mutton, and 'pretty little tiny kickshaws' is modest by gentry standards, but his precise call for short-legged hens reveals a modern interest in breeding improvements. These birds were domesticated for less aggression and more flesh than Bantam chickens, whose more muscular legs made them better for cockfighting, and were prized by the nobility (5.1.23). To be sure, human benefits are the immediate aim of such species variation (farming practices later cited by Darwin to demonstrate historical knowledge of natural selection; compare Shylock's Old Testament story of Laban's sheep-breeding in *The Merchant of Venice*, 1.3.73–87). But like Oliver's farm in *As You Like It*, there is a sense in this pre-industrial setting that both people and animals are cared for and living healthy lives. Within the context of England's early ecological crises, Shallow's neo-georgic practices balance human uses of nature with conservation of its structural integrity.[49]

Eco-cosmopolitanism

While this may be environmentally affirming, the spectacle of old men getting tipsy and swapping tales of their youthful sexual escapades is bound to appear trivial compared to the generational transfer of power at court and Hal's momentous rejection of Falstaff. Shakespeare appears to anticipate today's feelings that heritage farming can appear quaint in relation to the challenges of feeding modern urban masses. Gloucestershire's nostalgic marginality, however, may be Shakespeare's ecological point. Just as Henry V's accession and Falstaff's thousand-pound debt suddenly darken its future, Shallow's community is inescapably impacted by new military industries, trade, and imperial adventurism. Ursula K. Heise argues that this kind of involuntary re-situating of bioregional relations within transnational spheres of resource-use and production is a characteristic effect of 'eco-cosmopolitanism'. This is Heise's environmentally adapted version of cosmopolitanism, an approach towards questions of identity related to physical and imaginary border-crossing. Cosmopolitanism encourages spectators to think beyond compartmentalized cultures, ethnicities, or nations to imagine intersecting global attachments.[50] Until recently, however, cosmopolitanism, like other theories in literary and cultural studies, has concerned itself exclusively with human values. Heise expands the scope of these attachments to include more-than-human habitats and species relations across planetary ecosystems.[51] In *Henry IV Part Two*, emerging mechanized warfare undercuts georgic attempts to heal damage and distance the impacts of globalized modernity.[52]

Bioregional scenarios elsewhere in Shakespeare hint at similar eco-cosmopolitan tensions, beginning with the playwright's first georgic figure. In *Henry VI Part Two*, Alexander Iden's brick-walled garden and small-scale prosperity are conventional signs of Virgil's 'happy man', self-sufficient and detached from the turmoil of metropolitan politics (4.10). But Cade's invasion of his garden suggests Iden is unable to shield himself from authentic ecological problems expressed (in however burlesqued form) by Cade and his protesters: population growth, rising prices, dearth, displacement by new technologies, and the commodification of land and resources. Moreover, violent early modern controversies over tragedies-of-the-commons suggest why the starving Cade is unable to forage even a salad from public land before he desperately breaks into Iden's garden. In his famished state, Cade represents a more desperate version of the impoverished but still surviving Corin in *As You Like It*. Iden's bioregional (and, punningly, Edenic) idyll is nonetheless radically dislocated after he kills Cade and presents his head to the king. Henry commands Iden to join the court's world of factional intrigue and imperial crisis, whose entanglements Iden smugly assumed he could avoid.

War, the environment, and health

Gunpowder militarization also made public health an emerging aspect of eco-cosmopolitan awareness. Andrew Wear has shown how exploration and conquest of New World regions generated comparisons with

English climates and environments. The differences encouraged 'people to articulate their ideas of how to judge whether a [foreign] place was healthy or not', and to distinguish at home between healthy and unhealthy environments, particularly as urbanization and industrialization gathered pace.[53] One new risk to local health and subsistence, as I suggested above, was armament manufacturing's excessive consumption of fuel and food resources. In *Henry IV* their disordering effects are troped by persistent images of countrywide disease and illhealth. As these symptoms intensify in Part Two, Shallow's georgic programme of ecodynamic land-use, agrarian labour, and healthful food illustrates a pragmatic alternative.[54]

Shakespeare calls attention to Gloucestershire's health-restoring effects in a small but telling way when a bibulous Master Silence echoes Falstaff's Eastcheap sentiment, 'now comes in the sweet o'th'night' (2.4.362, 5.3.49–50). In the earlier scene the arrival of Bardolph and a dozen captains cancels Falstaff's anticipated dalliance with Doll. Equally elusive is the prospect of good health in turkey-starved, lame-horse, and coal-burning London. Falstaff's ageing body presents a mosaic of these debilities, and in Part Two they increasingly preoccupy him, beginning with his opening question about the state of his urine, and later in his references to Galen (1.2.1–2, 113–14). Galenic medical theory posited that human bodies composed of the four physical humours were susceptible to corresponding environmental influences such as locally ingested foods and ambient weather. Mary Floyd-Wilson describes this process of physiological exchange as 'geo-humoralism'.[55] Like the symbolic order of the body politic, both natural and political bodies needed to be kept in balance by disciplined consumption and controlled exposure to changeable environments.[56] In the light of these beliefs, it may at first seem odd that King Henry and Warwick should propose war as a means of restoring the country's health:

> HENRY
> Then you perceive the body of our kingdom,
> How foul it is, what rank diseases grow...
> WARWICK
> It is but as a body yet distempered,

Which to his former strength may be restored
With good advice and little medicine.
(*Henry IV Part Two*, 3.1.37–42)[57]

Their therapeutic reasoning is related to the cultural assumption that war will end naturally in a return to cultivation, but it comes from the other end of the homeopathic cycle. According to classical theories of war, extended periods of peace were thought to engender overconsumption and corruption which need to be corrected by blood-letting. George Gascoigne's 1575 poem *The Fruits of Warre* described the full circle as: 'Plentie brings pryde, pryde plea [i.e. quarrel], plea pine [i.e. war], pine peace, / Peace plenty, and so (say they) they never cease' (142[58]). Gascoigne's 'say they' alludes to classical writers such as Virgil, whose *Georgics* celebrates the peace-and-plenty phase after the epic 'pining' is over.[59] In sociable conversation with a passing Captain, Hamlet blandly refers to this commonplace as an explanation for Fortinbras's Polish aggression. But later in his 'How all occasions do inform against me' soliloquy, he privately questions it (Q2 *Hamlet*, 4.4.24ff). Falstaff typically parrots the idea to evade the Chief Justice's accusations (*Henry IV Part Two*, 1.2.71–73, 202). When it occurs elsewhere in Shakespeare, it is always in ironic military settings.[60]

Like Hamlet, Gascoigne dissented from traditional theories of self-balancing war based on Galenic homeopathy, but in his case owing to direct experience of modern warfare in the Netherlands. He recorded its horrors first in *The Fruits of Warre*, and then in his most influential news pamphlet, *The Spoyle of Antwerp* (1576). These writings described in graphic detail the destruction of people, animals, and environments during the notorious Spanish attack.[61] Gascoigne's war publications represented a new generation of eye-witness reports of gunpowder's calamitous levels of destruction. As Elizabethan England became more deeply embroiled in increasingly expensive and deadly wars in Normandy, Ireland, and the Netherlands, printed news galvanized resistance to enforced enlistment, as did the spectacle of mutilated and disabled men returning home. In *Pericles*, Bolt speaks from these conditions when he defends his job as a pimp as a rational alternative to becoming a soldier: 'What would you [Marina] have me do? Go to the wars ... where a man may serve seven years for the loss of a leg, and not have money enough in the end to buy him a wooden one?' (*Pericles*, 19.218–21).

Shakespeare alluded to certain passages in *The Spoyle of Antwerp* in both *The First Part of the Contention* (later *Henry VI Part Two*) and *Henry IV Part Two*,[62] and he also echoes Gascoigne's discomfort with justifying the anarchic cruelty and devastation he saw as providentially ordained ('War is [God's] beadle. War is his vengeance' [*Henry V*, 4.1.161–62)]. Whereas Williams and Bates critique Henry V's refusal to accept personal responsibility for his soldiers' deaths in battle, Gascoigne focuses on war's impersonal hostility to public welfare. Employing *occupatio* (wherein a subject is raised by denying it is being mentioned) to avoid the impression of sensationalizing, he argues that mechanized war has become a disproportionate therapy for 'effeminizing' peace:

I set not down the ugly and filthy polluting of every street with the gore and the carcasses of men and horses; neither do I complain that the one lacked burial, and the other fleeing until the air, corrupted with their carrion, infected all that remained alive in the town.   (C1r-v)

In contrast to Gascoigne, Henry V opportunistically threatens to turn this kind of miasma into a biological weapon:

> And those that leave their valiant bones in France,
> Dying like men, though buried in your dunghills
>   ... there the sun shall greet them
> And draw their honours reeking up to heaven,
> Leaving their earthly parts to choke your clime,
> The smell whereof shall breed a plague in France.
>   (4.3.99–104)[63]

Just as the indiscriminate effects of cannon slaughter threatened by Henry and reported by Gascoigne destroyed natural and built environments, resource degradation by gunpowder manufacturing undercut both the Virgilian ecology of war and the Augustinian theory of its morally chastening effects. Industrial militarization denatured traditional theories of catastrophe and regeneration, while opening up an urgent need for new ecological thinking.

Henry IV Part Two contributes to this process by asking questions and imagining alternatives. Falstaff's pre-tragedy before Henry V's public rejection may be his half-conscious recognition of the health-restoring effects of georgic humoralism. Like the play's military satire, this aspect of Gloucestershire's bioregionalism plays out on the comic-topical edges of the play's main political narrative. Falstaff's registers his intimations of Gloucestershire's regenerating powers at a distance, beginning with a series of choric prose commentaries. He condescendingly admires Shallow's upward mobility as an Elizabethan new man, now rich in 'land and beeves', which he promises to 'snap at' according to a Hobbesian 'law of nature' when he returns (3.2.312–16). But once back in Gloucestershire this superior attitude seems to vanish. He allows himself to become captive to Shallow's provincial hospitality and rustic dialogues with Davy, which he predictably mocks after they exit. Reducing their labours to the herd instincts of geese, he opines that 'It is certain that either wise bearing or ignorant carriage is caught as men take diseases' (5.1.67–68). Yet Shallow's unified and vigorous community stands in contrast to the subjective fears and destined extinction as cannon fodder that Falstaff imposes on local husbandmen. Consistent with his own Galenist outlook, Falstaff's physical being is contingent upon his environmental circumstances.

Our sense that Falstaff's outspokenness is somewhat muted by his position as Shallow's guest may also alert us to his susceptibility to Gloucestershire's thriving community. Because localities were thought to be humorally active, they could sympathetically transform porous living bodies. Falstaff ingests this possibility with Shallow's supper and dessert; temporarily, they graft him into Gloucestershire's bio-relations of soil, plants, and animals. His brief transformation perhaps explains the unexpected sincerity of his reply to Silence's 'sweetest morsel of the night'. Falstaff answers not with a jesting aside but a pledge of 'health and long life', which he and the company repeat—perhaps not just drunkenly—during their merry-making. Dramatically, their healths recast the hollow pledges of Prince John and the rebels in royally compromised Galtres Forest (4.1.298–335; see Chapter 1). In Gloucestershire, progressive images of agrarian well-being and sustainable prosperity briefly ring true because stewardship is in tune with seasonal rhythms.[64] The confrontation in Galtres, however, foreshadows the unstoppable changes of political and environmental modernity. The wistfulness of Shallow's community registers the passing of a traditional refuge in the face of the emerging negative effects of eco-cosmopolitanism.

In his classic manifesto, *Dwellers in the Land* (1979), Kirkpatrick Sale presents a neo-georgic vision of bottom-up liberation from distant, impersonal forces of 'agropolitan culture'. Shakespeare's Gloucestershire anticipates both Sale's bioregional response and subsequent ecocritical scepticism about this still sentimentally valued vision in a global domain of metropolitan values. *Henry IV Part Two* recognizes that provincial self-sufficiency cannot fully insulate people or ecosystems, because localism is not a privileged standard of ecological value (any more than globalism). When Pistol arrives with news of Henry V's reign, Shallow's incomprehension suggests a localism overwhelmed by deterritorializing forces it has avoided coming to grips with. Their immediate vanguard is Henry's gunpowder diplomacy and French resource appropriation by 'civil swords and native fire[power]' (*Henry IV Part Two*, 4.3.343–45, 5.5.104). They signal a familiar modern outsourcing of militarization's exorbitant carrying capacity.

Although Shallow's eco-localism remained more viable during England's first steps towards industrialization than it became in later centuries, it has already become an unwilling player in the environmental wagers of modern progress. Earlier in *Henry IV Part Two*, Bardolph predicts the rebels' chances of success after their losses at Shrewsbury in similar terms, except that he sees them even more wedded to the new irrational calculus of environmental risk for the sake of profitable gain:

> We all that are engagèd to this loss
> Knew what we ventured on such dangerous seas
> That if we wrought out life 'twas ten to one;
> And yet we ventured for the gain proposed,
> Choked the respect of likely peril feared,
> And since we are o'erset, venture again.   (1.1.179–85)

Bardolph's metaphor captures the early modern transition from traditional to reflexive risk. The dangers of shipwreck are natural because the earth's powers are recognized as being more powerful than humans' ability to control them; whereas the risks of gunpowder-enhanced warfare exemplified by Hotspur and Hal's generation are tolerated because they nurture dreams of conquering the world.[65]

The rise of gunpowder exploded classical theories of a naturally recurring alternation between swords and ploughshares. Resource consumption by armament manufacturing began to have similar effects on the environment and agrarian economies, albeit at a slower pace, as the destruction of war itself. It likewise upended promises of peacetime prosperity and security that traditionally justified wartime expenditures. Unintentionally, however, the ruin and displacements caused by gunpowder manufacturing in a globalizing marketplace also generated new ecological insights: that natural resources are finite; that excessive growth in one area (e.g. cannons and gunpowder) has negative environmental and social consequences in other areas (soil integrity, farming, and subsistence); that boundaries between resource-exploiting industries are not discrete but overlapping; that modern rates of consumption and production are interdependent on local, national, and global levels; and that structural conservation of the natural world and sustainable uses are essential to long-term public health and ecological resilience.

Gunpowder's darkening reputation as an aspect of European genius eventually led cultural theorists to expel it from the company of printing, compass navigation, and other inventions by the mid-seventeenth century.[66] Shakespeare's plays contributed to this rejection by connecting the grotesque glamour of 'seeking the bubble reputation in the cannon's mouth' to gunpowder's disruption of traditional ecologies of dwelling and well-being. In the second part of this chapter, I turn to *Macbeth* to explore how it associates these epochal and potentially catastrophic changes with the ingrained violence of Scotland's militarized culture.

'What visionary poet will lament vile, bloody-fingered dawn?'

Reporting the latest state of Scotland's wars early in *Macbeth*, the bleeding Sergeant compares Banquo and Macbeth's fury in repelling a Norwegian invasion to 'cannons overcharged with double cracks, / So they doubly redoubled strokes upon the foe' (1.2.37–38).[67] Earlier in his report, the Sergeant praises Macbeth as 'Valour's minion' (1.2.19). As Harry Berger pointed out in a seminal essay on the endemic violence of Duncan's Scotland, 'minion' refers to a culverin, or small cannon, as well as a favourite.[68] Like 'doubly redoubled', the Sergeant implies that Macbeth has become a martial cyborg, physically transformed by the mechanical rhythms of gunpowder warfare.

Duncan recognizes the ecological dangers of this violence. Presenting himself as the nation's good farmer, he vows to restore Scotland's productive fertility by 'planting' Macbeth to 'make [him] full of growing' (1.4.29–30). By taking Scotland's native ethos of competitive violence to gunpowder levels of aggression, however, Macbeth cuts off expectations of remedial cultivation. At mid-play, an unnamed Lord reintroduces these hopes:

> ... we may again
> Give to our tables meat, sleep to our nights,
> Free from our feasts and banquets bloody knives ...
> All which we pine for now.   (3.6.33–39)

And after defeating Macbeth and making promises similar to Duncan's, Malcolm seems to pick up where the latter left off: 'What's more to do / Which would be planted newly with the time...' (*Macbeth*, 5.7.94–95). Whether Malcolm will follow through depends partly on how we interpret his use of Birnam Wood and its contextual environmental ethics (of which more towards the conclusion of this chapter).

In a fine early ecocritical reading of *Macbeth*, Robert N. Watson argued that the play's metaphors of seasonal and generational renewal converge on Birnam as a 'heliotrope' of regenerative nature.[69] Whereas the Macbeths presume they can evade natural cycles which model familial and political orders, their opponents cooperate with such patterns to restore Scotland's lost organic unity. The premise of Watson's and other redemptive readings of Shakespeare's tragedy is that Macbeth's regicide represents an exceptional violation of cosmic myths and transcendent justice which normally validate social hierarchies and the rule of law. Preternatural screams, reports of horses eating each other, and other uncanny portents register the natural world's presumed outrage at the Macbeths' offenses. Macduff's and Malcolm's heroic vengeance ultimately reverses their breaches of nature.

Certain modern directors and critics, however, have questioned whether the Macbeths' dystopic violence has not been shaped more by Scotland's warrior culture than their personal demonic impulses. If Scotland's violence is seen to be culturally fixed and socially determining, its condition becomes homologous with the new reflexive risks of human and environmental disaster introduced by early modern gun-powder technologies and industrial militarization. Muriel Bradbrook was perhaps the first to observe that Macbeth's regicide and overthrow were typical of Scotland's monoculture of feudal rebellion and murder before and after the events represented by Shakespeare.[70] This polit-ical reality coincided, as Watson notes, with the deforestation of Scotland, including the royal forest of Birnam. Holinshed draws attention to Macbeth's overexploitation of the realm's resources and impoverishment of the nobility in his description of the extravagant building of Dunsinane Castle. Shakespeare shifts the emblem of his regime's excessive footprint to gunpowder. By relating military and environmental histories, Shakespeare opens possibilities of reading *Macbeth* ecocritically as a non-redemptive tragedy about long-term degradation of human and natural environments by militarized nation-states.

Roman Polanski's 1971 film points in these directions. Working with Kenneth Tynan's screenplay of Shakespeare's text, Polanski pre-sents the Macbeths not as uniquely evil albeit fascinating deviants, but as young and attractive representatives of Scotland's subjective culture of violence. Through graphic depictions of Macbeth's mechanized reflexes in killing Duncan, and Scotland's unconscious cruelty towards non-human animals, Polanski suggests that a new horizon of gun-powder warfare—imaginatively associated with the nuclear threats of the 1960s and '70s—destabilizes tragedy's traditional hopes of restor-ing 'measure, time, and place' through peacetime cultivation. The film ends famously with Donalbain seeking out the witches and presump-tively becoming the next Macbeth. Polanski thereby suggests that the normal alternation of war and peace is stuck in a self-destructive feedback loop. Although Polanski and Tynan's ending is an adapta-tion, its realism is supported by Shakespeare's continually blurred lines between authorized and deviant violence. These are categorical con-fusions that the equivocating Malcolm, and Macduff's 'industrious soldiership', seem unlikely to clarify.

Harry Berger substantiated this anti-Romantic interpretation with close readings of the ambiguous language of war in the play's early scenes. Like Polanski's film, his work implicitly suggests an ecological as well as ethical crisis at the heart of Scottish society. '[O]f the revolt / The newest state' suggests the beating of swords into ploughshares has been indefinitely postponed (1.2.2–3). The 'Strange images of death' Macbeth carves on the battlefield likewise 'palter in a double sense' to hint at such violence being redirected against Duncan. Macbeth's 'unseaming' of Macdonald 'from the nave to th'chops' eerily anticipates the news of Macduff's 'Untimely ripped' birth. Watson argues that Macduff's heroic correction of Macbeth's tyranny is attributable to their shared 'Caesarian' associations. They suggest Macduff carries a taint of ontological ambivalence that enables him homeopathically to drive out the larger corruption. Conversely, as Polanski's and Berger's focus on the irrepressible impulses of Scotland's warrior-thanes suggests (Ross in particular), Macbeth's infection is not isolated but viral. It may not be purged by the dissembling equivocations of the anglicizing Malcolm. Like Duncan's rule (and Richard III's and King John's before him), Malcolm's regime will be founded on coercive bloodshed and therefore open to future challenges—as in history was his rule and that of his successors. The deeper threat of Macbeth's regicide is to expose the nobility's lack of any serious alternative to Scotland's ecocidal polity.

That this culture seems unlikely to be reformed after Macbeth is overthrown is further suggested by the victors' praise for 'Seyward's son' and 'many unrough youths that even now / Protest their first of manhood' (5.2.9–11). Like Hal fighting at Shrewsbury in *Henry IV Part One*, rites-of-blood signal the younger generation's entry into a renewed order of martial competitiveness that calls into question their sublimation of ambitions into peacetime cooperation. Seyward's stoical reaction to his son's battlefield sacrifice affirms their legacy.[71] Although subsequent images of sickness and purging conventionally signal Macduff and his comrades' curtailing of the country's excesses (5.2.27–29), the play's representations of destroyed natural and human environments, combined with the arrival of Malcolm's foreign troops, indicates that warfare will continue to denature Scotland.

Enter three ...

Among modern authors writing about the end of conventional assumptions about nature caused by manmade changes to global environments, Michel Serres's work is suggestive for war and ecology in *Macbeth* because of his theatrical analogies. Serres observes that the

West has traditionally treated the natural world as a 'stage backdrop', or 'theatre of war', for its pursuit of technological progress through militarization. The subjected environment becomes a common enemy of unspoken military protocols between human competitors. The Captain's report of the battle between Macbeth and Macdonald hints at a re-materialization of this third-party axis:

> Doubtful it stood,
> As two spent swimmers that do cling together
> And choke their art.   (1.2.7–9)

The combatants are so caught up in their competitive violence that they 'forget' they are immersed in a physical entity that will overreach their efforts to dominate each other unless they respect it. Five hundred years after the emergence of gunpowder armaments and the related shift to a fossil-fuel economy, nature is no longer passive but elementally furious at modernity's obsession with endless growth and its mindless abuse of the planet and non-human species. When these unconscious outrages violate biospheric laws to the point where conventional nature has ended and 'nothing is / But what is not' (1.3.142–43), the earth's primordial interdependence pushes back, re-territorializing human history.[72] As Serres puts it: 'We've reached the end point of growth ... when ... objective [or environmental] violence, which is tragic in a new way ... involuntarily, replaces the useless vanity of [human] subjective wars, which ... multiply their devastation in longing pursuit of decisive victory'.[73] Oceans warming, habitats disappearing, and catastrophic typhoons, hurricanes, and ice-storms have become the planet's way of staging a global alienation effect.

Rachel Carson gave mid-twentieth-century readers a new way of recognizing this structural level of ecological disaster by demonstrating that civil offshoots of Second World War weapons manufacturing had released massive levels of pesticides and carcinogens into the biosphere and destroyed traditional farming practices (*Silent Spring*, 1962). The malignant effects of these presumed advances went unnoticed or seemed containable under complicit political oversight until Carson and other early environmentalists outed them. The Weird Sisters stage a similar ecocritique in *Macbeth*. Although their identity as real or mythical figures has been endlessly debated,[74] in one form or another the Weird Sisters have always represented a feminized threat to masculine dominance over the natural world. I want to suggest that the Weird Sisters materialize mechanized war's rampant destruction of the earth and its derangement of human subjectivities. In doing so they perform nature's third-party protest against the deformed ecologies of gunpowder warfare, which, as I have been suggesting in this chapter, serves as Shakespeare's trope for wider environmental dangers of early modernity, as well as an ecological meta-commentary on his plays' political conflicts. This dramatic project subverts traditional assumptions about the Weird Sisters' demonic origins in ways that parallel the defiance of Carson's chilling but accurate research against attacks on her as a female scientist questioning the benefits of the American military-industrial complex. Like Carson, the Weird Sisters' shows disrupt the human–nature dualisms of Western progress and startle audiences into a new awareness of imminent planetary extinctions.

Stirring the environmental pot

The Sisters' famous riddling chants and verbal enigmas establish a rationally estranging discourse[75] which opens imaginative space for a deep ecological equation between war's human losses and its abuses of non-human life and physical landscapes. Their 'thunder and lightening' hurly-burlys manmade and natural meteorological calamities. In early modern usage 'thunder' and 'lightning' doubled for the boom and flash of gunpowder weapons. The Jacobean stage enlivened these associations by using squibs to produce stage noise and fog. In his discussion of how the sound and smell of theatrical gunpowder insinuated historical memories into contemporary consciousness, Jonathan Gil Harris argues that the sulphurous cracks of *Macbeth*'s opening scene would have triggered transtemporal associations with outlawed Catholic theatre, the Gunpowder Plot, and other 'fair and foul' events.

Multi-temporality can also contemporize associations. When the Captain compares Macbeth and Banquo to overcharged cannons, the lingering whiff of stage gunpowder might have stimulated connections between Scotland's deep-sticking warrior culture and the ecological ruptures of emerging munitions industries. As we have seen, these included state-sponsored manufacturing of saltpetre in England and other European countries. But the Weird Sisters' pungent show of fiery sounds also modulates the environmental criticism of *Henry IV* and *Henry V* to a new level of eco-remonstrance. Their elemental associations suggest that global nature is invading the domain of transnational armament competition, as when the Captain later reports that 'Shipwrecking storms and direful thunders' follow Macbeth's smoking and bloody execution against Cawdor and the Norwegians (1.2.18, 26–28).

The Weird Sisters' appearances in gunpowder-spiked 'filthy air' likewise points to destabilized human and natural fault lines. Commentators tend to assume the Sisters are referring to some typical Scottish weather.[76] But the other context in which Shakespeare uses the word 'filthy', *Henry V*, is also an extreme battlefield environment (*Henry V*, 3.3.111). Both sites are thick with air-borne contagion from putrefying animal and human body parts, which in *Macbeth* the Weird Sisters ostentatiously display (4.1.12–38). Their 'filthy witnesses' spread through Macbeth's first-hand letter to his wife, infecting her with the viral incitements of Duncan's murder, and 'incarnadining' their entire worldview (2.2.46, 61–62).

Conventionally, the Weird Sisters' grotesque cookery is understood to be whetting ambitions for worldly power. It is worth remembering, however, that the play's on- and off-stage spectators do not see the Sisters act in any violent way. This allows for the possibility of understanding their incantations not as recipes for malice but as inventories of early modern and present-day military conflicts:

> Round about the cauldron go,
> In the poisoned entrails throw.
> … Eye of newt and toe of frog,
> Wool of bat, and tongue of dog…
>   Nose of Turk, and Tartar's lips …. (4.1.4–5, 14–15, 29)

Gleaning and recycling the global reflux of competitive state violence, the Weird Sisters perform dark invoices of bio-accountability. Items such as rats without tails seem to anticipate the physical mutations that Rachel Carson linked to the effects of DDT (1.3.8). The horizon of extinctions encoded by their ecological reckoning supersedes classical limits of therapeutic war alternating with bioregional cultivation. It also exposes the theatre's complacent presentation of the natural world as a backdrop for gunpowder-enhanced heroism, marketed as urban entertainment.

The Weird Sisters' story of the shipwrecked Sailor and his Wife varies their shows with a cautionary tragedy of ecological hubris, again associated with gunpowder manufacturing. Aleppo was a major entre-pôt for saltpetre from Bengal. Over the seventeenth-century India took over as the major outsource for European gunpowder-makers because of the NIMBY problem (i.e. 'not-in-my-backyard': new land-uses opposed by local residents because of their environmental haz-ards) of domestic production. This overseas relationship possibly explains why the husband is more cruelly punished than his chest-nut-hoarding wife. His profitable trading in Indian saltpetre, and possibly other spoils of South Asian imperialism, have evidently kept her well fed at home. The Weird Sisters refigure the ecological optics of the couple's consumption: the sailor's age-of-discovery journey shrinks to a 'fragile niche' from which there is no possibility of withdrawal or escape from hurricane-force winds. The Weird Sisters thus rescale the Sailor's commercial ambitions within clashing envir-onmental worldviews, anthropocentric and biospheric.[77] Only one is sovereign, and its lessons can be harsh. The Sailor's elliptical misfor-tune fills in the dots between Europe's expanding *matériel* culture and his Wife's obliviousness to stuffing herself in a physically finite and increasingly overexploited world. Moreover, as 'Posters of the sea and land', the Weird Sisters draw attention to human and non-human bio-relations as negotiated choices. The Witches exemplify this vision by identifying easily with both domestic and wild species ('I come Graymalkin. / Paddock calls' [1.1.8–9]). They mediate the dynamic tensions between Scotland's deterritorializing war culture and the natural world which materially supports but ultimately transcends it. As emissaries of global nature ('All the quarters . . . / I'th'shipman's card') they exercise the capacity to drain dry the overflows of human ambition, as the tempest-tossed Macbeth discovers when he exceeds its earthly afforded boundaries (3.4.20–25).

Had he heard it, one feels Banquo might have understood the Weird Sisters' ecological allegory. Although the Captain links him to Scotland's proto-mechanizing warfare with Macbeth, Banquo understands that the earth is a ball of animate physical properties which can overmaster human desires: 'The earth hath bubbles, as the water has, / And these are of them' (1.3.79–80). In his sceptical distance from the Weird Sisters, Banquo catches glimpses of future disasters originating in Scotland's militarized culture, Macbeth's rivers of blood, and environmental nemesis: 'There's husbandry in Heaven, / Their candles are all out' (2.1.5–6). Macduff, by contrast, reads the murder's aftermath in terms of a traditional ethos of providential retribution:

> . . . each new morn
> New widows howl, new orphans cry, new sorrows
> Strike Heaven on the face, that it resounds
> As if it felt with Scotland, and yelled out
> Like syllable of dolour. (4.3.4–8)

Interpreting this outcry from the geo-physical perspective of the Weird Sisters, however, one might question its call to restore a transcendent ideal of cosmic balance through righteous vengeance. It could suggest the planet's reflexive amplifying of war's ruptures which heralds an environmental threat to all of Scotland's mutually choking warriors. Although Macbeth is conscious of this threshold crisis,

> I am in blood
> Stepped in so far, that should I wade no more,
> Returning were as tedious as go o'er (3.4.137–39)

he cannot stop consuming human and natural capital in striving against nature's slower-evolving changes.[78] To recall Michel Serres again, Macbeth's dagger of the mind is the thinking of the parasite who ravens up life by following 'a flow moving [only] in one direction'.[79]

Even though they are formally absent from the ending of the play, the Weird Sisters' 'strange intelligence' frames our understanding of its final scenes to suggest why Scotland may not escape its ecocidal destiny by scapegoating the Macbeths. The ambivalent violence of Malcolm's accession unsettles the idealizing tropes of a natural transition to peacetime equilibrium. Like the fate of Richard's famous horse in *Richard III*, Scotland's destruction of non-human life and physical landscapes remains merely 'collateral' in the minds of its survivors.

In this respect Malcolm's use of Birnam Wood seems to cut both ways. Traditionally, his use of forest boughs as camouflage suggests that providentially ordered nature authorizes human retaliation against the Macbeths' desecrations. As Robert Pogue Harrison puts it, 'the moving forest of Birnam comes to symbolize the forces of natural law mobilizing its justice against the moral wasteland of Macbeth's nature'.[80] *Richard III* presented an earlier scenario for this redemptive retaliation when the grieving widows in Act Four and the ghosts of Act Five seem to channel their wrath through Richmond's tide-turning victory at Bosworth. In *Macbeth* the Weird Sisters' outrage might be similarly devolved onto Macduff, Malcolm, and Banquo's descendants as the agents of an environmental turn away from Scotland's militarized culture with the cooperation of their English allies. Its pacific icon would be the Weird Sister's last apparition of '*a child crowned, with a tree in his hand*' (4.1.100 SD).

In keeping with this outlook, Malcolm's order to cut only 'a bough' from Birnam's trees indicates limited rational use rather than clear-cutting (5.4.4–5). His borrowings from nature may remain within the sustainable limits of the natural cycles Robert Watson identifies. Moreover, the Messenger's description of the rebels' army as 'a moving grove' (5.5.38) suggests the re-establishment of a renewable woodland economy which anticipates Malcolm's final promises to rebalance military drawdowns through sustainable husbandry. Malcolm might therefore be seen as a kind of conservation biologist in Birnam, making a necessary but controlled intervention to regenerate a landscape that has been savagely degraded by Macbeth's violence. Although he does not qualify as a deep ecologist, Malcolm could be said to exemplify a reform environmentalism which aims to ameliorate excessive human disturbances. In this reading of Birnam Wood, Malcolm and his English allies might also analogize the kind of multilateral cooperation needed today to prevent crossing the mid-century 2°C threshold into extreme disorder predicted by the researchers of 2013 report of the Intergovernmental Panel on Climate Change. In Chapter 4, I shall read *Cymbeline* along these more hopeful lines as a story of transnational cooperation and environmental altruism.

In Macbeth's time, on the other hand, Birnam Wood was a royal domain. Like Windsor Forest in *The Merry Wives of Windsor*, this status placed it outside the jurisdiction of the common law. Owing to this legal anomaly, as Robert Pogue Harrison has shown, royal forests are associated in literary history with vigilantism and outlawry, which were the dark obverse of the monarch's absolute power. From this perspective Malcolm's chopped and discarded boughs may signal the continuation of Scotland's culture of belligerence towards nature, which resulted in Birnam's and Scotland's deforestation. Polanski and Tynan's film invites such a reading by showing Malcolm's soldiers hacking down whole young trees, thereby suggesting, along with Young Seyward's death, that generational renewal is not returning to Scotland anytime soon. And in his allusions to gunpowder warfare, as I have argued, Shakespeare suggests the country's history of progress seems to be defined more by emerging horizons of technologically enhanced conquest than by environmental reciprocity. Absent reliable signs of such cultural change, Scotland stands as it did, its militarized sorrows ecologically rooted rather than regenerated.

Biospheric Ecologies in Cymbeline

> I'th'world's volume
> Our Britain seems as of it but not in't,
> In a great pool a swan's nest.   (3.4.138–40)

Cymbeline makes a theatrical virtue of continually echoing dialogue and scenarios from Shakespeare's previous plays. Earlier critics were doubtful about this recycling, wondering whether Shakespeare was not falling back on re-runs to make up for failing inventiveness towards the end of his career. These opinions tended to overlook his return to writers such as Boccaccio and Holinshed for fresh material, as well as his projection of personal conflict into new geographic contexts, in the manner of *All's Well That Ends Well* and his other late romances. Modern stage productions have capitalized on these signs of imaginative vigour, however, by embracing *Cymbeline*'s retrospective recreation as cheeky, knowing humour, particularly in the final scene of over-packed revelations and entwining narratives.

Cymbeline's multiple storylines create a polygeneric experience characteristic of Shakespeare's plays in general and his romances in particular. Steve Mentz has observed that *Cymbeline* and other 'polyglot' romances are well suited to staging modern narratives about the natural world's tendencies to interdependence, adaptation, and biodiversity.[1] Every main character in *Cymbeline* has his or her own environmental attachments (e.g. Innogen and Britain, Giacomo and Italy, Lucius and the Roman empire, Cymbeline and 'Lud's Town', Belarius, Arviragus, Guiderius and Wales, Posthumus and Milford

Haven).[2] Each of these place-identities represents a different physical and cultural worldview, so when they shift and/or interweave, they suggest dynamic networks operating at multiple levels of planetary space and time.[3] These webbed relations raise modern questions of environmental ethics and practice. Which plane of ecological relations suggests the best way of dwelling responsibly in the world? Which life-challenge might analogize a resolve to reduce excessive consumption and reverse human harm? (e.g. cultivating the local allotment garden? travelling to fewer conferences? preserving boreal forests?).

Following trends in postmodern and postcolonial studies, ecotheorists observe that environmentalism has tended to privilege local attachments and modes of dwelling as the common ground for resistance to degrading forces of economic globalization.[4] Pioneering ecocritic Jonathan Bate, for example, celebrated regional and village-focused writers such as William Wordsworth and John Clare.[5] By contrast, Lawrence Buell, Ursula K. Heise, and Timothy Clark all question the priority of locally based models of understanding as either incipiently essentializing or too narrowly focused to address problems such as climate change and deforestation that transcend local concerns and national boundaries. Their point is not to discount the value of the local (which, as I have tried to show in earlier chapters, was a transformative reference point in Shakespeare's age and continues to be a necessary ecological paradigm), but to integrate it meaningfully within nested scales of environmental relations. As the Sierra Club's slogan originally captured it: 'Think globally, act locally'.[6]

This has proved to be more easily said than done. Global interactions, Heise observes, are not normally experienced directly like day-to-day relationships. They are known through cultural media and technological representation. One such platform for conceptual world-making in the early modern period was the new science of cartography. Its impact on Shakespeare's geographic imagination is reflected in a range of allusions to New World maps and regions (e.g. *Twelfth Night*, 3.2.73–74). The equivalent technologies today are digital tools such as Google Earth. Scalable images of shrinking ozone layers, polar ice sheets, and global woodland expand our environmental awareness beyond personal experience, opening minds and hearts to shared responsibilities for planetary well-being.[7]

In Shakespeare's time a complementary vehicle for world-making was the London playhouse;[8] and from *Cymbeline*'s original performances we have suggestive evidence of the theatre's ability to generate eco-cosmopolitan consciousness. (Eco-cosmopolitanism, as I mentioned in Chapter 3, is Heise's term for the modern condition of cultural and environmental exchange across local and national borders; chapter 3 pp. 94–5.) Simon Forman recorded his impressions of a performance of *Cymbeline* on 8 September 1611, probably at The Globe theatre. They included details of the historical dispute between Rome and Britain over the payment of tribute, and of the romance wager that grows out of the worldly banter in Philario's house in Italy, before shifting to urban London and back again to Italy with Giacomo. From a performance without mimetic scenery, Forman looked out through his mind's eye to Belarius's mountain cave, Welsh woods and fauna, and Milford Haven as a portal to British, European, and classical worlds. Implicitly these sites related Forman's London reality to their environmental and historical diversity.[9] As with other playhouse accounts by Forman, we would love to know more about this performance of *Cymbeline* and what he thought of it. Although we cannot be certain to what extent his environmental self-awareness was affected, we can infer from The Globe's stage mediation that he perceived connections among the play's dramatically embodied geographical identities. This meant seeing the 'global' ecologies of imperial Rome working through the thoughts and behaviours of ancient Britons, and these bio- and cultural relations working further into London urban and Welsh rural landscapes. Simultaneously, *Cymbeline*'s Welsh and British energies radiate outwards to France and Rome. Shakespeare's structural mechanism for making this environmental interdependence 'visible' is the nested design of *Cymbeline*'s far-flung stories and mobile characters. In spatial terms, their interfitted structures may in some ways resemble a hierarchy, like a descending array of Russian dolls, or the pyramid model of a terrestrial food web (a few carnivores at top, lots of plants, worms, and insects at the bottom). But in ecological terms the relationships are horizontalized ones of competitive and cooperative exchanges.[10] There is no difference in biological priority or evolutionary value. A wren's eye in Wales is as precious as a lion's whelp in Rome.

Nested patterns are familiar to biologists and ecologists but new to ecocritical discussions of Shakespeare. In this chapter they will serve as

my ecocritical framework for exploring *Cymbeline*'s transnational relations. I shall begin by examining the play's antitype of cosmopolitanism: the artificially compartmentalized ecology of Cymbeline's court.
By suppressing biological and cultural diversity, Cymbeline and his
Queen simultaneously weaken England's resilience and increase its
vulnerability to regime change and extinctions. The middle sections of
this chapter will shift attention to the play's Welsh scenes. There I will
return to James Gibson's idea of ecological affordance, while also
revisiting one prominent Shakespearian scenario that *Cymbeline*
recycles from *King Lear* and several other plays explored in this
book: the reshaping of inner identities by lively contact with local
environments which encode woodland, neo-georgic, and/or bioregional relations. The daily life of Belarius, Arviragus, and Guiderius
in Wales converges all these modes of dwelling. In keeping with the
wider horizons of Shakespeare's romances, however, as well as his
earlier explorations of bioregionalism in *As You Like It* and the English
histories, *Cymbeline* reveals both the environmental virtues and the
provincial limitations of an 'ethics of proximity'.[11] As *Cymbeline*'s
dispersed personal trajectories reconnect at the international cross-
roads of Milford Haven, British and Roman worldviews re-engage
through the environmentally afforded victories of Posthumus and his
Welsh comrades, and the transformative encounter between Innogen
and Lucius. *Cymbeline*'s final reconciliations reintegrate these individuals and their environmental identities in a multipolar world. The
political and environmental altruism of the play's ending is suggestive
of today's need to merge regional and national interests with multilateral political action to avert global dangers such as rising sea levels and
eroding biodiversity.[12]

Bad farming

Cymbeline begins in the middle of an ecological as well as a dynastic
crisis. The King's banishment of Posthumus and persecution of his
daughter Innogen after their unauthorized marriage disrupts the process of peacetime regeneration which followed Britain's earlier war
with Rome. The play's opening images of cultivation bring into focus
Cymbeline's suppression of fertility that reflects the kingdom's reversion to a regime of exploitation. The First Gentleman recalls how the

king initially cared for the orphaned Posthumus by giving him 'all the learnings that his time / Could make him receiver of', so that 'in's spring became a harvest' (1.1.43–46). The education-as-husbandry metaphor suggests that a vital relationship between cultural memory and productive agriculture has been broken. Cymbeline must redis-cover this logic to put the country's prosperity back on a sustainable footing and fulfil his closing promise of 'peace and plenty' (5.3.459).

The Gentleman also tells us how Cymbeline's former generosity towards Posthumus sought to enrich the court's experiential capital— and now, we might add, the health of its gene pool—by integrating people from diverse social backgrounds and environments. By doing so Cymbeline continued the inclusive traditions of his father, Cassibelan, who befriended Posthumus's father Sicilius Leonatus after they had fought as enemies. In her psychoanalytical reading of the play, Cop-pélia Kahn observes that Cymbeline formerly acknowledged the desir-ability of balancing masculine-constituting rivalry with co-dependent emulation of his Roman opponents. The collective identity of the older generation—Cymbeline, Sicilius, Cornelius, Belarius, and pos-sibly Pisanio—has been shaped by grafting Roman technology and civil values onto British strength and resourcefulness.[13] The richness of this social fabric implies that Britain also fortified its ecological resilience by cultivating biodiversity. Resilience is the structural capacity of an ecosystem to absorb and recover from environmental disturbances— such as the early modern climate and demographic pressures I outlined in my introductory overview that have much in common with today's global challenges. Resilience resists and diffuses environmental shocks so that biological integrity is preserved and openness to survival and evolutionary adaptation continues.[14]

Innogen also reminds the king that her choice of husband origin-ated in the common trust nurtured by the court's pluralism: 'You [Cymbeline] bred [Posthumus] as my [non-royal] playfellow' (1.1.146). But when she acts to sustain these values into future gen-erations, Cymbeline banishes Posthumus, and court relationships become rigidly stratified and closed off ('You do not meet a man but frowns' [1.1.1]). The king aggressively asserts patriarchal ownership of his daughter, goaded by the Queen's desire to match Innogen with her yobbish son Cloten. Her wicked-stepmother ambitions throw the court's sustainability narrative off-message. Cymbeline expresses this

generic conflict in his erratic behaviour and poor judgement. His
volatility continues until nearly the end of the play, when the play's
converging personal and environmental experiences finally restabilize
his political authority and Britain's ecological integrity. Antoni
Cimolino's 2012 Stratford Festival production suggested these ruptures working at an unconscious level by opening the performance
with a scene of Cymbeline in bed being tormented by nightmares.
Their waking effect is an ill-conceived policy of top-down resource
management that reduces Britain's collective ability to adapt.[15] To put
this in terms of the First Gentleman's agricultural metaphors, Cymbeline orients the country towards monoculture in eradicating any
species deemed to be unprofitable. But the absence of internal diversity
leaves England vulnerable to invasive disease and extinction. These
dangers are aggravated by the King's regression to an enclosure men-
tality. Like Oliver and Frederick in *As You Like It*, Cymbeline has
seized Belarius's lands on the basis of false rumours of the latter's
confederacy with the Romans (3.3.103). His reactions recall the
doomed possessiveness of King Lear: Cymbeline treats everything
and everyone in his kingdom as personal property without respect
for their independent needs or integrity. He only belatedly notices
Innogen's absence after rashly 'pen[ning] her up' (1.154; 3.5.43–51).

Extinctive nationalism

Eric Heinze is the latest critic to observe that Cymbeline has cut
himself off from a robust ethos of global interdependence by adopting
the tribal nationalism of the Queen and her son.[16] Like the behaviour
of some governments today towards the United Nations, the King's
refusal to pay Rome tribute strikes a superficially patriotic note but is
revealed to be the public face of his denaturing behaviour towards his
family, and environmental ignorance of his own country. His court's
resort to the rhetoric of mythical patriotism (viz. a campaign to reverse
Rome's alleged suppression of Mulmutius's rule of law and native self-
government) represents an early modern version of what environmental sociologist Ulrich Beck calls 'methodological nationalism'. This is
the tendency of modern political discourses to conceive of environmental problems in terms of defensive national borders rather than
worldwide ecologies: 'While reality is becoming more thoroughly

cosmopolitan, our habits of thought and consciousness...disguise the growing unreality of nation-states'.[17] The nested actions of *Cymbeline* move towards breaking down these isolationist tendencies. Reflecting James I's personal attempt to refashion British identity in terms of Continental peacemaking rather than militant Protestantism, Cymbeline ultimately re-embraces political and social inclusivity at the play's conclusion (it helps, of course, that the British are victors). Anticipating this resolution, Shakespeare is careful to have Cymbeline treat the Roman envoys with detached courtesy. Cloten and his mother, by contrast, speak for the court as blaring jingoists. Their tabloid belligerence recycles the hoary island-nation rhetoric which Shakespeare had satirized in Elizabethan plays such as *King John*. Echoing the latter's final hollowed-out speech by the Bastard, the Queen declares:

> Remember sir, my liege,
> The kings your ancestors, together with
> The natural bravery of your isle, which stands
> As Neptune's park, ribbed and paled in
> With oaks unscalable and roaring waters.... (3.1.16–20)

The court tries to legitimize this all-too-modern discourse of bristling frontiers and xenophobia through historical revisionism. Cloten rejects the legal effect of Julius Caesar's conquest of Britain on the questionable grounds that 'Our kingdom is [now] stronger than it was at that time'. The Queen puffs up his shirtiness with the (unconsciously deflating) image of 'Britons strut[ting] with courage'. She and the King imagine a national cult of blood and soil as the basis for the triumphing will of a 'warlike people' (3.1.21–23, 33–35, 51).[18] Absent from her selective account of how Caesar's shipping cracked 'Like eggshells...'gainst our rocks' is the fact that British regionalism never remained immune to external change, and that Rome's cosmopolitan influence was not unbeneficial (3.1.22–29). Post-war tribute was mutually negotiated by Caesar and Cassibelan, as Lucius's and the Queen's arguments silently acknowledge. While offensive to parochial pride, the convergence of British and Roman interests produced greater internal resilience for both parties; only Cymbeline's blinkered court now sees it as an insulting compromise which detracts from its North Korean–like fantasy of pristine isolation and miraculous prosperity. This self-delusion represents just one of many instances of failed vision in *Cymbeline* noted by Peggy Muñoz Simonds.[19] Collectively they draw attention to the court's rejection of altruism as the real basis of (re)productive, social, and environmental fitness, or what Richard Dawkins calls, in relation to genetic sustainability, the 'survival of the stable'.[20] Cymbeline's resistance to a regional–global axis analogizes today's difficulties of avoiding a future 2°C-rise in global temperatures in the face of petty national interests. Ulrich Beck sums up the challenge of contextualizing planetary environmental problems at day-to-day levels:

nothing which happens on our planet is only a limited local event; all interventions, victories and catastrophes affect the whole world, and we must reorient and reorganize our lives and action, our organizations and institutions [accordingly].[21]

Cymbeline's court tries to avert its eyes from the reality of this scaled interconnectedness, retrofitting Britain within the straits of its 'salt-water girdle'. The play's environmentally afforded boundary crossings (of which more in the next sections) expose the futility of the court's protectionism.

In *A Sand County Almanac*, Aldo Leopold observes that people often unwittingly break vital chains of bio-dependency in their misguided desires to conquer nature. Yet 'the conqueror role is eventually self-defeating' because it knows nothing about 'just what makes the community clock tick, and just what and who is valuable'.[22] From the court's perspective, and again to recall the play's husbandry metaphors, it seems that the only thing that can grow in Cymbeline's Britain is hothouse absolutism. As the wicked widow, stepmother, and witch, the Queen's arrogance towards the kingdom's creatures and environment exacerbate her husband's ecological myopia. Her little show of flower-gathering ('To make perfumes, distil, preserve' [1.5.13]—often burlesqued in modern performances) fools nobody about her real interest in poisons; it also contrasts with the use of preserving and regenerating herbs and flowers used to grace Fidele's grave in Wales (4.2.284–88). When Cornelius questions the Queen's motives, she hides behind a bogus version of the heuristic empiricism advocated by scientific rationalists such as Francis Bacon and practised by experimental physicians such as Helena's father in *All's Well That Ends Well*:

> Having thus far proceeded,
> Unless thou think'st me devilish, is't not meet

> That I did amplify my judgement in
> Other conclusions?   (*Cymbeline*, 1.5.15–18)

Cornelius is already aware, however, of the Queen's lack of scruples in aiming to subject 'higher' victims to her pseudo-science, which he thwarts by secretly substituting a non-lethal sleeping drug for her poison. The Lords' thinly veiled mockery of Cloten, and Pisanio's moral courage in shielding Innogen, present similar acts of covert resistance to the royal family's viciousness. Their actions mirror the bottom-up insights of Arviragus, Guiderius, and Posthumus in Wales. On the other hand, when Cloten himself tries surreptitiously to enter Innogen's chamber, he figures himself as a predatory Acteon stalking Diana. He cynically assumes her 'rangers', or ladies-in-waiting, are all corruptible, just as he slavers at the idea of his musicians 'fingering' Innogen's body (2.3.12–14, 63–68). Giacomo echoes his misogyny in reducing Innogen to an exchange commodity in his efforts to humiliate Posthumus. His language is part of the globalizing trade-and-contract rhetoric which both men aggressively distort in their competitive wager over Innogen's chastity (1.4.36ff).[23] Treating women as a resource-playground, all three men caricature Western masculine attitudes towards the natural world.[24]

Cymbeline and his officials fail to foster any meaningful relations with the land, or to convey any authentic sense of British belonging. Huw Griffiths argues this is owing to Cymbeline's literal inability to see his own country; for despite the court's location in London, the word 'England' is never spoken in the play. Its absence leaves both the physical reality and political identity of Britain underdetermined. Cloten, as usual, unconsciously parodies this situation by being peevishly distressed when he travels into unfamiliar Wales, yet obsessed with Londoners' opinions when he arrogantly confronts Guiderius (4.1.1–2, 4.2.101). An impaired sense of place-identity also temporally afflicts the victims of Cymbeline's aggression. Posthumus's Cloten-like tendencies cripple his ability to see through Giacomo's specious evidence of Innogen's infidelity. Even Innogen briefly loses sight of Milford Haven when journeying into Wales.[25]

But unlike Cloten, Innogen and Posthumus are transformed by their Welsh experiences—or, more precisely, by the Welsh landscape, which engenders their rediscovery of diversity and adaptability on local and global levels. Recalling Falstaff's temporary physiological transformation in Gloucestershire (discussed in Chapter 3), Innogen and Posthumus journey separately into environmental symbiosis with the Welsh landscape, from where they connect in different ways with Roman cosmopolitanism. Together with Arviragus and Guiderius, they collectively regenerate Cymbeline's deracinated kingdom and Britain's mutually beneficial relationship with Rome. The contribution of Wales to the kingdom's renewal leads Huw Griffiths to argue that, despite the play's ambiguous geography, 'Britain['s heterogeneous identity] *has* to be produced on its Celtic margins, since that is what distinguishes it from England'.[26] Griffiths's main concern is the cartographic ambiguity that reflects the shifting political symbolism of Milford Haven (a site of division and unity in *Richard II* and *Richard III* respectively). My interest is in how Welsh landscapes and habitats allow the play's younger generation to recognize the sustaining value of local and global relationships. Their environmentally afforded discoveries resemble the ways Pericles grows in eco-cosmopolitan knowledge from his sea voyages to diverse Mediterranean cities and regions, and Prospero matures from his island encounter with Caliban. While *Cymbeline*'s bioregionalism compliments the new British identity of King James's court, Shakespeare insists it is a mosaic within a composite planet.

Living like a Welsh mountain

We learn the backstory to the crisis at Cymbeline's court at the play's midpoint (3.3). Years earlier Belarius had virtuously abducted Cymbeline's two infant sons, Guiderius and Arviragus, to the mountains of Wales in order to raise them away from the factionalism of the post-war court. His outlaw dissent recalls the court-and-country oppositions of *A Midsummer Night's Dream*, *Henry IV Part Two*, *As You Like It*, *King Lear*, and *Timon of Athens*, in which pastoral, georgic, or wilderness perspectives critique stifling court hierarchies. Shakespeare juxtaposes the bioregional integrity of Belarius's Welsh refuge against Cymbeline's destruction of fertile relationships. Bioregional in this case means not only subsisting autonomously, but also being forced to adapt to living with non-human species in a physically challenging landscape. Shakespeare's recreates his earlier woodland settings as an interactive space of globalization from below in the face of Cymbeline's faltering ethic of hyper-managed growth.[27]

Belarius's successful escape to Wales confirms Cymbeline's isolation from any real physical knowledge of his kingdom. Once in its hinterlands, Belarius can elude detection for decades, 'fear[ing] no poison which attends / In place of greater state' (3.3.77–78). In the vividly imagined environment which made a strong theatrical impression on Simon Forman, 'Morgan', 'Polydore', and 'Cadwal' recall the honourable outlaws in *Two Gentlemen of Verona* who shadow the dysfunctional court with the promise of social renewal. *Cymbeline's* exiles live off deer-meat, roots, and simple herb broths. Their diet reflects that of William Harrison's idealized Welsh Britons in his *Description of England*.[28] In his regard for personal attachments to local habitats as morally improving and environmentally virtuous, Belarius echoes both early modern and twentieth-century back-to-the-land movements:

> To apprehend thus
> Draws us a profit from all things we see,
> And often to our comfort shall we find
> The sharded beetle in a safer hold
> Than is the full-winged eagle.   (3.3.17–21)

Like Duke Senior and his courtly exiles in *As You Like It*, Belarius represents an older generation which imposes a pastoral idealism on the Welsh landscape to reinvent physical exile as a spiritual haven.

Belarius's attitudes to the land are not limited to high-minded complaints or nostalgia, however, and *Cymbeline's* landscape suggests links between physical dwelling and distributed agency that are more active than in Shakespeare's earlier forest plays. James R. Gibson's concept of environmental affordance, which I discussed in Chapter 1, clarifies these interactions. To recall Gibson, humans, like other animals, interact with their environments not as detached objects in 'empty' space (the classical view of Cartesian ontology and Newtonian physics) but relationally, as immersive physical mediums (e.g. air, water) and shifting perceived shapes and surfaces (plains, rocks, trees, mountains, and living creatures). The landscape's interfaces continually alter the living being's positioning and movements. Through these dynamic perceptions and responses, physical environments continually determine thoughts and behaviours and shape evolutionary adaptation.[29] Since this potential holds true for both human and non-human animals, shared reliance on environmental prompting levels their relationship from one-way subject and object, to co-dependent life forms. Becoming conscious of this non-traditional ontology opens the possibility of humans returning the animal gaze in what Chris Danta and Dimitris Vardoulakis call a 'double gesture', and Laurie Shannon terms 'cosmopolity'. At social levels it creates inroads for animality in political institutions, as Bruno Latour imagines in his eco-allegorical 'Parliament of Things'.[30]

Belarius thus prefers the 'flats' and 'valleys' of his locality not just because he is older and less agile. The lie of the land also shapes his potential movements and environmental worldview. As a human animal he perceives its flatter surfaces offer him faster opportunities for escape if threatened. Upon his arrival, Belarius grasped that a low-roofed cave 'i'th'rock' offered shelter and security. In terms of animal memory, the landscape reactivates the safety-seeking instincts of him and his sons as potential prey, much like the ferally transformed Edgar in *King Lear*, who 'Escape[s] the hunt' in the 'happy hollow of a tree' (*King Lear*, 7.167–68). While raising Polydore and Cadwal with their nurse Euriphile ('lover of the earth'), Belarius valued their cave's low entrance for teaching them ethical humility as well as perceptual wariness. In both senses the landscape grounds his georgic ethos of retirement from the city, and sharpens his juxtapositions between former 'warlike feats' and the 'usuries', slanders, and factions of the court. These stories have unintended effects on Polydore, however, firing his imagination with a different behavioural script, which he tests by '[putting] himself in posture / That acts [Belarius's] words' (3.3.94–95).

Even though Belarius is mildly disconcerted by these responses, they reflect the formative influence of the Welsh climate and mountain landscape. Cadwal and Polydore have grown up immersed in its ecosystem, scrambling up hills and mimicking its animals through both gentle zephyrs and 'the rud'st wind / That by the top doth take the mountain pine / And make him stoop in'th'vale' (4.2.172–73, 175–77). Gibson observes that non-human animals offer people the most richly variable objects of behavioural affordance because their surface shape continually changes while retaining essentially the same outlines: 'What the other animal affords the observer is not only behavior but also social interaction. As one moves so does the other, the one sequence of action being suited to other in a kind of behavioral loop.'[31] The unpredictable movements of non-human animals express an independent intelligence that challenges supposed human superiority, as sceptical early modern humanists such as Montaigne understood when he famously asked, 'When I play with my cat, who knows if I am not a pastime to her more than she is to me?'[32] Cadwal and Polydore have entered into the thought-patterns and movements of local animals, and collectively they have all perceived their shared habitat as dynamically evolving. This partly suggests why the two brothers regard their 'pinching cave' as a 'cell of ignorance'. Unlike Belarius they do not value stasis either physically or morally, since they are used to thriving in an environment they perceive to be reciprocally alive:

> What should we speak of
> When we are as old as you? . . .
> We have seen nothing.
> We are beastly: subtle as the fox for prey,
> Like warlike as the wolf for what we eat.
> Our valour is to chase what flies; our cage
> We make a choir, as doth the prisoned bird,
> And sing our bondage freely.   (3.3.35–44)

Arviragus's complaint implies that he and his brother have routinely seen and returned the animal gaze, exchanging subject positions as both prey and predator in the fluid landscape. Living relationally with animals has set up the kinetic equivalent of a double-gestured language which Shakespeare represents textually in their animalized diction ('We'll browse on that' [3.6.38][33]).

Environmental symmetries

The constant need to forage for food makes hunting a preoccupation in Wales.[34] John Vaillant illuminates Polydore and Cadwal's interdependence with local fauna as subsistence hunters in his account of a highly intelligent but wronged male Siberian tiger.[35] He was killed by overwhelming human force after he made a series of justifiable revenge attacks in the Primorski Krai region of pacific Russia in 1997. As Vaillant shows, modern technology aside, traditional hunters of the region transform themselves into animal predators who cultivate—or, at a deeper level, rediscover—the ability to insert themselves imaginatively into the minds and bodies of tigers. They likewise have to envisage 'successful hunting scenarios by adapting to, and manipulating, random events within a constantly shifting environment' (164). To realize such affordances, they used empathic thinking, 'even to the point of disguising [themselves as prey] and mimicking [their] behavior':

> It was our ancestors' skill at not only analyzing and imitating that nature of a given animal, but identifying with it, that enabled them to flourish in dangerous environments, both physically and psychically. In hunting societies, such as the Udeghe, the !Kung, the Haida, or the Sioux, animals were not merely food, they were seen as blood relatives, spiritual companions, hunting guides, and sources of power and connection to the surrounding world.   (164)

The Shakespearian character who most vividly represents this kind of trans-species understanding is another ancient Briton, Edgar, in *King Lear*. As a wilderness outcast, he becomes sensitized to the relationship between human and non-human life and its shared natural habitats. Disguising himself as a beggar, Edgar eventually immerses himself in animality, yet without becoming bestialized.[36] His experience anticipates an ordeal Vaillant relates of German geologists Henno Martin and Hermann Korn in 1940–43. Having fled persecution to Africa from Nazi Germany, they escaped into the Namibian desert with their dog Otto to avoid capture by South Africans. For two and half years all three lived as fugitives in the barren gorges of the Kuiseb River system, foraging for scarce water and food with other local wildlife. Like Edgar or Polydore and Cadwal, Martin and Korn patiently adapted their daily thoughts and physical rhythms to the lives of their non-human neighbours. In the process they 'rediscover[ed] skills and instincts that had lain dormant since the Stone Age'.[37] As Edgar's bare and needy body imitates the feeding habits of other animals, he enters elementally (or darkly, as Timothy Morton's ecology would have it) into their struggle to survive:

> Poor Tom . . . eats the swimming frog, the toad, the tadpole, the wall-newt and the water[-newt]; . . . eats cowdung for salads, swallows the old rat and the ditch-dog, drinks the green mantle of the standing pool. . . .   (11.115–19)

How much this and his other speeches during the storm scenes are Edgar's performance of 'madness' or his real experience as a 'forked animal' who 'eats, but where he is eaten', is uncertain.[38] At some points, however, non-human animals begin to colonize his imagination, transforming him into the kind of hybrid creature Belarius is fearful of becoming (e.g. 'hog in sloth, fox in stealth, wolf in greediness, dog in madness, lion in prey' [11.83–84]). Edgar's mind seems temporarily to cross over at the survival level of subconscious language and reflexive actions. Like Martin and Korn, he discovers the visceral insights recognized by Russian taiga hunters, Charles Darwin, and modern geneticists: that human and non-human species co-exist 'handy-dandy' by virtue of their shared evolutionary instincts. These forces drive the ever-renewing cycle of death-in-life with which Edgar, like Posthumus, synchronizes himself: 'Ripeness is all'; 'The action of my life... I'll keep, / If but for sympathy' (*King Lear* 23.11; *Cymbeline* 5.3.243–44).

Having absorbed the region's competitive and cooperative conditions of animal survival, Guiderius and Arviragus likewise understand there are adaptation and reproductive advantages to venturing beyond their present range. Hence their temptation to discard 'meal and bran' (4.2.27) when a new human creature—Fidele—wanders into their habitat and becomes part of their community: they know 'nothing' and potentially 'everything' about her.

Belarius attributes his 'son's' inveterate restlessness to a romance convention: the 'invisible instinct' of their royal birth. He sees this motive emerging when Guiderius fearlessly kills Cloten and both he and his brother decide to abandon hunting in order to care for the sick Fidele ('O thou goddess... how thyself thou blazon'st / In these two princely boys!' [4.2.170–72]). Belarius's imagery complicates the conceit of hidden nobility—the early modern equivalent of genetic determinism—by suggesting that the region's blustery weather has shaped their physical movements and, by extension, their knowledge of living in a world of environmental fluctuations.[39] To apply the phrase associated with Aldo Leopold's biocentrism—an ethos that challenges human-centred superiority—Guiderius and Arviragus think like a mountain because the Welsh climate, terrain, and organic life have educated their perceptions of the earth as a shared dwelling of multi-scaled and interdependently changing relationships.

Ultimately the bioregional affordances of Wales transform Britain's national and global outlooks because Guiderius and Arviragus apply their resilience-enhancing adaptability to the task of defending Britain from the tribute-denied Romans. Their success re-legitimizes Cymbeline's and their own dynastic heritage, and re-entwines it culturally with Roman civilization. Before considering how these nested levels come together in the play's finale, I would like to examine a bit further how the Welsh landscape shapes the play's battle sequence, and thus the eventual transformation of British ecological identity.

After audiences have witnessed the combat action largely in mime (5.2), Posthumus gives an unusually detailed report of the setting: a 'narrow lane', 'ditched, and walled with turf' (5.3.14ff). Jodi Mikalachki and Coppélia Kahn have each observed that this restricted and sexualized space intensifies the masculine competitive rivalry that has defined the relationship between Britain and Rome in the past and is now replayed over the symbolic terrain of Innogen's body.[40] Shakespeare has actually transferred the geographic details from an unrelated battle narrative in Holinshed. He also broadens the meaning of 'lane' from a passage-way through enemy troops (the word's usual meaning in the English history plays) to a natural corridor in the landscape. The subsurface lane prevents the Romans from attacking from above, despite their spatial and numerical advantage. Instead the combatants are forced to confront each other on level ground. This allows the Britons to range themselves 'athwart', preventing lateral movements and re-establishing a sense of themselves mentally and physically as a threatened pack, after the rest of Cymbeline's army has fled in disorder. Although the lane is blocked at one end with British corpses, the 'old man, and two boys' use the landscape's 'ecological optics' to transform a potential trap into a strategic opening.

Posthumus's account stresses that British success depended on the kind of animal intelligence learned from hunting and scavenging in their Welsh habitat. This follows early modern theorists who believed that hunting skills were directly transferrable to combat in war.[41] Having noted the place's possibilities of 'accommodation', they managed to reverse the role of prey and predator:

> [They be]gan to look
> The way that they did and to grin like lions

> Upon the pikes o'th'hunters. Then began
> A stop i'th'chaser; a retire; anon
> A rout, confusion thick.   (5.3.37–41)

The embedded stage direction in this passage elaborates spatially on Belarius's defiance towards his retreating comrades: 'Stand, / Or we are Romans, and will give you that / Like beasts which you shun beastly' (5.3.25–27). He calls on the Britons to act like beasts not in terms of perceived viciousness (e.g. 'Lolling the tongue with slaught'ring' like the Romans, or like the anthropomorphized tigers Henry V exhorts his soldiers to imitate at Agincourt), but of panoramic intelligence. In other words they should behave like real animals, not debase themselves with gratuitous ferocity below the level necessary for survival. Ultimately it is the Romans who are symbolically translated down the chain of being from eagles to chickens, teaching them a lesson in the limits of transnational power over local subjectivities (5.3.41–42).

After Posthumus finishes his story, Shakespeare repeats his career-long habit of poking fun at the artifice of his dramatic fictions by having the Lord mock Posthumus's outlandish tale. Having rescued the endangered king by joining forces with Guiderius and Arviragus (5.2), however, the 'poor peasant' angrily takes ownership of the factual truth of his story. He repositions the Lord's courtier cynicism as a shallow attempt to deflect his own cowardice on the battlefield, and reaffirms the political agency of this bottom-up environmental refashioning of British history.[42]

Innogen's nests

Within the play's rapidly unfolding series of threats, Innogen is preserved by Cornelius's substitution of a sleeping drug for poison, Pisanio's loyalty, and Welsh hospitality. Her adaptive and regenerate body symbolizes the ecological reclamation of Cymbeline's Britain, while structurally its transmutations anticipate the dynamic effects of the environmentally afforded battle at Milford Haven. Shakespeare builds up early impressions of Innogen's relationship to the natural world through indirect associations such as Giacomo's invasion of her bedchamber, where he compares the 'natural notes about [Innogen's] body' to delicately observed lilies and cowslips (e.g. 2.2.15–16, 37–39).

The aubade which Cloten has performed to break through Innogen's resistance works in a similarly ambivalent way ('Hark, hark, the lark at heaven's gate sings'). Cloten's vulgar puns serve only to distance him from the song's simple conceits of sensual awakening to 'chaliced flowers' and 'winking Mary-buds' (2.3.22–23).

Innogen's relationship to the traditional natural world also runs through Ovid: from her bedside reading of the 'tale of Tereus', which analogizes Giacomo's voyeuristic rape, to the biomorphic, or shape-shifting, transformations that characterize her travails in Wales.[43] Yet unlike classical metamorphoses, British plant and animal life and the Welsh landscape are autonomous agents of physical change rather than epiphenomena of the gods. Materially they afford the wider play's journeys into new ecological knowledge and action, with the dramatic pivot beginning in the woodland burial of Innogen's supposedly dead body:

> GUIDERIUS
> If he be gone he'll make his grave a bed.
> With female fairies will his tomb be haunted,
> (*To Innogen*) And worms will not come to thee.
> ARVIRAGUS
>   With fairest flowers
> Whilst summer lasts . . .
> . . . Thou shalt not lack
> The flower that's like thy face, pale primrose, nor
> The azured harebell . . .
> The leaf of eglantine . . .
> . . . The ruddock would
> With charitable bill . . .
>   . . . bring thee all this,
> Yea, and furred moss besides, when flowers are none,
> To winter-ground thy corpse.   (4.2.217–30)

The worms Guiderius mentions may refer to maggots more than earthworms—although early modern distinctions between the two blurred easily (as we shall see further in Chapter 5). Like other non-human animals, however, these worms are capable of identifying non-threatening creatures such as Innogen. They demonstrate the kind of rational intelligence which commended them to Darwin, especially in comparison to faulty human observers such as Posthumus. Guiderius and Arviragus's lament implies that humans could afford to learn ecological ethics from animals, and more generally from the natural world's relational ethics. Ironically it is Giacomo who consciously glances at this insight in his self-divided reactions on first meeting Innogen. Although he intends to puzzle her with his asides, they confess his recognition that human wickedness does not derive from any shared biological nature with animals, but from a false idea of superiority:

> It cannot be i'th'eye—for apes and monkeys,
> 'Twixt two such shes, would chatter this way and
> Contemn with mows the other .... (1.6.39–41)

Anticipating the burials of Ophelia and Ferdinand's father in the biomorphic ooze of their respective river- and sea-beds (*Hamlet*, 4.7.155–58; *The Tempest*, 1.2.401–402), Innogen's fern-like body merges with the wildwood soil to receive and later produce the flowers and foliage her unknown brothers lay on her grave.[44] Shakespeare intensifies the lyricism of the brothers' lament with dialectic signatures. 'Ruddock' is a Warwickshire name for robin, and 'winterground', as Oxford editor Roger Warren notes, is the playwright's coinage. Earlier Arviragus admired Innogen's ability to balance 'grief and patience' like 'mingled spurs' or tree roots—another Warwickshire term (4.2.59–60).[45] Guiderius's suggestion that Fidele should be 'laid beside their mother Euriphile' completes the convergence of death and life in 'quiet consummation'.

This echo of the *Book of Common Prayer* burial service stands out in a dramatic setting that Shakespeare otherwise takes care to mark as pre-Christian.[46] From a religious perspective, 'consummation' suggests the soul's release from physical mortality. Its redemptive ethos animates Christian universalism, whose historical origins the Jailer alludes to in his wry attempts to cheer up the condemned Posthumus (5.3.251–64). But Innogen is only sleeping, and in the context of the play's woodland burial Guiderius and Arviragus's imagery also points to the biocentrically patterned identities on display throughout the Welsh scenes. Their cumulative significance suggests Fidele's 'brothers' are celebrating another variation on naturally afforded biodiversity: an organic transformation into humus and soil that fertilizes new life. Their theory of burial is naturally metabiotic: it presumes that Innogen will live beyond death not by transcending physical nature but by becoming biologically reintegrated into its perpetually renewing cycles and evolutionary adaptations. Chapter 5 will explore the idea of metabiosis at greater length in *Hamlet* and *Antony and Cleopatra*.

After Innogen awakens and comes to terms with the excruciating reality of Posthumus's apparent death, Lucius offers to repurpose her life in the hopeful direction signified by her alias. His empathetic gesture foreshadows the dramatic convergence of Posthumus's return to his native British loyalty, his and Giacomo's renunciation of masculine arrogance, and the final personal and transnational reconciliations at court (2.4, 5.1, 5.4). Unsurprisingly, the first thing that catches Lucius's eye is not Innogen but the 'trunk.../ Without his top' (4.2.354–55). More unusual, however, is his instant admiration: 'The ruin speaks that sometime / It was a worthy building' (355–56). On a naturalistic level his remark confirms why Innogen could have mistaken Cloten's body for her husband's. In cultural terms it reveals the cosmopolitan values Lucius infuses into Welsh eco-localism to regenerate Cymbeline's Britain. In his discussion of the poetics of regeneration in *Cymbeline*, Barry Thorne notes that Lucius's sudden entrance represents the 'breaking in of one world upon another'.[47] Lucius expresses this worldview by allowing the muscular appearance of Cloten's body, rather than its physical horror or possible moral implications, to shape his first impressions. His homosocial regard recalls that which Shakespeare's other male soldiers, such as Old Clifford and York (*Henry VI Part Three*), the earlier Lucius and the Goths (*Titus Andronicus*), and Coriolanus and Aufidius (*Coriolanus*) have for their enemies' bodies. Their mutual respect affirms a cross-cultural aesthetic and adapted trait of masculine prowess. In *Cymbeline*, Lucius's esteem recalls the former admiring competition between British and Roman soldiers that has been cut off by the English court's bellicose provincialism, whose stage emblem is Cloten's stinking body.[48] Because Lucius's worldly sensibility can nonetheless transfigure that body into something rare and admirable, he is able to empathize with Innogen's bloody grief over her husband. His empathy affirms the authenticity of her local needs by finding connections to his own Roman worldview.

A similar exchange occurs in the Jailer's prophetic application of Christian universalism to Posthumus's miseries at the historical moment that the play's British events coincide with yet-to-be written biblical ones. The Jailer's and Lucius's parallel gestures suggest such imaginative flexibility can be shaped by situations and environments from below as well as above. Greg Woolf has shown that Christianity's future hegemony was enabled by the systemic scalability of Roman political governance. Social and economic relations in Rome and Italy were successfully shifted to overseas imperial administrations because their internal structures, or 'ecosystems', retained their integrity as local operations went global, and vice versa. The retention of a sustainable integrity in the process of adaptation partly explains the longevity of the empire's cultural genes.[49] Innogen's changing views of British regional wilderness embrace a similar nested vision:

> Our courtiers say all's savage but at court;
> Experience, O thou disprov'st report!
> Th'imperious seas breeds monsters; for the dish
> Poor tributary rivers as sweet fish. (4.2.33–36)

Lucius's double-gestured response to Innogen reminds us of Arviragus and Guiderius's adaptation to Welsh habitats. The coming-together of their outlooks indicates that deeper ecological principles of diversity and resilience will mutually strengthen British and Roman communities.

These worldviews shift the prejudices of Cymbeline's court away from hard-shell provincialism towards multi-polar cooperation. The play's fashioning of an organically rooted but globally receptive British identity continues in the spectacular dream-riddle Jupiter reveals to Posthumus:

... and when from a stately cedar shall be lopped branches, which being dead many years, shall after revive, be jointed to the old stock, and freshly grow, then shall Posthumus end his miseries .... (5.4.234–37)

The play's Soothsayer, Philharmonus, explains that the branches represent Cymbeline's two sons, originally cut off from the royal family tree but 'recycled' by Belarius to regenerate the sterile court (5.4.454–59). The riddle's catalysing hinges include allusions to hybridizing plants and trees as metaphors for cosmopolitan nodes. Not surprisingly, the Soothsayer does not explain the riddle's philosophical implications, but his comments do look forward to a related moment in *The Winter's Tale* when Perdita and Polixenes debate the ethics and utility of grafting

(4.4.79ff; see Introduction pp. 25–7). Both plays suggest that interventions of human technology in the natural world need not be disruptive if they are synchronized to long-term preservation of genetic diversity. As Polixenes explains, all human uses of nature—even Perdita's cultivation of wild or non-hybridized breeds which she believes avoid varietal adaptation—gradually modify the natural world in ways that are part of, rather than separate from, 'great creating nature'. Like the Delphic oracle in *The Winter's Tale* or the vision of Artemis in *Pericles*, the temporality of Posthumus's riddle reorients Cymbeline's Britain to timelines of incremental change and adaptation.

The cascading personal revelations and narrative coincidences of *Cymbeline's* long final scene create a structural analogy for biodiversity's sometimes hidden or unrecognized interdependencies. By emulating Posthumus's forgiveness of Giacomo, in which the former recognizes the latter's competitive misogyny in himself, as well as Lucius's worldly compassion towards the nearly broken Innogen, Cymbeline abandons monocultural obsessions and avoids dynastic extinction. On both sides Britain and Rome rediscover the mutualism necessary for long-term organic and sociable relations. Cymbeline's reconciliations point to today's need to rebalance national interests with multilateral action in order to tackle imminent environmental disasters.

Cymbeline represents diversity both geographically and environmentally through a virtuoso reuse of Shakespearian scenarios and genres. As was the case for the success of the Chamberlain's Men at The Globe, recycling vitalized Shakespeare's powers of creative reinvention as well as his horizons of ecocritical enquiry. It also offers today's audiences a metacritical commentary on the current shift away from older green readings of Shakespeare as the poet of cosmic and natural harmonies, towards evolutionary models of ecology based on sustainable adaptation to natural and human-generated forms of change.

5

'I wish you joy of the worm'

Evolutionary ecology in Hamlet *and* Antony and Cleopatra

[T]his evening there is no mention of the ghost that walks the terrace by night. The light of the moon suddenly falls upon an earthworm sliding under a stone, and Hamlet asks his friend:

'Did you know, Horatio, that without earthworms men could not create civilisations?'

With characteristic scorn Horatio answers sarcastically:

'Until now I thought that earthworms were destined to destroy the last traces of human civilisation, devouring men's corpses and swallowing their buildings'.

To which Hamlet replies once more:

> *There are more things in heaven and earth, Horatio,*
> *Than are dreamt of in your philosophy.*[1]

Disaffected from the court and shaken out of conventional assumptions about human nature by the Ghost's revelations, Hamlet begins to think of comparisons with non-human life, beginning with his father as 'old mole' (1.5.170).[2] Later he turns to worms, and his attention suggests a willed strategy of existential and ecological discovery, since worms occupied a place diametrically opposite to humans in the traditional hierarchy of life. Renaissance Humanists often used the perceived inferiority of worms and other animals to define human uniqueness. Their gradations of being, by extension, justified human mastery of the earth represented in *Hamlet* by Claudius's modernizing transformation of Denmark into a military-industrial state.[3] Adopting a worm-oriented perspective (wryly imagined by conservation ecologist André Voisin in my epigraph), Hamlet begins to question his own conventional Humanist reflexes, such as those on display in his opening soliloquy (e.g. 'O God, a beast that wants discourse of reason / Would have mourned longer' [1.2.150–51]).

Recent critics have shown how analogies between social behaviour and animals in *Hamlet* and other Shakespeare plays reflect the rediscovery of classical scepticism towards human superiority by Humanists such as Michel de Montaigne, before René Descartes and other Enlightenment philosophers elevated mind and soul into essential qualities of human nature. As in other areas of ecology and environmentalism discussed in this book, early modern reflections such as Hamlet's look forward to today's post-Cartesian and post-human enquiries into human, animal, and cyborgian crossovers.[4] In this chapter I want to align these pre-modern and present-day horizons with the scientific revolution that links them: evolutionary biology's tracing of human origins to the shared creaturely and genetic life of the planet. Worms will be my trope for Hamlet's attention to what Giorgio Agamben calls a 'zone of indeterminacy' between human and animal life, and what Andreas Höfele identifies as the complex doubleness of similarity and difference that runs through all of Shakespeare's animal–human relations, beginning with the comic dialogues of Crab and Lance in *The Two Gentlemen of Verona*.[5] Hamlet's dramatic challenge to human exceptionalism anticipates the rationale of Charles Darwin's life-long fascination with earthworms. For Darwin, worms were an icon of the co-dependency between humans and their non-human ancestors (caricatured by the famous Punch cartoon, 'Man is a Worm', Figure 5.1).

Hamlet's recognition of the way worms recreate nature and culture prompts him to question the Ghost's command as a principled response to abused justice and a practical reaction to human transience. Observing the labour of worms prompts Hamlet to resituate his revenge task within the larger adaptive timelines of evolutionary nature. Rather than a terminal condition requiring myths of heroic redemption or modern ironic detachment, judging the death of humans from the perspective of worms invites Hamlet to contextualize

PUNCH'S ALMANACK FOR 1882.

MAN·IS·BVT·A·WORM·

Figure 5.1. 'Man is But a Worm', *Punch Almanack* (1881). <http://commons.
wikimedia.org/wiki/File:Man_is_But_a_Worm.jpg>.

his personal loss and grief within wider structures of ecological and
cultural sustainability. In dramatic terms, they invite him to think
beyond short-term tragedy to long-term tragicomedy.

Hamlet and *Antony and Cleopatra* are obviously different types of
plays—one an existential revenge tragedy, the other a doomed epic
romance.[6] But Cleopatra shares Hamlet's interest in non-human animals and species interdependency as an imaginative framework for
acting out her shifting relationships with Antony and Caesar. One of
the many ways Shakespeare distinguishes Cleopatra's Egypt from Rome

is through their different attitudes towards non-human animals and the value of biodiversity. Cleopatra's cultural reflexes tend to be playfully self-depreciating rather than dismissive or superior:

> O, Charmian,
> Where think'st thou he is now? . . .
> . . . is he on his horse?
> O happy horse, to bear the weight of Antony!
> Do bravely, horse, for wot'st thou whom thou mov'st?—
> The demi-Atlas of this earth . . . .   (1.5.18–23)[7]

More broadly, in opposing the competitive individualism that characterizes Roman political leadership, Cleopatra and Egyptian culture socialize the personal insights of Hamlet's worm-inspired scepticism about human exceptionalism, and thereby prefigure Darwinian ideas of life's shared biological pathways. Mary Thomas Crane has explored the conceptual implications of differences between Roman and Egyptian ways of talking about nature. She observes that Romans refer to their environment as a 'world' of cultural artefacts, and they regard themselves (ideally) as physically impervious to nature's vicissitudes. Egyptians, by contrast, see themselves as physiologically embedded in the earth's organic cycles of material change, rebirth, and transmutation. Thomas Crane relates these opposing experiential outlooks to opposing atomic and elemental ways of understanding the physical world that were, respectively, emerging and passing away in Shakespeare's time. His sympathetic portrayal of Egypt in *Antony and Cleopatra*, she argues, exhibits nostalgia for 'the pre-seventeenth-century cosmos of elements and humors that rendered subject and world deeply interconnected'.[8] The issue of interdependency in Thomas Crane's distinctions between Roman 'world' and Egyptian 'earth' also point to divergent ecological epistemologies. Shifting the scientific framework from physics to natural history, Egypt's elemental-humoral worldview may be seen not as residual but as anticipating the evolutionary web of life that challenges classical and later Cartesian anthropocentrism epitomized by Caesar as 'universal landlord'.

Conflicting Roman and Egyptian knowledge of the natural world presents new opportunities to explore Antony's tragically divided identity from ecocritical perspectives. Cleopatra is also divided, but in more complex ways that reach beyond human paradoxes to encompass what Michel Serres calls the 'third position' of the earth and its non-human inhabitants.[9] In suicide she overreaches Caesar while aspiring to romantic redemption with her poetically transfigured 'husband'. In the same moment, however, the worms of Nilus reunite Cleopatra with the ecodynamic forces that shaped her bioregional identity. Cleopatra stages a ritual show of earthly transcendence for Caesar and Western posterity that is simultaneously contested by a biocentric, or species-levelling, journey back into local cycles of regenerative nature. Her triple-turning suicide clarifies Hamlet's less clearly resolved choices between heroic revenge violence, which in theory will redeem the deficit in providential creation caused by his father's murder, and worm-oriented redemption in nature's food webs.

Cleopatra's conflicting desires for spiritual, romantic, and metabiotic forms of transcendence reveal the difficulties of authentically accessing the wildness of nature. From an ecocritical perspective, her situation mirrors current tensions between neo-Romantic and post-Darwinian orientations of environmentalism. Cleopatra analogizes the former outlook in aspiring to a pure and direct connection with the natural world, not excluding its traditional spiritual values. At the same time, her suicide enacts a (proto-)evolutionary acceptance of biological recombinations within ever-changing physical realities. Humans may choose to interact positively or negatively with these recreations, but can never absolutely dominate them.[10] Hamlet comes to recognize the unconditional 'modesty' of this evolutionary condition before his self-possession is situationally ruptured by the final duel's spiral into deadly violence and Fortinbras's symbolic restoration of 'natural' law.

Although Cleopatra's 'worms' are different from those that capture Hamlet's imagination, the pre-scientific categories of early modern natural history were loose and disputed. In Shakespeare, 'worm' could refer multilaterally to maggots, snakes, earthworms, caterpillars and other kinds of creeping animals. When Cleopatra asks the rural fellow who brings her asps, 'Will [they] eat me?' (5.2.270), she has in mind, as Michael Neill notes, the 'worms of the grave'. At the same time, her desire for a 'gentle grave' and her reaction to the worm's love-bite as 'sweet as balm, as soft as air, as gentle' uses 'gentle' as a term for maggot.[11] The capaciousness of this grouping resembles the taxonomic inflation of today's so-called megafauna, or 'flagship species'. These are aesthetically appealing animals, such as harp seals, killer whales (orcas), and giant pandas, who 'evolve' through sentimentalizing media or institutional appropriation into glamour species used to raise emotions and cash for conservationist agendas.[12] Darwin was a meticulous taxonomist and rigorously unsentimental, but he was not immune from endowing earthworms with megafaunic charm, in the same way that Shakespeare showcased Crab in *The Two Gentlemen of Verona*. Darwin's research demolished traditional prejudices by demonstrating the biological, evolutionary, and cultural importance of worms. And like his other human–animal homologies, Darwin's celebration of worms demonstrated that *Homo sapiens* is not uniquely intelligent. In this chapter I shall use 'worms' as a flagship trope for exploring both Hamlet's and Cleopatra's evolutionary attitudes towards animal–human relations.

In the midst of death, we are in life

In *The Formation of Vegetable Mould, Through the Actions of Worms, with Observations on their Habits* (1881), published six months before his death, Darwin focused on one small but mighty actor in the drama of evolution, *Lumbricus terrestris* (the common earthworm), originally native to Europe but now found around the world in moderately humid conditions. From decades of close observation and experiments, Darwin concluded that earthworms work the earth to an average depth of seven to eight feet, sifting and digesting an astonishing ten tons of organic and mineral matter per acre per year, which they recycle to the surface as fertile soil, or vegetable mould as it was called in Darwin's day.[13] In southern England, Darwin calculated that over five years earthworms add one inch of mineral nutrients to the topsoil.[14] Their actions naturally renew the earth's fertility and continually reshape its physical contours. Although the landscape seems fixed, it is kept constantly in motion yet stable by worms (among other natural agents).[15] By sustaining all organic life on land, worms attain an ecological significance that entirely belies their traditionally low cultural status and negative associations with bodily death and corruption.

More controversially, Darwin argued that worms bring to bear a form of natural, though non-tendentious, intelligence on the environment. He observed that worms routinely plug up the entrances of their burrows with fallen leaves for warmth, and line the walls to avoid direct contact between their bodies and the cold soil. In doing so, they rely not only on instinct but are also capable of decision-making and even of going against their preferred habits when presented with an advantageous choice. Darwin demonstrated this capability by offering worms 303 irregularly shaped triangles of paper with which to plug their burrows. Instead of choosing sides randomly, the worms judged which end of the triangle was best to pull in, selecting the narrow apex nearly two thirds of the time to save themselves effort. They thereby acted 'in nearly the same manner as would a man under similar circumstances'.[16] Darwin concluded that, despite their low standing in the scale of species organization, worms are able to experiment, respond flexibly, and make decisions.[17] In putting forward these daring claims, the wider though typically understated agenda of Darwin's book emerged. Worms exemplify the biocentric implications of his earlier *On the Origins of Species* (1859) and *The Descent of Man* (1871) which challenged the traditional position of human beings at the top of the chain of being, and, from religious and Cartesian perspectives, as a uniquely created species superior to all other life forms. Darwin's worms anticipate post-human efforts to rewrite the animal–human relationship in order to give non-human creatures rights and interests of their own.

Adam Phillips has explored the cultural implications of Darwin's revolutionary thinking in *Darwin's Worms: On Life and Death Stories* (1999). He suggests that *The Formation of Vegetable Mould* revalued the relationship between death and life. As agents of natural transience and biotic regeneration, worms embody ethically neutral forces of rebirth and continuity as well as decay. From their perspective, suffering and loss are natural (though humanly mournful) experiences within larger interactions of fertility and reproduction, extinction and adaptation. Darwin's treatise thus substituted a non-redemptive myth of sustainability-within-death—nature as 'contingently hospitable' Phillips calls it—for utopian notions of human transcendence over physical mortality. These dreams are the conceptual framework for traditional ideas of natural law. Its justifications for revenge conventionally include legitimating retaliation to redress personal injuries, and bringing the ideal of worldly equilibrium back into moral balance within an eternal providential order. Darwin's and Phillips's worms raise the possibility of an alternative evolutionary theory of Shakespearian tragedy.

Looking at life from the ground up, in the manner of Darwin, causes Hamlet to notice the ways in which worms and people interact in mutually beneficial ways. Without the assumption of a human essence detached from animal life or physical nature, Hamlet questions revenge as a heroic affirmation of metaphysical laws reflected in the social order. These laws find their symbolic counterpart in medieval and Renaissance theories of harmoniously unchanging nature. Such ideals still colour outdated models of steady-state ecology and sentimental environmentalism.[18] Worms instead orient Hamlet towards the temporal and epistemological horizons of Darwinian ecology, in which non-teleological transience binds human and non-human life in shared cycles of reproduction, death, and metabiotic regeneration.

Levelling the food and species chains (1): *Hamlet*

Worms become visible in *Hamlet* when the prince, having hidden Polonius's corpse, confronts Claudius with a sardonic extrapolation of the courtier's physical afterlife:

> CLAUDIUS Now, Hamlet, where's Polonius.
> HAMLET   At supper.
> CLAUDIUS At supper? Where?
> HAMLET   Not where he eats, but where he is eaten.
> A certain convocation of politic worms are e'en at
> him. Your worm is your only emperor for diet. We fat
> all creatures else to fat us, and we fat ourselves for
> maggots. Your fat king and your lean beggar is but
> variable service—two dishes, but to one table. That's
> the end.
> CLAUDIUS Alas, alas!
> HAMLET   A man may fish with the worm that hath eat
> of a king, and eat of the fish that hath fed of that worm.
> CLAUDIUS What dost thou mean by this?
> HAMLET   Nothing but to show you how a king may go a
> progress through the guts of a beggar.   (4.3.17–31)

Hamlet plays with the proverbial reputation of worms as gothic creatures exercising a trivial yet fearful agency in the world. By modern standards the taxonomic language is slippery. As elsewhere in Shakespeare, the word 'worm' could refer to both the earthworm (class Oligochaeta) or to other creatures resembling them. The simultaneous

sense of earthworm and maggot is present, for instance, in Prince
Henry's send-off to the dying Hotspur in *Henry IV Part One*:

> HOTSPUR   No, Percy, thou art dust
> And food for—   *He dies*
> PRINCE HENRY   For worms, brave Percy.   (5.4.84–86)

Like 'dust', 'worms' serves as a proverbial metonym for physical
decomposition combined with a *contemptus mundi* valence of spiritual
release.[19] This is their traditional significance in Luis de Granada's *Of
Prayer, and Meditation* (1582), long recognized as a source-text for the
Gravediggers' scene in *Hamlet*, but hitherto undiscussed in relation to
the wider play.[20] In two chapters (2, 7) on the 'horror and loathsome-
ness of our Graue' (Aa8r-v, Cc2v), Granada invokes a medieval
commonplace by recalling the body's end in becoming 'meate for the
wormes and maggottes of the earthe',[21] and contrasting this destiny
with the delusions of 'gaye pompe':

> In steede of his multitude of delicate dishes, and waiting seruinge men, he
> must haue there such an infinite number of crawling wormes, and fylthie
> maggottes feedinge vpon him, he cannot chuse . . . but merveill to see vnto how
> base a condition such a noble creature is now come, and to consider with
> whom he must now keep companie there, euen fellowe, and fellowe like.
>
> (Aa8r-v)

In Hamlet's exchange with Claudius, worms likewise dethrone
humans as privileged consumers at the top of the food pyramid,
resituating them in a circular relationship with other life forms. But
while Hamlet picks up on Granada's eating and dining metaphors, he
also shifts the function of worms from that of moralizing symbols to
biological agents of ecological reintegration. Reigning in supreme
omnivorousness, the worm is 'your only emperor for diet', a punning
reference to the 1521 Diet, or council, of Worms, where Martin
Luther defended his radical attacks on the Catholic Church.[22] Hamlet's
topical wit veils his seditious dig at Claudius that worms reduce social
hierarchies to biological routines of feeding, digestion, and excretion.
Anticipating Darwin, Hamlet turns worms into essential creatures
of georgic labour. Nature's cycles are neither constrained nor evaded
by the individual's death but enriched by its material translation into
long-term common benefit—'variable service' for the life of 'one

table'—as worms ultimately feed all terrestrial life by maintaining soil fertility. As fellow animal organisms, worms also interact with humans to sustain other local species. Their work challenges the human-centred economies of animal husbandry and artificial selection implied by Hamlet's wry remark, 'We fat all creatures else to fat us' (4.3.22–23). Implicitly the exchange also destabilizes hierarchical polities embedded as generic features of classical and Renaissance tragedy, such as royal families, tyrannical rulers, and heroic revengers.[23]

Although Hamlet's jibes at differences in social rank are proverbial, his apparently flippant tale of Polonius's afterlife responds in unexpected ways to Granada's question, 'what becomes of the physical body after death?':

If it were so, that the bodie in this separation [from the soul] shoulde ende in some thinge that were of anie price or proffit, it woulde be some kinde of comfort vnto vs. But this is a thinge to be wondered at, that so excellent a creature shall ende in the most dishonorable and lothsome thing in the worlde.
(Aa8v)

Granada maintains that dead bodies yield nothing of value, and he illustrates this opinion by recalling Job's contrasting story of the afterlife of a felled tree, which

after it is cut, hath hope to reuiue, and springe againe, and if the roote of it doe rott in the grownde, and the stocke be dead in the earth, yet with the freshnes of water it springeth againe, and bringeth forth leaues, as if it were newlie planted. But man after he is once dead, withered, and consumed, what is become of him?   (Bb1r; Job 14 [original marginal note])

Although the example of Job confirms the human body's inability to regenerate itself, it also inadvertently sets up a positive turn. The regenerating tree he and Granada describe is a real phenomenon, and we now know that earthworms play a part in its revival.[24] As Shakespeare was aware, the ability of cut trees to grow back supported the traditional woodland practice of coppicing (see Chapter 1, p. 41). Coppiced timber had a market value and sustained the lives of local commoners and tenants in places such as the forests of Windsor and Arden. Hamlet sees the positive effects of worms on Polonius's body in a similar light to Granada's regenerating tree-stock. In both cases worms create mutualistic relationships.[25]

In tracing the feeding pathways of Polonius's afterlife, Hamlet identifies their links to larger food webs and more complex nutrient cycles.[26] Worms enable him to re-theorize human mortality as a transitional stage of ongoing ecological interdependency rather than terminal physical closure. Recognizing that the value of his and every other human action will be radically redefined by this biological metadrama, Hamlet begins to reconsider revenge tragedy's underlying assumption that heroic retaliation is the obvious or obligatory remedy for wrongful death.

Comparing de Granada's moral reflections with Hamlet's imaginative performances on Polonius's corpse also reveals the protagonist's evolving attitudes towards metaphysical destinies. From the viewpoint of worms, the relationship between death and life is not ethically fraught. It has no need of symbolic belief-systems that disembody human life to affirm some kind of eternal essence. Instead, Hamlet's physical interactions with Polonius's body—violently convulsed, then slowly draining back into the earth's life—prompt him to look downward and take upon him the mystery of things from below. From there he perceives that all physical matter passes through the bodies of worms to be reborn in new biodynamic relationships. Hamlet's intuition of these natural but non-teleological laws lays the imaginative groundwork for Darwin's evolutionary procedures of reproduction, natural selection, and descent with modification.[27]

Levelling the food and species chains (2): *Antony and Cleopatra*

A worm-oriented perspective reveals that Antony's personal and political conflicts are marked by the same kind of shifting ecological claims that Hamlet perceives in mortal bodies becoming part of the food web. As the play opens, Antony has become partly a creature of Egyptian organicism, or holistic relations, but remains divided by desires to transcend it through heroic passion. The longing for transcendence represents merely a change of object from his more deeply cultivated Roman ambitions for worldly conquest:

> Let Rome in Tiber melt, and the wide arch
> Of the ranged empire fall! Here is my space.
> Kingdoms are clay. Our dungy earth alike

> Feeds beast as man. The nobleness of life
> Is to do thus, [embracing Cleopatra] ...
>   when such a mutual pair,
> And such a twain can do't – in which I bind,
> On pain of punishment, the world to weet
> We stand up peerless.   (1.1.35–42)

As Cleopatra later observes, echoing both Antony and Hamlet, worms maintain Egypt's fertility by converting dung and other matter into nourishing soil that feeds both beggars and Caesar. Along these lines, Edward J. Geisweidt has shown how *Antony and Cleopatra*'s detrital webs of excrement and decomposition represent the universal movement of life forms into productive cycles of decay and growth.[28] Egyptians' view of the earth as dungy also reflects pre-modern and proto-scientific knowledge that the physical environment is in the truest sense alive at all levels:

> Much is breeding,
> Which, like the courser's hair, hath yet but life,
> And not a serpent's poison.   (1.2.191–93)

Egypt's prominent associations with earth and water have led critics to assume that these elements dominate its ecosystems. Mary Floyd-Wilson has demonstrated, however, that Galenic theorists believed all four elements were always reshaping human and animal life—as when Cleopatra feeds herself 'delicious poison' by juxtaposing Antony's description of her as a 'serpent of old Nile' with her present body, sunburnt and wrinkled by 'amorous' Phoebus (1.5.25–29).[29] Although age does wither Cleopatra, her behavioural fitness springs from an awareness of more-than-human connections with Egypt's humoral and physical diversity, whereas Antony's adaptive efforts are invested in trying to reverse his declining virility.[30]

Fertile transience (1)

Gabriel Egan has suggested that Antony and Cleopatra pit themselves against 'the Earth's reproductive principles' because their love is not motivated by having children'.[31] I would read Antony's claim (in his opening speech, cited above) differently because Cleopatra immediately ridicules it: 'Excellent falsehood! / Why, did he marry Fulvia and not love her?' (1.1.42–43). The comma in this line is editorial, so Cleopatra's objection could be a rhetorical question ('Did he not also love Fulvia when he married her?') or a mocking barb ('What was the point of marrying Fulvia if not to have children?'). The second of these inferences suggests that, for Cleopatra, erotic love and fertility are inseparable. (By contrast, Antony's marriage to Fulvia is lawful but apparently childless, and he disingenuously claims to have 'Forborne the getting of a lawful race' by Octavia in order to please Cleopatra [3.13.107–9].) When Cleopatra tries to mollify Antony's jealousy after he has had Thidias whipped, she pledges, 'the next Caesarion smite, / Till by degrees the memory of my womb, / together with my brave Egyptians all, / . . . Lie graveless, [and] the flies and gnats of Nile / Have buried them for prey' (3.13.163–68). This does not mean that Cleopatra ties sex and offspring to the Roman ethos of legitimizing male heirs through marriage. As many critics have observed, Cleopatra expresses a desire to become Antony's wife only after he is dead. At that point her aims are complicated by her determination to thwart Caesar's plan to display her as a prisoner in Rome. Caesar himself snidely notes that Antony and Cleopatra have shamelessly celebrated 'all the issue [of] their lust' in public ceremonies (3.6.1–8). His further sneer that these children included 'Caesarion, whom they call my father's [Julius Caesar's] son' underlines the point that Cleopatra's sexual charisma and political ambitions have always been partly dynastic, which is why they threaten Octavius's authority, since he was not Julius Caesar's biological heir. From Octavius's perspective, Cleopatra's reproductive goals also confuse masculine social imperatives, in which the body's physical claims must be mastered. 'Let's grant it is not / Amiss to tumble on the bed of Ptolemy', Caesar remarks less-than-sincerely to Lepidus, 'yet must Antony / No way excuse his foils when we do bear / So great weight in his lightness' (1.4.16–17, 23–25). Recreational sex is fine off-duty to 'foil', or set off, Antony's paramount identity as a Roman general. 'But to confound such time / That drums him from his sport' not only snubs Caesar but also demeans Rome's ideal of transcending animal instincts by rationally disciplining the body (a theory Iago maliciously inverts to ensnare Othello).

After Messengers bring news of Pompey's maritime attacks on Italy, Caesar expands on this view in a lamenting reproof about Antony's extreme diet as an exiled soldier:

> When thou once
> Was beaten from Medina...
> ...at thy heel
> Did Famine follow, whom thou fought'st against—
> Though daintily brought up—with patience more
> Than savages could suffer. Thou didst drink
> The stale of horses, and the gilded puddle
> Which beasts would cough at. Thy palate then did deign
> The roughest berry on the rudest hedge...
> It is reported thou didst eat strange flesh,
> Which some did die to look on. And all this...
> Was borne so like a soldier that thy cheek
> So much as lanked not.   (1.4.54–71)

Antony consumes horse urine and putrifying flesh too repellent to think about even in extreme starvation. He thereby overcomes environmental adversity by becoming more beastly than beasts yet rising above natural instincts. By situating himself on the lowest rungs of the food chain with maggots, worms, and the 'beetle' in 'his shards', or dung (3.2.20), Antony paradoxically proves his exceptional adaptability as a Roman, which consists not of integrating himself into the natural world but shaping it according to his will.[32] Caesar is also careful to signal that Antony's role, like his own, remains a cultural performance and expresses no genuine identification with nature. As the civilized teller of the story, Caesar distances himself from its contaminating details by aestheticizing them (e.g. the 'gilded puddle', Antony's 'palate'), thereby preserving the superiority of their shared Roman education ('daintily brought up'). Enobarbus deploys a similarly engaged deflection when he mythologizes Antony's submissive encounter with Cleopatra at Cydnus in order to immerse his interlocutors in the Queen's sensuality while shielding himself from its emasculating power. Although audiences may be glad to be seduced by his poetic affects, Caesar's man Agrippa tersely undercuts Enobarbus's strategy by banalizing Cleopatra as fertile dirt: '[Julius Caesar] ploughed her, and she cropped'.

When Antony uses similar agricultural imagery to try to make sense of his conflicting loyalties, he reveals an understanding of Egyptian webs of love, play, and work. The bioregional emblem of these networks is the Nile, with its seasonal rhythms of flooding, fertility, decay, and regeneration:

> ANTONY
> Thus they do, sir: they take the flow o'th'Nile
> By certain scales i'th'pyramid; they know
> By th'height, the lowness, or the mean, if dearth
> Or foison follow. The higher Nilus swells,
> The more it promises: as it ebbs the seedsman
> Upon the slime and ooze scatters his grain,
> And shortly comes to harvest.   (2.7.17–23)

As Antony eggs on Lepidus's drunken recollections of Egypt's pro-verbial wonders such as spontaneously generating crocodiles, he begins to sound like a parody of an animal-rights activist: '[Your crocodile] is shaped, sir, like itself, and it is as broad as it hath breadth. It is just so high as it is, and moves with it own organs. It lives by that which nourisheth it, and the elements once out of it, it transmigrates' (2.7.41–44). Antony's humorous variation on the Pythagorean theory of transmigrating animal souls prefigures molecular and genetic levels of kinship. That Shakespeare, like Darwin, could have intuited such possibilities without knowing their cellular mechanisms is suggested by the changes he made to his natural history source material. In *A Geographical History of Africa* (1600), Leo Africanus makes the reason-able claim that moderate flooding of the Nile generates optimal fruitfulness—an environmental golden mean—whereas excessive inun-dations suppress fertility. Antony instead reports that the greater the river's flooding, the richer Egypt's harvests (Neill n. to 2.7.17–23). If this is not simply a bibulous hyperbole, Shakespeare takes a Darwinian turn away from treating the effects of death and life as opposing values and instead merges them in sustainability-in-death relationships. The engulfing Nile suggests layers of interconnectedness that produce more complex biodiversity and, in turn, greater ecological resilience—the ability to withstand and productively diffuse disturbances.

Early in one of the play's messenger scenes, in which Shakespeare uses the reception of bad news to draw out Antony's and Cleopatra's charac-ters, Antony commands the Messenger not to spare his sensibilities:

> Name Cleopatra as she is called in Rome...
> ... and taunt my faults

> With such full licence as both truth and malice
> Have power to utter. O, then we bring forth weeds,
> When our quick winds lie still; and our ills told us
> Is as our earing.   (1.2.106–111)

Antony's meaning remains clear until 'O, then...' when the logical relationship to his preceding thoughts becomes murky. Switching once more to an agricultural metaphor based on his exposure to Egyptian soils and environments, he likens 'minc[ing]' Roman public opinion to the sprouting of 'weeds', and he prefers unvarnished reports of the truth to ploughing ('earing') the soil. By contrast, a coil of opinion is brought forth when 'quick winds', or natural processes of germination—like those stirred by the Nile's annual flooding—are absent. Antony thus associates plain truth with organic diversity over monocultures, and he values biodynamically attuned production over maximally efficient growth, which erases political and ecological wisdom. Antony has learned these distinctions from the life-sustaining effects of Egypt's environment on his own body, since Galenic theories of physiology posited that living creatures were susceptible to mental and corporeal changes brought about by what Mary Floyd-Wilson calls 'geo-humoralism' (see Chapter 3, p. 96).[33]

Goaded by his rivalry with Caesar, however, Antony retreats to the imaginative refuge of imperial ecology after his humiliating defeat at Actium and Mardian's false report of Cleopatra's suicide. Hastening to bridge the chasm between his past glories and present disgraces, he recalls:

> I...with my sword
> Quartered the world, and o'er green Neptune's back
> With ships made cities....   (4.15.57–59)

Antony's near-Eastern conquests paved the way for Roman urbanization and technologies to spread throughout the known world (as far away as Britain, through Antony's predecessor Julius Caesar and successor, Claudius, as Shakespeare reminds audiences in *Cymbeline* [Chapter 4], and which Darwin discovered first-hand while investigating earthworms; see below in this chapter). Early modern colonialism revived these ambitions as overseas discoveries expanded geo-physical and political borders, and scientific innovation spurred Western hopes of extracting ever-greater human benefits from global resources. In both periods the ecological consequences of imperial growth were excessive carrying capacities, in which consumption of resources outstripped supplies and undermined long-term sustainability. In Antony's time, one particular challenge was supplying food for Rome's expanding legions, including the squandering 'waste' with which Caesar feasts them to secure their loyalty after capturing Egypt's storehouses (4.1.15–16). These excesses made gaining control over grain supplies in client states such as Egypt essential, as Pompey confirms when he mentions the obligation to send 'Measures of wheat to Rome' from Sicily and Sardinia that was part of his post-civil-war agreement with the triumvirate (2.6.37). The long-term environmental effect was the deforestation and erosion of the Mediterranean basin, resulting in the semi-desert landscapes that still dominate the region today.[34]

Fertile transience (2)

Extinction rather than genetic inheritance is the biological norm of Shakespearian tragedy, and it is sharply gendered. Unlike comedy, which gives women central roles in peopling the world, tragedy represents what Linda Woodbridge calls a 'triumph of sterility' through the childlessness and/or deaths of its women characters. In *Titus Andronicus*, *Romeo and Juliet*, *Othello*, *King Lear*, and *Macbeth*, reproduction fails to happen or is cut off, and family lines fail. 'Except in the Roman plays,' Woodbridge notes, 'Shakespeare kills off every woman prominent enough to have appeared in a tragedy's last scene'.[35] In *Antony and Cleopatra*, the Queen's dynastic hopes are extinguished by Caesar. In *Hamlet* this 'anti-fertility agenda' is represented chiefly by Ophelia. Dismissed by Hamlet to a nunnery,[36] she expresses the shock of her father's death in bawdy songs and laments (4.5). Conventionally these signal a frustrated sexuality that ends, according to Gertrude, in ambiguous suicide:

> Her clothes spread wide,
> And mermaid-like awhile they bore her up;
> Which time she chanted snatches of old tunes,
> As one incapable of her own distress,
> Or like a creature native and endued

> Unto that element. But long it could not be,
> Till that her garments, heavy with their drink,
> Pulled the poor wretch from her melodious lay
> To muddy death.   (4.7.150–58)

Gertrude at first elegizes Ophelia as a mermaid-swan, floating sky-wards and chanting like the angels who will later sing Hamlet to his rest. The image gestures at an Ovidian refiguring of bodily decay as sublime metamorphosis. Gertrude then shifts direction, however, with Ophelia's physical descent into the river's mud. From the perspective of dramatic tragedy, and Shakespeare's tragic women in particular, this is a typical moment of isolation prior to death and lost fertility. But from the perspective of the river's ecosystem it looks different. The brook recalls the scene of Hamlet's fisherman in the Polonius passage I cited earlier, and hence a reversion to the fertile matrix of wild nature. To recall Hamlet again: 'A man may fish with the worm that hath eat of a king, and eat of the fish that hath fed of that worm' (4.3.27–28). This time it is Ophelia's body that becomes food for worms and other micro-organisms which feed the fish, which the man catches using the worms who have eaten Polonius. The worms recycle Polonius's body-as-nutrients back into the soil to nourish the herbs and flowers Ophelia distributes during her songs, and which Gertrude later strews on her grave.

Reimagining John Everett Millais's continually adapted image of Ophelia as riparian detritus (Figure 5.2) represents the kind of dark ecological turn which Timothy Morton argues is necessary for envir-onmentalism to move beyond Romantic aesthetics of nature.[37] Real organic decay may offend decorum and be personally painful, but as genetically progressive interactions of fertility, reproduction, and bio-diversity, it is morally and biologically neutral. The natural world's seeming 'indifference' to our feelings as bereaved creatures of memory invites us to relativize our proper grief within a metabiotic perspective like the one Ariel suggests to Ferdinand in describing his supposedly drowned father in *The Tempest*:

> Full fathom five thy father lies,
> Of his bones are coral made,
> Those are pearls that were his eyes;
> Nothing of him doth fade,

Figure 5.2. Sir John Everett Millais, *Ophelia* (1851–52). Reproduced by Permission of the Tate Gallery.

> But doth suffer a sea-change
> Into something rich and strange.   (1.2.397–402)

In the final paragraph of *The Formation of Vegetable Mould*, Darwin points out that only corals surpass worms as foundational agents of biological transformation.[38] Both not only preserve but also remake the physical world ('Nothing of him doth fade'). Corals live only in tropical zones, however, whereas the range of worms is now much wider. Their labour was visible to Darwin as well as Shakespeare in their beloved gardens. A lifetime of admiring study explains their privileged appearance in the final famous paragraph of *Origin of Species*.[39] There worms negotiate Darwin's diplomatic transition between older and newer scientific and cultural horizons—between the opening pastoral imagery of singing birds and flitting insects, and the ending's counter-elegiac conclusion in which ecologically entangled growth, inheritance, and 'variable service' flourish out of the struggles for life.[40]

Gertrude's mythologizing of Ophelia gently reorients spectators away from the impossible goal of 'transcendental objectivity' implied by the revenge quest, now taken up fiercely by Laertes, towards a neo-Darwinian aesthetic.[41] She introduces a new conception of symbiotic networking within the immanent vitality of organic life. Her story also suggests a shift in personal convictions from her earlier 'common' assurance to Hamlet that 'all that lives must die, / Passing through nature to eternity' (1.2.72–73); that is, rise from material nature into metaphysics. Gertrude's evolved ecological outlook prepares audiences imaginatively for Hamlet's continued revisioning of the revenge imperative in the fifth act's biotropic sequence of the Gravediggers' skulls and Ophelia's funeral. Hamlet's alternatives are clarified, I think, by the actions of another mudbound tragic hero, Cleopatra; so I will consider her journey first.

Follow the slime: Pathways of extinction and survival

Earlier I suggested that Antony expresses his desire for Cleopatra partly by drawing on his new knowledge of Egyptian terrains and ecosystems ('Here is my space'). Because of his shallow roots in Egypt, however, this environmental identity fails to displace his Roman impulses to master nature, epitomized by the mythology of Herculean overcoming that personifies his dedication to an idealized masculine individualism. Antony's destruction by these competing ecological and political value-systems stands in contrast to Hamlet's gradual renegotiation of the Ghost's duty of self-sacrificing revenge, which he juxtaposes against patterns of natural transience and non-transcendent redemption by worms. His internal debate coincides with his father's receding presence in the dramatic action, from the Ghost's appearance to Hamlet alone in Act Three, to his complete disappearance thereafter.

Cleopatra, on the other hand, surpasses her lover's bungled attempt to salvage his Roman identity through suicide. Her final performance juggles political and ecological desires for respective transcendence from, and deepest kinship with, Egypt's webs of life. The country's regenerative values become visible in earlier moments such as the Soothsayer's fortune-telling (1.2). There Charmian's bawdy dream-play burlesques the language of early modern wonder-ballads (e.g. 1.2.26–30) to uncover 'nature's infinite book of secrecy' (associated in learned Renaissance circles with 'Egyptian' hermetic writings). In *A Midsummer Night's Dream*, *The Winter's Tale*, and other plays,

Shakespeare parodies ballad reports of extreme weather events and 'freaks' of nature which moralists seized on as providential warnings about sinful behaviour. By contrast, the Nile's marvels of elemental (re-)generation infuse the reproductive fantasies of Charmian, Alexas, and Iras with unabashed pleasure. Their bawdy thrusts and ripostes reciprocate Antony and Cleopatra's more rhetorically decorous performances of desire. In both cases the speakers display a range of gesture and affect shared with non-human animals. In *The Expression of the Emotions in Man and Animals* (1872), Darwin documented this kind of crossover repertoire, showing how it encodes interactive choices of sexual selection. Its absence in the marriage negotiations over Octavia foreshadows the extinctive future of her union with Antony.

Roman observers, on the other hand, regard Cleopatra's court as decadent and bestial. Its perceived laxity offends not only proto-Augustan 'family values' but also Roman self-identification with epic mythologies of human nature. Twelve people eating eight roasted boars for breakfast confirms the prevailing Roman image of Egyptian excess, even though this hospitality intentionally flatters imperial Roman appetites. It also hints at human digestive physiology being monstered (2.2.186–87). Whereas Cleopatra's playful substitution of salt- for fresh-water fish at the end of Antony's gullible line mimics the benign human–animal humour of her attendants, Antony existentia-lizes such boundary crossings in increasingly tragic terms. His 'doting mallard' routine at Actium, the scapegoating desertion of his legions, and his corporeal vulnerability to Caesar's 'penetrative shame', transform him into a 'savage cause' like the 'hornèd herd' of Bashan (3.13.128–29). Eventually he teeters psychologically on the brink of hypermorphosis:

> Sometime we see a cloud that's dragonish,
> A vapour sometime like a bear or lion,
> A towered citadel, a pendant rock,
> A forkèd mountain, or blue promontory
> With trees upon't.... (4.15.2–6)

Behind Antony's dissolving identity lurks an Ovidian nightmare of primordial biomass, or non-differentiated organic life in aggregate, which the Roman world associated with reversionary states of wild

nature such as primeval forests, shipwrecking oceans, or the submer-
sive Nile.[42] Antony tries to redirect his collapsing identity into a
post-hoc affirmation of human essence through suicide (4.16). Only
the allegorically figured Eros is able to play out this dream, however.
What we and the apparently shaken Cleopatra see on stage is the
human vitality bleeding uncontrollably out of Antony's body. The
precarious efforts of hauling him up to Cleopatra's monument, and
her inattention to his repeated cries of dying, create theatrical tur-
bulence which makes it difficult to read his death either as romantic
transcendence by a now swordless 'bridegroom in ... death' (100) or
as benign transience.

Forewarned of Caesar's intentions to humiliate her in Rome,
Cleopatra aspires to overreach him. 'Proportioned to our cause', her
performance must be 'as great / As that which makes it' and 'after the
high Roman fashion' (4.16.5–6, 88). But behind these aspirations,
initially, is an underlying plan for biological and political afterlife
through her surviving family. Commentators routinely observe that
Shakespeare ignores Plutarch's description of the fate of Cleopatra's
children, including Caesar's murder of Caesarion. Shakespeare likewise avoids the contemporary sentimental colouring of Cleopatra as a
soon-to-be bereaved mother found in Robert Garnier's *Marc Antoine*
(1578), the Countess of Pembroke's translation, *The Tragedy of Antony*
(1595), and Samuel Daniel's *The Tragedy of Cleopatra* (1594). Instead
Shakespeare places primary emphasis on Cleopatra's personal queen-
ship and suicide.

Although this makes good thematic and structural sense, I would
say that the presence of Cleopatra's children is something more than
'purely nominal' (Neill n. to 5.2.130–33). Cleopatra hopes to preserve
'the circle of Ptolemies for her heirs' (3.12.19). 'If [Caesar] please / To
give me conquered Egypt for my son', she says later to Proculeius,
whom Antony has advised her to confide in, 'He gives me so much of
mine own as I / Will kneel to him with thanks' (5.2.18–21). She
covertly persists in this hope after Caesar threatens her children if
she takes her own life (5.2.128–33). Stewart Cole argues that this hope
would have been more apparent to early modern spectators in the
context of increasing non-aristocratic attention to the valuation and
transmission of material property through inheritance laws. These
historical conditions focus attention on the double meaning of

Cleopatra's bold avowal before her treasurer Seleucus of the exact 'money, plate, and jewels / I am possessed of', with 'nothing' secretly reserved 'To myself' (5.2.138–44). The subtext is that she has kept aside the rest of her wealth for her heirs, appropriately prioritizing her children's well-being and her family's dynastic future.[43] Seleucus's unexpected failure to corroborate the finely distinguished truth of her loyalties (and pronouns) incenses Cleopatra. Thus betrayed, her improvised half-admission of keeping 'some nobler token' for Livia and Octavia (of all people!) succeeds in deflecting attention away from her original plan to save her children and their bequeathed wealth. Seleucus, for his part, may be pragmatically switching sides to Caesar's rising fortunes. Both his double-cross and Dolabella's subsequent disclosure that Caesar intends to display Cleopatra and her children in Rome (5.2.200–2) cancels her hopes of outdoing personal death through lineal inheritance. She leaves her children to their fate, which educated early modern spectators would have accepted with a sense of irony in relation to Caesar's historical role as a herald of 'universal' Roman and Christian 'peace' (4.6.4).

Cleopatra's other option consists of transcending fate downward:

> Rather a ditch in Egypt
> Be gentle grave unto me! Rather on the Nilus' mud
> Lay me stark naked, and let the water-flies
> Blow me into abhorring!   (5.2.57–60)

She converges this physical transformation and the political humiliation of Caesar with the help of the 'pretty worm / Of Nilus', whose biting is in both senses of the word 'immortal' (5.2.242–43, 245–46, 280). Naively refusing to soften his account of the worm's lethalness, the Clown emphasizes the physical pain suffered by its most recent female victim. He thereby underlines the creature's autonomy as it pursues its own interests: 'the worm will do his kind' (261–62). Cleopatra recognizes that she cannot dominate but only synchronize her life with the worm's own instincts. Initially it refuses to be co-opted as a surrogate object of romantic and maternal desire, just as Crab stubbornly refuses the family roles Lance thrusts upon him in *The Two Gentleman of Verona*. Cleopatra's command, 'Poor venomous fool, / Be angry, and dispatch', indicates that the worm is taking its time, even though it cannot be entirely itself (5.2.304–5). Eventually, however, it becomes alarmed by Cleopatra's handling and gives her its distress signal. The Queen makes their embrace culturally legible under the ritual signs of the fertility and animal goddess Isis. The arriving Caesar and his officers ignore this symbolism, however. Instead they Romanize the event by distancing it from its material significance. Caesar detaches the scene from his now-dashed plans of triumph by authorizing its interpretation as a romantic sacrifice (glancing back dramatically to Shakespeare's *Romeo and Juliet*). Against this image Dollabella and the First Guard juxtapose an autopsy of Cleopatra's venting body, itemizing the material remains of Cleopatra's interspecies encounter and unconsciously blazing her pathway back to Egypt's bioregional matrix:

> This is an aspic's trail, and these fig-leaves
> Have slime upon them, such as th'aspic leaves
> Upon the caves of Nile.   (5.2.349–51)

Recalling Hamlet's down-to-earth orientations with the Gravediggers, audiences recognize that this semiotically overflowing moment represents more than forensic diligence or an inert backdrop for Caesar's mythologizing. Worms do not simply release Cleopatra's spirit from this 'knot intrinsicate' to 'catch another Antony / In her strong toil of grace' (*Antony and Cleopatra*, 5.2.303, 345–46). They also transpose her body into the sustaining life of the Nile's food webs and Egypt's evolutionary becomings.

Shakespeare enriches Cleopatra's ecological reunion with contextual valences of fertile transience beyond death. She reclaims what is normally lost in culture's separation from nature through her paradoxical identification with Antony. He becomes both the romantic source of her natural 'oblivion', and 'nature's piece 'gainst Fancy, / Condemning shadows quite' (1.3.91, 5.2.99–100). Imagining Antony 'past the size of dreaming', Cleopatra inverts Philip Sidney's celebration of human creativity over transitory nature and history. Metabiosis, or the regenerating diversity of organic matter, she implies, is more sublime than the poet's golden world. Cleopatra also refigures Antony in her own image by describing his delights as 'dolphin-like' (5.2.89). Commentators usually explain this phrase as Cleopatra's mythical elevation of Antony, troped by the dolphin's proverbial reputation for saving people from drowning (e.g. Sebastian in *Twelfth Night*,

1.2.14). Yet as Shakespeare observed elsewhere, the dolphin is biologically amorphous—'neither fish nor flesh'. It playfully exceeds the
epistemological boundaries of traditional natural history and outdoes
Romantic *liebestod*.[44] In following Cleopatra's example, Charmian
aspires to both this ecocentric horizon and her mistress's natural
ecstasy (literally, ex-stasis) when she offers to mend her crown 'and
then play' (5.2.232, 317).

Viewed from the perspective of dolphin and worm, Cleopatra's
performance as Antony's 'wife' redeems his failed Roman suicide by
turning him into a hybrid creature. Her identification with the elements
of fire and air conventionally juxtapose soul and body after the manner
of moral commentators such as de Granada. Yet like her sea-mammal
Antony, she rejoices in water and earth as well, characterizing them not
as obliterating or alien mediums but as pathways of natural consummation (anticipating Arviragus and Guiderius's integration of Innogen's
body into their Welsh ecosystem; see Chapter 4, pp. 128–31):

> Have I the aspic on my lips? Dost fall?
> If thou and nature can so gently part,
> The stroke of death is as a lover's pinch
> Which hurts, and is desired.   (5.2.292–95)

As gentle (i.e. maggoty) as balm and air, flyblown burial wings
Cleopatra back to the Nile's infinite recombination of life forms, on
which she models her megafaunic identity as an inexhaustible lover
(5.2.310). If we chose to see beyond tragedy's conventional antagon-
ism between culture and nature, and beyond anthropocentric categories of knowledge and being, Cleopatra's symbiosis redefines death as
post-human tragicomedy. In *Antony and Cleopatra* Shakespeare adds a
pre-Darwinian dimension of ecological temporality to the glorious but
fleeting consolations of romantic transcendence over youthful extinction staged in *Romeo and Juliet*. *Hamlet* gestures towards similar nested
timescales, even if its dramatic bias of revenge-killing, and the final
triumph of top carnivore Fortinbras, theatrically overshadows them.

Until we meet again, Alexander

Ophelia's journey into nature reported by Gertrude is doubled by
her land-burial in the second half of the Gravediggers' scene (5.1).

The funeral is one of the play's often-discussed 'maimed rites'.[45] It gives little comfort to Ophelia's survivors, fails to bring the community together, and is ambiguous as a symbolic separation of corrupt body and incorruptible spirit, in the manner de Granada idealizes. Beforehand, the Gravediggers parody the coroner's inquest that ostensibly resolves whether Ophelia was a suicide. When Hamlet and Horatio arrive to get caught up in their irreverently literalizing humour, it first suggests to them that the First Gravedigger has 'no [proper] feeling of his business' (5.1.64–65). But after he heaves up a skull, Hamlet begins to imagine a more authentically redemptive process than Ophelia's funeral: natural burial by worms:

> HAMLET   This might be my Lord Such-a-one ... might
> it not?
> HORATIO   Ay, my lord.
> HAMLET   Why, e'en so, and now my Lady Worm's,
> chapless, and knocked about the mazard with a sexton's
> spade. Here's fine revolution, if we had the trick to
> see't.   (5.1.80–86)

Hamlet's apostrophe could mean 'my Lady Worm's skull', like the generic 'Lord Such-a-one's', and it could also mean the skull and body of the lady have become food for worms, like Polonius and Ophelia earlier. Similarly 'revolution' could mean the cycle from soil to food to body to worm and back to soil, as well as a biocentric translation of the Lady's social status to the level of worm. (Revolution has not yet acquired its modern sense of a violent break from the previous political order.) Hamlet recognizes that whichever meaning we attribute to the skull as a metonymic sign—the traditional one of human mutability, or the worm-oriented one—depends on having the will to observe closely the environmental processes happening underground.[46] There, decomposition does not mark the end of materiality, which is limited neither to human perceptions of its physical state nor to its dialectic value in the human realm of social relations.[47] Hamlet's empirically focused thoughts about mortality gradually accept the viewpoint of the Gravedigger from below, that burials are not for separating the quick and the dead but for converging their states in the eco-drama of metabiosis, like that towards which the worms of Nilus usher

Cleopatra, and the Welsh winter-ground 'composts' Innogen. Hamlet pursues this insight in imagining the physical afterlife of Alexander, in down-to-earth prose:

> HAMLET   To what base uses we may return, Horatio. Why, may not the imagination trace the noble dust of Alexander till he find it stopping a bung-hole?
> HORATIO   'Twere to consider too curiously to consider so.
> HAMLET   No, faith, not a jot; but to follow him thither with modesty enough, and likelihood to lead it. As thus: Alexander died, Alexander was buried, Alexander returneth into dust. The dust is earth, of earth we make loam, and why of that loam whereto he was converted might they not stop a beer-barrel?   (5.1.193–202)

This understanding of terrestrial ecology recalls Timon's description of the earth (its cynicism aside) as 'a thief', whose life-renewing processes of feeding and breeding originate in a detrital 'composture stol'n / From general excrement' (*Timon of Athens*, 14.441–42). Although the 'uses' of physical decay appear to be degrading, in Polonius Hamlet has already glimpsed death productively transformed by the activities of worms. Here his insights continue to evolve. Riffing off the Gravedigger, Hamlet's rhetorical cadence of death, burial, and dust inverts the 'thrasonical brag' of Alexander's Plutarchian counterpart, Julius Caesar: 'I came, I saw, I conquered' (or 'overcame'). Hamlet extends the ecological horizons opened up by Polonius and Yorick, reconstructing Alexander's exceptionalism as another earthbound journey through worms, this time into loam and a stopper.[48]

What kind of stopper depends on two possible meanings of 'loam' in Shakespeare's day. It could signify a mixture of clay, sand, and dung, hardened to make plaster (*OED* 1a, 2). Or it could mean fertile soil digested by worms (*OED* 1b, 3), and thus imply the humus for cork trees that supplied the other common material used for stoppers.[49] Alexander's rebirth as a barrel cork sardonically undercuts his imperial ambitions while recalling Hamlet's eco-networking of Polonius, fish, and angler. There is also a nice irony of justice, because Alexander was notorious for killing his best friend

Cleitus in a drunken rage (a story Fluellen refers to in *Henry V*, 4.7.35).

Hamlet's juxtaposition of classical empire-builders and worms raises another shared connection with *Antony and Cleopatra* and Darwin which relates to the breaking-down of the culture and nature divide. In the fourth chapter of *The Formation of Vegetable Mould*, Darwin describes his visits to various places around southern England where the remains of Roman Britain were being excavated. Having shown in an earlier chapter the 'Amount of Fine Earth Brought Up By Worms To The Surface', Darwin was curious to measure the thickness of the vegetable-mould layer at these sites, and to observe 'The Part Which Worms Have Played In The Burial Of Ancient Buildings' (ch. 4, title). This apparent digression amplifies Darwin's overall contention that worms are life-directed makers of the world. Their digestive labours not only nourish terrestrial evolution but also preserve the material artefacts of human culture. Although they are only following nature's laws, without preconceptions or intentions, Darwin regards worms as natural historians, collaborating with archaeologists and antiquarians to bring back the past into the present as both social difference and continuity.

Darwin was first alerted to this role for worms after reading about iron arrow-heads from the battle of Shrewsbury (best known in Darwin's time, perhaps, from Shakespeare's *Henry IV Part One*). These turned up in a grassy field outside the town that was ploughed to lie fallow and naturally regenerate itself (the human-evolved equivalent of worms' preparation of soil to become turf). After a local antiquarian wrote about the discoveries, Darwin was inspired to visit other excavation sites of Roman towns. His discussions with local workers confirmed that worms had penetrated the pavements and stone walls of buildings so that they subsided or collapsed. In other words, the worms had buried them in their habitual action of casting up soil. They also conserved human skeletons in hypocausts, the hollow spaces under ancient floors used to accumulate heat for houses or baths. Worms therefore literally undermined the Roman world, but also preserved it. Although the Romans are now gone, memory of their civilization survives through the material collaboration of worms with the cultural work of historians such as Plutarch and dramatists like

Shakespeare. Worms similarly feed Hamlet's imaginative regeneration of the physical past through his rhetorical and dramatic inventions.

The afterlife of sparrows

As the scene shifts to Ophelia's funeral proper, commentators often remark that Hamlet's political declaration, 'This is I, / Hamlet the Dane' (5.1.247–48), and his breezy description of Rosencrantz and Guildenstern 'go[ing] to it' (5.2.13–60), signal a change in tone and outlook. Out of these experiences of 'rash' and 'indiscrete' action, Hamlet forthrightly states, 'There's a divinity that shapes our ends, / Rough-hew them how we will' (5.2.10–11). He also claims that heaven was 'ordinant' in the deaths of his erstwhile friends (5.2.49). To many actors and critics, these categorical remarks suggest Hamlet has made peace with the idea of human action directed by the will of providence, or that he goes into the final duel as a fatalist. He puts a Christian gloss on these sentiments at the end of his conversation with Horatio by alluding to Matthew 10.29: 'There's a special providence in the fall of a sparrow' (5.2.167–86). Contextually this seems to say that, since divine grace and a higher purpose guide life's apparent randomness, one need not bother trying to determine the outcome of events that may at any time end in the spirit's liberation from 'solid flesh'. Hamlet therefore puts aside the illness he feels about his heart (5.2.159)—possibly a premonition that the coming duel with Laertes will be fatal—and concludes, 'Let be' (5.2.170, Quarto 2 only). But as critics and performers have often felt, the play's final actions—the duel's accidental calamities, the excessive deaths, and Fortinbras's conquest—seem difficult to square with Hamlet's unwonted metaphysical confidence, or the affirmation of providential justice, or any conscious fulfillment of the Ghost's commands.

Alternatively, Hamlet's reflections on the worm-assisted labour of organic transience suggest that the convergent lives of fallen sparrow and tragic hero do not end in flights of angels or existential irony. Hamlet points to a different horizon of expectations in describing the sparrow's fall as the sign of a 'special providence'. Unconditionally determining in itself, providence does not require the tautological qualifier 'special'. This logical wobble opens the possibility that Hamlet is redefining absolute reality in something other than conventional metaphysical terms. Ewan Fernie's stimulating reading of *Hamlet* is suggestive in this regard. He argues that Hamlet's meditation on the sparrow's fall results in an ethical commitment to radical spontaneity in the present moment which seeks to realize a Kierkegaardian 'metaphysics of rashness'. In the play's final scene Hamlet belatedly enacts his heroic role with a 'militant indifference' that transcends the material constraints of the revenge-quest and detaches him from political and symbolic orders. Fernie's interpretation of Hamlet's self-surrender to radical contingency is compelling, but I would reorient it from metaphysics to the biodiversity Hamlet has been discovering in worms and food webs. They signify a human-and-beyond, but non-transcendent, regeneration which redefines the absolute as metabiosis. What becomes clearer to Hamlet in the graveyard is not a turn away from material alterity—'a mode of opposition to what is' (to continue from Fernie's reading).[50] Instead Hamlet discovers a shared desire for environmental belonging that dissolves social constructions of difference in an integration of human consciousness and webs of organic life. This hypo-physical condition is not alien to human difference but an evolved knowledge of its buried truths of absolute dwelling, including mortality, decomposition, and fertile (re)birth. In a world where worms recreate human life as an eighth age of man, *Hamlet* challenges revenge tragedy's metaphysical violence and self-consuming desires by resituating them in relation to the non-linear rhythms of evolutionary nature. Hamlet's imaginative journey with Alexander leads to an understanding of the 'modesty' and 'likelihood' of these interactions (5.1.198).

Although his tone and situation are different from Hamlet's, Timon of Athens again echoes this reconception of nature as a biospheric 'domestication' of metaphysics:

> Why should you want? Behold, the earth hath roots;
>> Within this mile break forth a hundred springs;
>> The oaks bear mast, the briers scarlet hips.
>> The bounteous housewife nature on each bush
>> Lays her full mess before you. Want? Why want?
>>> (14.417–421)[51]

In *Hamlet* the fertilizing labour of worms indicates that after the sparrow falls to the ground, its natural history continues. Like Polonius, Ophelia, and Alexander, its contribution to sustaining the earth is of no less value than that of living human beings, despite the biblical discourse that privileges them (Matthew 10.31), and neo-Romantic readings that celebrate the irreplaceable singularity of the tragic hero. The biodiversity of 'great creating nature' (*The Winter's Tale*, 4.4.88) is ready to absorb and recycle them all to new reproductive uses. The sparrow's and Hamlet's shared destinies, like those of Cleopatra and her worm, are not tragic isolation and disintegration—with a special escape clause for the human soul—but physical translation into the accidentally estranging but nested diversity of the natural world. Such assimilations may be painful in terms of personal human loss, but are morally neutral and ecologically desirable as pathways of genetic inheritance and adaptation. And unlike the sparrow (we presume), Hamlet possesses the human privilege of becoming conscious of this process through language. He knows that when it is his turn to fat worms which 'fat all creatures else', his life will have served a bio-dynamic purpose.

Near the end of his section on Darwin's worms, Adam Phillips asks: 'What would our lives be like if we took earthworms seriously, took the ground under our feet rather than the skies high above our heads, as the place to look, as well, eventually, as the place to be?' (60–61). Hamlet, I've been suggesting, focuses attention in the same direction, problematizing the redemptive teleology imposed on him as 'the son of a dear father murdered' with an underground narrative of organic transience. This story dispenses with human myths of triumph over mortality, and gestures generically in the direction of what Joseph Meeker calls the comedy of survival.[52] 'Let be' acknowledges an ecological reality that challenges the still-common view of Shakespearian tragedy as the representation of human error and loss symbolically redeemed by heroic suffering and transcendent self-consciousness.

Can intuited awareness of the deep vitality of micro- and macro-biological symbiosis cure a grieving son's heartache for his murdered father? Probably not entirely, because, as Cleopatra's tussles with the asp show, humans do not simply live in nature, but outside it too. But arguably Hamlet's insights about worms and death propose some measure of imaginative comfort—or hospitable restitution, to use Phillips's terms—for the pain of personal grief. Nor does this recognition imply abandoning justice. On the contrary, the levelling and interdependent labour of worms, as Darwin perceived, suggests collaborative models of social and political organization that are entirely relevant to the cooperation necessary to confront today's environmental crises. By (re)discovering these paradigms for us, Hamlet also corrects the distortions of social Darwinism—'survival of the fittest' and the ideology of aggressive competition—homologized by Fortinbras's outlier individualism and hostile takeover of Denmark.[53]

Epilogue

Shakespeare and Ecology in performance

Shakespeare's plays reflect early modern awareness that relations between human and non-human life and their physical environments were changing. Their direct or contextual representation of new threats such as climate change, population growth, deforestation, biologically degrading cultivation practices, and gunpowder militarization clarified the presence of real but sometimes distant and complex new disturbances to daily lives. Shakespeare's vivid perceptions of micro- and macro-networks of organic life also invited audiences to compare local or regional English environments with the period's empirically expanding boundaries of global nature. By registering these multi-scaled conditions of dwelling and natural history, Shakespeare anticipated today's similarly fluid state of ecological knowledge and its leading paradigm of interdependence. His plays also construct imaginative bridges between post-Darwinian ontologies and post-humanist ethics by reflecting pre-Cartesian ideas about the shared mental and physical capacities of human and non-human animals. As I have tried to suggest in this book's selectively focused discussions, the scope for exploring such connections further remains richly open.

Because Shakespeare wrote professionally as a playwright and poet, rather than as a natural historian, he wove his age's nascent understanding of ecology as both science and environmental politics into the metaphoric textures and situational dynamics of his dialogue, often under the veil of humour and irony. His creative approach to early modern ecologies licenses critical practices that extend the limits of his period's geophysical knowledge, and that suggest productive analogies with our own ecological challenges. Recent ecocritics have been seizing such opportunities to help us rethink environmentally destructive economic and social paradigms (see Further Reading).

Shakespeare's greatest possibilities for becoming our eco-contemporary, however, arguably lie not in academic discourse but in performance. Part of this potential comes from Shakespeare's extraordinary global reach and seemingly inexhaustible capacity for reinvention, whether in local shows, regional and worldwide tours, or proliferating digital platforms. In theatre productions specifically, but perhaps other mediums as well, audiences see and feel a physical space shaping the bodily interactions of players, characters, and audiences—in-the-moment relations which Shakespeare often asks us to notice within his dramatic fictions. These spatial and kinetic feedbacks implicitly convey an environmentalist ethos: that actual or imagined environments are not decorative or utilitarian backdrops for human-centred relations, but have independent agency and determining energies of their own. Further, because Shakespeare in modern performance continues to appeal to a wide range of hearts and minds, his plays wield affective and imaginative power for shifting personal convictions and behaviours in ways that pioneering ecologists such as Aldo Leopold recognized were essential for stirring up environmental complacency and motivating progressive action.

Yet so far relatively few professional productions have experimented with making Shakespeare our eco-contemporary. Whatever the reasons for their hesitancy, this situation seems likely to change. The imaginations of future directors and actors will almost certainly reflect the growing pressures of climate change, habitat destruction, and species loss in twenty-first-century public discourse and international relations (which may include conflict over shrinking resources such as water). Today's astonishing range of linguistic and cultural adaptations also make Shakespeare more globally open than ever to staging either historically derived or contemporary threats to local landscapes, regional watersheds, and global oceans. (I have not said much about Shakespeare's seascapes in this book, partly for reasons of space and partly because they are the subject of excellent recent work by Steve Mentz, Daniel Brayton, and Lowell Duckert; see Further Reading.)

I'd like to illustrate the possibilities of ecocritical Shakespeare in performance with a suggestive example: Rupert Goold's 2006 Royal Shakespeare Company production of *The Tempest*, designed by Giles

Cadle and starring Patrick Stewart.[1] This production broke radically with the vaguely Mediterranean or balmy New World settings of conventional productions, yet its fiercely environmental ethos was coherently attuned to Shakespeare's original ecological insights. Goold made a harsh polar and/or post-catastrophic landscape an active 'character' in his recreated story of adaptive survival against environmental adversity. He also reinvented the protean identity of Shakespeare's island by interweaving material and metaphoric signs of contemporary eco-narratives into the play's main tale of Prospero, a usurped and exiled Milanese Duke who uses magical arts to bring his enemies into his power but ultimately forbears punishing them violently.

Goold avoided the perennial problem of trying to hear the opening scene's dialogue of shipwreck through the simulated noise of a raging sea-storm by projecting the image of a 1960s marine transmitter onto a translucent stage-screen. While the audio broadcast a series of fishing and weather bulletins, the radar dial flashed the sweep of an approaching storm. The dial then turned into a porthole-lens showing a grainy black-and-white video of *The Tempest*'s Mariners fighting a losing battle with roiling waves and pelting winds (scenes recalling the documentary scenes of Derek Jarman's 1979 film of the play—another strongly environmental though not overtly environmentalist production). Images of the capsizing ship finally broke up into a transmission blizzard. As the screen rolled up, it transitioned into the stage's jagged, snow-blasted landscape with two slanting walls of Prospero's clapped-up shack of wood and metal detritus. Gloomy light and feeble heat radiated from a smoking oil can. Standing with his back to the audience completing his shipwreck spell, Prospero appeared to perform an evolutionary metamorphosis: from bottom-feeding exo-skeleton, to shaggy humanoid creature of skins and furs, to a slightly stooped old man wearing a simple rough jacket and baggy trousers. Some spectators thought he looked like an aboriginal shaman journeying through animal and human spirit-worlds. Others were reminded of human wreckage from Franklin's or Scott's polar expeditions, or a crossover monster of Inuit or post-human fantasy.

The time-travel quality of Goold's production suggested that Prospero's shipwreck was not only setting up Alonso's court party for revenge, but also re-inflicting a memory of his own traumatic

experiences twelve years earlier for the express purpose of not forgetting.
Similarly, the magic-lantern radar show and inhospitable landscape
reflected both Prospero's calamities as well as a warning about our
own environmental recklessness. Although the eclectic anthropological
details and fearless anachronisms of Goold's production put off some
spectators, their artful jumble made sense in a globally trashed world.
The charred oil can and arctic desert suggested various environmental
endgames, such as the devastation of a worldwide, possibly nuclear, war
over dwindling fossil-fuel. Alternatively, the radio's shipping forecasts
and Prospero and Miranda's primitive living conditions hinted at the
aftermath of a zero-sum showdown over ocean resources. The idea of
overfishing later became explicit during the banquet-torment of Alonso,
Antonio, and Sebastian, when Ariel exploded from the belly of a
harpooned whale as a bloody Harpy (Figure E.1). His speech of tribu-
lations ('You three men of sin . . .' [3.3.53–68]) retained Shakespeare's
original images of elemental payback for human abuses of the natural
world that had clearly inspired Goold's environmentalist vision (and
were reminiscent of the Witches as eco-feminist heralds of biospheric

Figure E.1. *The Tempest*, dir. Rupert Goold, Royal Shakespeare Company, 2006.
Photograph by Manuel Harlan © RSC. Reproduced by Permission of the Royal
Shakespeare Company.

nemesis in *Macbeth*; see Chapter 3). Following implosions of Western technology and overconsumption, Prospero and Miranda had been forced—a bit like Belarius, Arviragus, and Guiderius in Wales in *Cymbeline*—to relearn their animal dependence on primordial nature for existence. They must compete for their island's now diminished resources with an abused and abusive Caliban. Yet in their struggle to survive, Goold's production suggested, human culture was also being reconstituted by collaboration with the unnamed island as a common habitat, rather than by dominion over it. This meant discovering the primacy of the island's physical ecology as a new, if temporary, home, and overcoming impressions on arrival of 'natural' desertedness and civilizing impulses that typically morph into imperial myths.[2] Stretching more tentatively beyond the confines of Shakespeare's text, the overdetermined mix of aboriginal tools and clothing, although strictly flawed, suggested that Prospero and Miranda, wherever on earth they had landed, had relied for survival on the hospitality and dwelling techniques of 'unseen' indigenous inhabitants, just like the first colonizers in Virginia and elsewhere in the New World (Figure E.2). It was this knowledge, intensified by localized spirits of Juno, Ceres, and Isis chanting a wedding vision to Miranda and Ferdinand as they knelt together blindfolded, that the new generation would bring back to Italy, possibly to rewrite its cultural and environmental assumptions.

In keeping with the production's reversals of Prospero's normally grumpy but sage authority, Goold played down the power of his magic. Patrick Stewart came across instead as a recovering supremacist. Having apparently absorbed the humbling lessons of global as well as personal shipwreck, he appeared 'yearning to be free of the responsibility of ruling an island he has [inadvertently] come to oppress' (*Mail on Sunday*, 13 August 2006). When he finally threw away his magic staff, the exploding oil can which demolished his shack signaled repudiation of the Faustian bargain of techno-mastery, and the beginning of a more respectful relationship with both human and non-human nature.

The paring back of Prospero's usual dominance threw greater attention on Julian Bleach's darkly symbolic Ariel. Many reviewers felt his stage presence rivalled that of Stewart, and some saw him as the defining spirit of Goold's production. Popping up white-faced out of Prospero's oil can like Becket's Nagg, Bleach's black

Figure E.2. *The Tempest*, dir. Rupert Goold, Royal Shakespeare Company, 2006. Photograph by Suzanne Worthington © RSC. Reproduced by Permission of the Royal Shakespeare Company.

apparel, sinister looks, and predatory gait gave him the appearance of a 'cadaverous ghoul' (*The Independent*, 13 August 2006). The hour-glass he carried around counted down Ariel's approaching freedom from Prospero. In terms of the production's tropes of environmental disaster, it also suggested the earth's clock ticking towards a sixth, but this time human-generated, mass extinction, which Prospero's chastened clemency towards the planet, his enemies, and Caliban would possibly avoid. Goold suggested by way of Shakespeare that that option is also open to us.

ECOLOGICAL MODERNITY IN SHAKESPEARE: AN OVERVIEW

1. *English Professional Theatre, 1530–1660*, ed. Glynne Wickham, Herbert Berry, and William Ingram (Cambridge: Cambridge University Press, 2000), 376–9; S. Schoenbaum, *William Shakespeare: A Documentary Life* (Oxford: Clarendon Press, 1975), 153.
2. James Shapiro, *1599: A Year in the Life of William Shakespeare* (2005; New York: Harper Perennial, 2006) 1–7, 112.
3. According to the Burbages, the £700 cost of building The Globe was the same amount their father James spent in 1576 on The Theatre. But in 1599 this sum *excluded* the amount they had saved by reusing The Theatre's timber and wood. So the cost of building The Globe with all new materials would have been about double that of The Theatre (*English Professional Theatre*, 493, 496–7). By contrast, the contract for building Philip Henslowe's rival Fortune Theatre in 1600 specified the use of 'good stronge and substancyall newe timber'. This attests to Henslowe's greater wealth, and, as Julian Bowsher and S.P. Cerasano suggest, implicitly criticizes The Globe's use of recycled timber, although Henslowe did not employ new timber when constructing The Hope theatre ('The Deed of Partnership in the Rose Playhouse,') <http:www.henslowe-alleyn.org.uk/essays/rosecontract.html>
4. J.U. Nef, 'The Timber Crisis', *The Rise of the British Coal Industry*, 2 vols. (London: Routledge, 1932) i. 156–64; John Hatcher, 'From Abundance to Scarcity: Fuel Shortage and the Rise of Coal, 1550–1700', *The History of the British Coal Industry*, ed. Michael W. Flinn and Roy Church, 5 vols. (Oxford: Oxford University Press, 1984–93), i. 31–55.
5. Carlo M. Cipolla, *Before the Industrial Revolution: European Society and Economy, 1000–1700* (New York: W.W. Norton & Company, 1976), 134, 265–9.
6. Ken Hiltner, 'Renaissance Literature and Our Contemporary Attitude toward Global Warning', *Interdisciplinary Studies in Literature and the Environment* 16.3 (Summer 2009), 429–41, cit. 432, citing *Calendar of State Papers, Domestic Series*, Elizabeth I (1578), 612.
7. *Poly-Olbion*, in *The Works of Michael Drayton*, ed. J. William Hebel, 5 vols. (Oxford: Basil Blackwell, 1931–41), iv. 279, ll. 164–6.

8. William Howarth, 'Some Principles of Ecocriticism', *The Ecocriticism Reader: Landmarks in Literary Ecology*, ed. Cheryll Glotfelty and Harold Fromm (Athens, GA and London: University of Georgia Press, 1996), 69–91.

9. Donald Worster, *Nature's Economy: A History of Ecological Ideas*, 2nd edn (1977; Cambridge: Cambridge University Press, 1994), 37, 52, 333–5, and *passim*.

10. Bruno Latour, *The Politics of Nature: How to Bring Sciences into Democracy*, trans. Catherine Porter (Cambridge, MA: Harvard University Press, 2004); 1–25; Timothy Clark, *The Cambridge Introduction to Literature and the Environment* (Cambridge: Cambridge University Press, 2011), 5.

11. J.U. Nef, 'The Early Industrial Revolution', *The Rise of the British Coal Industry*, i. 165–89; 'Prices and industrial capitalism in France and England, 1540–1640,' *Economic History Review* 7 (1936–37), 155; E.L. Jones, 'Agricultural Origins of Industry', *Past & Present* 40 (July 1968), 58–71.

12. Daniel Botkin, *Discordant Harmonies: A New Ecology for the Twenty-First Century* (Oxford: Oxford University Press, 1990); Michel Jeanneret, *Perpetual Motion: Transforming Shapes in the Renaissance from da Vinci to Montaigne*, trans. Nidra Poller (Baltimore and London: Johns Hopkins University Press, 2001).

13. Malcolm L. Hunter Jr, *Fundamentals of Conservation Biology* (Cambridge, MA: Blackwell Science, 1996); Richard Mabey, *Beechcomings: The Narratives of Trees* (London: Chatto & Windus, 2007); IPCC report: <https://www.ipcc.ch/report/ar5/wg1/#.UyB17yhkg20>

14. Jonathan Bate, 'The Boy from the Greenwood', *Soul of the Age: A Biography of the Mind of William Shakespeare* (New York: Random House, 2009), 30–52.

15. Ursula K. Heise, 'Science and Ecocriticism', *American Book Review* 18.5 (1997), 4. For an overview, see Richard Kerridge, 'An Ecocritic's *Macbeth*', *Ecocritical Shakespeare*, ed. Lynne Bruckner and Daniel Brayton (Farnham, Surrey, and Burlington, VT: Ashgate, 2011), 193–210.

16. Deborah E. Harkness, *The Jewel House: Elizabethan London and the Scientific Revolution* (New Haven and London: Yale University Press, 2007).

17. Edward O. Wilson, *Consilience: The Unity of Knowledge* (New York: Vintage, 1999), 7.

18. Stacey Alaimo, 'Sustainable This, Sustainable That: New Materialisms, Posthumanism, and Unknown Futures', *PMLA* 127.3 (2012), 558–64.

19. Clark, *Literature and the Environment*, 2.

20. 'Summer's Lease: Shakespeare in the Little Ice Age', *Early Modern Ecostudies: From Florentine Codex to Shakespeare*, ed. Thomas Hallock, Ivo Kamps, and Karen L. Raber (New York and London: Palgrave Macmillan, 2008), 131–42.

21. Cicero, however, discounts Casca's similar assumptions with the classical scepticism that early modern writers such as Montaigne had rediscovered, and Shakespeare represents in characters such as Edmund, *King Lear*, sc. 2. See note 21.

22. According to Edmund, Gloucester's namesake in *King Lear* similarly believes recent solar and lunar eclipses foretell the court's divisions.

23. This reversal suppressed Atlantic westerlies bringing warm air from the Gulf Stream and increased cold south-easterly winds from the North Atlantic and Scandinavia. Brian Fagan, *The Little Ice Age: How Climate Made History 1300–1850* (New York: Basic Books, 2000), 23–32, cited in Markley, 'Summer's Lease', 135.

24. Other references to rough weather include *Love's Labour's Lost*, 1.1.99–100, *As You Like It*, 2.5.41, and *Macbeth passim*. For 'devouring' tidal surges, see *King John*, 5.6.40–41.

25. Joan Thirsk, 'Enclosing and Engrossing', *The Agrarian History of England and Wales*, ed. H.P.R. Finberg and J. Thirsk, 8 vols. (Cambridge: Cambridge University Press, 1967–2000), iv. 221, 233; Shapiro, *1599*, 109–11, 233–4.

26. 'Strange Weather in *King Lear*', *Shakespeare* 6.2 (2010), 139–52.

27. Andrew McRae, *God Speed the Plough: the representation of agrarian England, 1500–1660* (Cambridge: Cambridge University Press, 1996), 13, 58–9.

28. Between 1520 and 1690, London's share of the national population grew from 2 to 11 per cent. And whereas London grew ten-fold, the number of people in England only doubled. Stephen Inwood, *A History of London* (London: Macmillan, 1998), 269; Charles Nichols, *The Lodger: Shakespeare on Silver Street* (London: Allen Lane, 2007), 100–8 and *passim*.

29. Victor Skipp, *Crisis and Development: An Ecological Case Study of The Forest of Arden 1570–1674* (Cambridge: Cambridge University Press, 1978), 7 and *passim*.

30. *Poly-Olbion*, ed. Hebel, iv. 279, l. 165.

31. Alec Ponton, 'Editorial', *The Pherologist* 4.3 (2001), 2, discussed in Patrick Curry, *Ecological Ethics*, 2nd edn (London: Polity, 2011), 254.

32. Mathis Wackernagel and William E. Rees, *Our Ecological Footprint: Reducing Human Impact on the Earth* (Philadelphia: New Society Publishers, 1996), discussed in Curry, *Ecological Ethics*, 254.

33. E.H. Phelps Brown and Sheila V. Hopkins, 'Wage-rates and prices: Evidence for Population Pressure in the Sixteenth Century', *Economica* 2 (November 1957), 289–306.
34. Vertue's drawing of New Place is discussed in S. Schoenbaum, *William Shakespeare: A Compact Documentary Life* (New York: Oxford University Press, 1977), 234–7.
35. James J. Gibson, *The Ecological Approach to Visual Perception* (1979; Hillsdale NJ: Lawrence Erlbaum Association, 1986), 2 and *passim*.
36. Garrett Hardin, 'The Tragedy of the Commons', *Science* 162 (13 December 1968), 1243–8.
37. Kirkpatrick Sale, *Dwellers in the Land: The Bioregional Vision* (1985; Philadelphia and Gabriola Island, BC: New Society Publishers, 1991), 43.
38. '[T]he diversity of life in all its forms and at all levels of organization', Malcolm L. Hunter Jr, 'Biological Diversity', *Maintaining Biodiversity in Forest Ecosystems*, ed. Malcolm L. Hunter Jr (Cambridge: Cambridge University Press, 1999), 3–21, cit. 3.
39. *As You Like It*, 2.1.16; the Soothsayer's 'nature's infinite books of secrets', *Antony and Cleopatra* 1.2.9.
40. Keith Thomas, *Man and the Natural World: Changing Attitudes in England 1500–1800* (1983; Oxford: Oxford University Press, 1996), 211, 226; Harkness, *The Jewel House*, 38–9; Rebecca Bushnell, 'Experience, truth, and natural history in early English gardening books', *The historical imagination in early modern Britain: History, rhetoric, and fiction, 1500–1800*, ed. Donald R. Kelley and David Harris Sacks (Cambridge: Cambridge University Press, 1997), 179–209.
41. *The Description of England* (1587), ed. Georges Edelen (Ithaca, NY: Cornell University Press for the Folger Shakespeare Library, 1968), 265–9; Harkness, *The Jewel House*, 52–5.
42. Charles Darwin, *The Variation of Animals and Plants Under Domestication* (1868), *The Works of Charles Darwin*, ed. Paul H. Barrett and R.B. Freeman, 29 vols. (London: William Pickering, 1988), xix–xx.
43. Jennifer Munro, 'It's all about the gillyvors: Engendering Art and Nature in *The Winter's Tale*', *Ecocritical Shakespeare*, ed. Lynne Bruckner and Daniel Brayton (Farnham, Surrey and Burlington, VT: Ashgate, 2011), 139–54.
44. Harkness, *The Jewel House*, 49–51.
45. Conservation biologist Malcolm Hunter, for instance, notes that not a single complete inventory of a forest ecosystem has ever been made because the complexities of microbial life escape taxonomy. They remain in the domain of nature's alterity or 'wild' (see n. 51 below). See Hunter,

'Biological Diversity', 6, citing V. Torsvik, J. Goksoyr, and F.L. Daae, 'High Diversity in DNA of soil bacteria', *Applied and Environmental Microbiology* 56 (1990), 782–7. Hunter also illustrates the gap in the number of species described by modern scientists and the number believed to exist: 1.7 million versus 10 to 1000 million ('Biological Diversity', 6, citing Edward O. Wilson, *The Diversity of Life* [Cambridge MA: Harvard University Press, 1992]).

46. Giorgio Agamben, *The Open: Man and Animal*, trans. Kevin Attell (Stanford: Stanford University Press, 2004), 14–38.

47. Erica Fudge, *Brutal Reasoning: Animals, Rationality, and Humanity in Early Modern England* (Ithaca, NY: Cornell University Press, 2006), 84–122; Stephen Greenblatt, *The Swerve: How the World Became Modern* (New York: W.W. Norton & Company, 2011), 188–91.

48. *Antony and Cleopatra*, ed. Michael Neill (Oxford: Oxford University Press, 1994), 81–5, cit. 82.

49. *The Winter's Tale*, 4.1.9–11, 4.4.475; *King Lear*, 9.8, 14.83; Robert Pogue Harrison, *Forests: The Shadow of Civilization* (Chicago: University of Chicago Press, 1992), 46, 50; Agamben, *The Open*, 58; Gilles Deleuze, 'Desert Islands', *Desert Islands and Other Texts, 1953–1974*, ed. David Lapoujade, trans. Mike Taormina (2002; Los Angeles, CA: Semiotext(e), 2004), 9–14. Also see Further Reading.

50. To cite examples just from *A Midsummer Night's Dream*, which 'gestures at the multiplicity of the nature of Diana' (ed. Peter Holland [Oxford: Oxford University Press, 1994], 32): 'Hecate' (5.1.375); 'glimmering' (unique to *MND*, 2.1.77, 3.2.61, 5.1.382); 'glow-worm' (3.1.61); 'Dian's bud', *Artemisia vulgaris*, or mugwort, used for women's diseases (4.1.72).

51. Harrison, *Forests*, 19–30.

52. Thoreau, *Walden, or Life in the Woods* (1854), discussed in relation to wild by Clark, *Literature and Environment*, 30–4; Mabey, *Beechcombings*, 260. Also 220, 234–36.

53. Dolphins, *Twelfth Night*, 1.2.15; porpoises, *Pericles*, 5.65; otters, *Henry IV Part One* 2.1.95, 75; and apes, *As You Like It*, 3.3.121. See Steve Mentz, 'Half-fish, Half-flesh: Dolphins, the Ocean, and Early Modern Humans', *The Indistinct Human in Renaissance Literature*, ed. Jean Feerick and Vin Nardizzi (London and New York: Routledge, 2012), 29–46.

54. Andreas Höfele, *Stage, Stake, & Scaffold* (Oxford: Oxford University Press, 2011); Bruce Boehrer, *Animal Characters: Non-human beings in Early Modern Literature* (Philadelphia: University of Pennsylvania Press, 2013); Laurie Shannon, *The Accommodated Animal: Cosmopolity in Shakespearean Locales* (Chicago: University of Chicago Press, 2013).

55. Agamben, *The Open*, 13–31.
56. Darwin recognized his predecessors in later editions of *On the Origin of Species* (1859), although they did not include Shakespeare, whom Darwin knew in the context of his nineteenth-century reputation as a proto-Romantic poet of nature. See Rebecca Stott, *Darwin's Ghosts: In Search of the First Evolutionists* (London: Bloomsbury, 2012).

CHAPTER 1

1. Lawrence Buell, *The Future of Environmental Criticism: Environmental Crisis and Literary Imagination* (Oxford: Blackwell Publishing, 2005), 62–76.
2. Rachel Carson's *Silent Spring* (Cambridge, MA: Riverside Press, 1962) is the iconic text of first-wave, and especially American, environmentalism. For 'ethic of proximity', see Ursula K. Heise, *Sense of Place and Sense of Planet: The Environmental Imagination of the Global* (New York: Oxford University Press, 2008), 33–6.
3. Hunsdon brought a retinue of 300 servants to Windsor to display his power and worthiness as a recipient. It is reasonable to assume that Shakespeare and his company would have been among this group.
4. Jonathan Bate and Dora Thornton, *Shakespeare: Staging the World* (Oxford: Oxford University Press, 2012).
5. Bate, *Soul of the Age*; Shapiro, *1599*.
6. Edward S. Casey, 'How to Get from Space to Place in a Fairly Short Time: Phenomenological Prolegomena', *Senses of Place*, ed. Steven Field and Keith H. Basso (Santa Fe, NM: School of American Research Press, 1996), 13–19; Buell, *Environmental Criticism*, 63.
7. Alexander Koyré, *From the Closed World to the Infinite Universe* (New York: Harper and Brothers, 1958).
8. Shapiro, *1599*, 240–1.
9. 'Diuerse new sorts of Soyle not yet brought into any publique vse, for manuring both of pasture and arable ground,' Part Two of Hugh Plat's *The Jewel House of Art and Nature* (1594, A1r-H4v); Skipp, *Crisis and Development*, 3, 39, 41.
10. Andrew Watkins, 'The Woodland Economy of the Forest of Arden in the Later Middle Ages', *Midland History* 18 (1993), 19–36, cit. 22.
11. Tanners used oak bark, a product of woodland husbandry. Oliver Rackham, *Ancient Woodland: its history, vegetation and uses in England*, new edn (1980; Colvend, Kircudbrightshire: Castlepoint Press, 2003), 154.
12. Through his father's glove-making and related tanning, Shakespeare also knew about animal husbandry and its counterpart trade, butchery. These

material roots of his poetic imagination were mythologized in John Aubrey's apocryphal anecdote of Shakespeare declaiming 'in the high style' while his father killed a calf. See Samuel Schoenbaum, *Shakespeare's Lives*, new edn (Oxford: Clarendon Press, 1991), 66. (The anecdote may have derived from the frequent images of vulnerable animals being butchered in Shakespeare's history plays.)

13. Arthur Standish, *The Commons Complaint Wherein is Contained Two Special Grievances. The first is, the generall destruction and waste of woods in this kingdome, with a remedy for the same: ... The second grieuance is, the extreame dearth of victuals* (1611); *New Directions of Experience by the Author for the Planting of Timber and Firewood* (1613); Rooke Church, *An Olde Thrift Newly Revived VVherein is declared the manner of planting, preserving, and husbanding yong trees of diuers kindes for timber and fuell. And of sowing acornes, chesnuts, beech-mast, the seedes of elmes, ashen-keyes, &c.* (1612); Harrison, *The Description of England*, ed. Edelen, 275–6, 281–2.

14. W.G. Hoskins, 'The Rebuilding of Rural England', *Past & Present* 4 (November 1953), 44–59.

15. Built 1590–97. Eleanor S. Godfrey, *The Development of English Glassmaking 1560–1640* (Oxford: Clarendon Press, 1975), 205 and plate IVf.

16. *The History of Windsor Great Park and Windsor Forest* (London: Longman, Green, Longman, Roberts and Green [*sic*], 1864).

17. All quotations are from T.W. Craik's Oxford Shakespeare edition (1990).

18. Raphael Holinshed, *The Chronicles of England ...* (London: J. Johnson *et al.*, 1807), iv. 329, cited by Godfrey, *English Glassmaking*, 30.

19. Billets were standardized logs made from large underwood trees cut to regular lengths (3.5 feet long by 9–12 inches in width) for various uses as firewood (e.g. they fit the andirons in Innogen's chimney, *Cymbeline*, 2.4.80–82, 88–91). Rackham, *Ancient Woodland*, 140, 142–3.

20. Typically for three years. Godfrey, *English Glassmaking*, 50–1.

21. Henry Percy, *Advice to his Son*, ed. G.B. Harrison (London: Benn, 1930), 81–2, cited by Godfrey, *English Glassmaking*, 48. Godfrey also refers to the example of Knole House, Kent, another estate that established a revenue-generating glasshouse. It used 1000 cords a year at 3s 4d in 1585. Twenty years later the price had risen to 4s 2d a cord. By 1615, when wood use for glasshouses was banned, the price had again nearly doubled (Godfrey, *English Glassmaking*, 191–2).

22. Godfrey, *English Glassmaking*, 60–75; John Hatcher, 'Towards the Age of Coal', *History of the British Coal Industry*, i. 6–15.

23. Shakespeare's awareness of coppicing is attested by *Love's Labour's Lost* 4.1.9–10. See Rackham, *Ancient Woodland*, 413–38; Mabey, *Beechcomings*,

67–72: 'The coppice is the original renewable resource, producing rough wood for whatever you need' (69).

24. *An Olde Thrift Newly Revived* (1612), A3r.

25. The glasshouse ruins which survive today in Virginia represent the most complete evidence of a seventeenth-century glass factory. See J.C. Harrington, *A Tryal of Glasse: The Story of Glassmaking at Jamestown* (Richmond VA: The Dietz Press, 1972), 29 and *passim*; Charles E. Hatch Jr, 'Glassmaking in Virginia, 1607–1625', *The William and Mary Quarterly*, 2nd ser., 21.2 (1941), 119–38, citing William Strachey's *The Historie of Travaile into Virginia* (published 1612 but circulated before and believed to be known by Shakespeare), who mentions the presence and location of the glasshouse (Hatch, 121, 123; Harrington, 10).

26. Stephano at one point claims he made the bottle 'from the bark of a tree with mine own hands, since I was cast ashore' (2.2.123–24). This ambiguous claim could be a comic allusion to the failed venture of the Virginia Company glassmakers.

27. Whether James took his own advice is unlikely. Godfrey, *English Glassmaking*, 67, 69.

28. 'Sustainable development—concept and action'. <http://www.unece.org/oes/nutshell/2004-2005/focus_sustainable_development.html>

29. Leopold, 'The Land Ethic', *A Sand County Almanac And Sketches From Here and There* (1949; New York and Oxford: Oxford University Press, 1987), 201–26; Andrew Dobson, *Green Political Thought*, rev. edn (London: Routledge, 2007); Bill McKibben, *Eaarth: Making a New Life on a Tough New Planet* (New York: Times Books, 2010). All discussed by Curry, *Ecological Ethics*, 94–7, 231–2.

30. Alaimo, 'Sustainable This, Sustainable That.'

31. Leopold, *A Sand County Almanac*, 173–4, 209–10.

32. Steve Mentz, 'After Sustainability', *PMLA* 127.3 (2012), 586–91.

33. G. Hammersley, 'The Crown Woods and their Exploitation in the Sixteenth and Seventeenth Centuries', *Bulletin of the Institute for Historical Research* 30 (1957), 136–61, cit. 149.

34. Hammersley, 'Crown Woods', 150–1; Godfrey, *English Glassmaking*, 48.

35. Menzies, *Windsor Great Park*, 3, 44, citing *Calendar of State Papers* but giving no detailed reference.

36. Oliver Rackham estimates that the average ratio of physical 'forest' (i.e. woodland 'vert') to legal forest (i.e. the landscape mosaic of woodland, pasture, tilled land, industrial use) was about 1 to 5. The Great Park (containing Herne's Oak) was a relatively small part of Windsor Forest's original woodland area of about 25,000 acres. By the Elizabethan period it had become a typical landscape mosaic like the Forest of Arden

(see Chapter 2). Rackham, *Ancient Woodland*, 185, 303. Windsor Forest survived legally until 1817.

37. John Norden's 1607 maps mark the sites of saw pits operating in Windsor Forest. Reproduced in Menzies, *Windsor Great Park*, as fold-out illustrations.

38. Enlarged in 1598 as *A Treatise and Discourse of the Lawes of the Forest* and reprinted several times.

39. The forests in *Two Gentleman of Verona* and *A Midsummer Night's Dream* nominally represent royal forests. But they are primarily landscapes of literary romance and Ovidian transformation rather than early modern woodland. Like Arden, Windsor is a mix of both. For an interpretation of *Merry Wives* through the lens of early modern poaching, see Jeffrey Theis, 'The "ill kill'd" Deer: Poaching and Social Order in *The Merry Wives of Windsor*', *Texas Studies in Literature and Language* 43.1 (Spring 2001), 46–73.

40. The challenge to forests and the royal prerogative which supported them also came from common-law judges and theorists such as Edward Coke. He vigorously opposed the Crown's attempts to restrain the rights of property owners, and fought a long-term jurisdictional battle against the prerogative courts of equity, which included forest courts. See Allen D. Boyer, 'Coke, Sir Edward (1552–1634), lawyer, legal writer, and politician', *Oxford Dictionary of National Biography*. The material interests of Windsor's middle-class citizens are aligned historically with the legal and political defenders of private property against arbitrary alienation by the Crown.

41. Watkins, 'The Woodland Economy of the Forest of Arden', 27–31.

42. Thomas Gill, 'Forest of Galtres', in *Vallis Eboracensis, Comprising the History & Antiquities of Easingwold and the Forest of Galtres* (1852; Easingwold, Yorkshire: G.H. Smith and Son, 1974), 37–52; Rackham, *Ancient Woodland*, 148.

43. Harrison, *Forests*, 69–80.

44. Richard Marienstras, 'The forest, the wild, and the sacred: a study of *A Treatise and Discourse of the Lawes of the Forest* by John Manwood', *New Perspectives on the Shakespearean World*, trans. Janet Lloyd (Cambridge: Cambridge University Press, 1985), 11–39; J.H. Baker, 'Manwood, John, (d. 1610), legal writer', *Oxford Dictionary of National Biography*; John St John, *Observations on the Land Revenue of the Crown* (London, 1787), Appendix.

Manwood's personal stake in the defence of forest laws and royal authority over purlieus was ambiguous. As a lawyer trained at Lincoln's Inn, he was aware of contemporary opposition to royal prerogatives that infringed common-law rights. Professionally, his allegiance was with political

defenders of the alienation of Crown land by judges and private landowners
such as Coke. He was also a 'new man' and an improver like Justice Shallow
(if we take Shallow's 'biography' in *Henry IV Part Two* as more definitive
than the boaster in *Merry Wives*). Manwood's estate near Chelmsford was
inherited from Church property confiscated by Henry VIII, and he later
submitted a treatise advocating agrarian enclosure to Sir Julius Caesar in
1609. Its arguments supported the profitable private conversion of forest
waste land that his *Treatise of the Lawes of the Forest* deplores.

45. In the Armada period Elizabeth feared that invading Spaniards would cut
off precious timber supplies by destroying the royal forest of Dean (Menzies,
Windsor Great Park, 3).

46. Between 1530–1600 the price of oak timber rose 1.25*d* to approximately
6.75 per cu. feet, more than a 400 per cent increase. Rackham, *Ancient
Woodland*, 163–4.

47. Thomas, *Man and the Natural World*, 100–20. A parallel situation existed
in the case of stray dogs. Named dogs with identifiable owners were safe
from dog catchers, who otherwise treated unnamed, unattached animals
ruthlessly. See *Much Ado*, 2.3.83–84: 'An he had been a dog that should
have howled thus, they would have hanged him'.

48. An image of an alleged fragment of Herne's Oak—inscribed in a way
resembling Orlando's verse-carving on Arden's trees in *As You Like It*—
was given to the British Museum by Queen Victoria and is reproduced in
Bate and Thornton's *Shakespeare: Staging the World*, 84. There is no
reliable evidence to prove that the Herne legend predates Shakespeare
or that he had in mind a specific local tree, despite indefatigable attempts
to do so by eighteenth- and nineteenth-century writers; e.g. Robert
Richard Tighe, *Annals of Windsor, being a history of the castle and town;
with some account of Eton and places adjacent*, 2 vols. (London: Longman,
Brown, Green, Longmans and Robert, 1858); i. 666–705. For the play's
relationship to historical attempts to trace the origins of Herne's Oak, see
Adam Zucker, 'Shakespeare's green materials: Windsor Forest and *The
Merry Wives of Windsor*', *The Places of Wit in Early Modern English
Comedy* (Cambridge: Cambridge University Press, 2011), 1–53.

49. Gibson, *Visual Perception, passim*.

50. 'Felling Falstaff in Windsor Park', *Ecocritical Shakespeare*, ed. Lynne
Bruckner and Daniel Brayton (Farnham, Surrey, and Burlington, VT:
Ashgate, 2011), 123–38, cit. 127–8, referencing *Henslowe's Diary*, ed.
R.A. Foakes and R.T. Rickert, 2nd edn (Cambridge: Cambridge University
Press, 2002), 319–21; '"Come, will this wood take fire?": *The Merry Wives of
Windsor* in Shakespeare's Theatres', *Wooden Os: Shakespeare's Theatres and
England's Trees* (Toronto: University of Toronto Press, 2013), 59–83.

51. 'Felling Falstaff', 124.
52. Peggy L. Fiedler, Peter S. White, and Robert A. Leidy, 'The Paradigm Shift in Ecology and Its Implications for Conservation', *The Ecological Basis of Conservation: Heterogeneity, Ecosystems, and Biodiversity*, ed. S.T.A. Pickett et al. (London and New York: Chapman & Hall, 1997), 83–92, cit. 91–2.
53. Leopold, *A Sand County Almanac*, 209–10.
54. Leopold, *A Sand County Almanac*, 174. Invoking a Darwinian pre-microbiological model, Leopold describes an 'ethic, ecologically, [as] a limitation on freedom of action in the struggle for existence' (202).

CHAPTER 2

1. All quotations are taken from Alan Brissenden's Oxford Shakespeare edition (1993).
2. Leopold, 'Thinking Like a Mountain', *A Sand County Almanac*, 129–37; Sale, *Dwellers in the Land*, 43.
3. '*Poly-Olbion: A Chorographicall Description of Tracts, Riuers, Mountaines, Forests, and other Parts of this renowned Isle of Great Britaine*' (original title page), *Works of Michael Drayton*, ed. Hebel, iv. 276. Also discussed by Shapiro, *1599*, 242–3.
4. Rackham, *Ancient Woodland*, 177–85.
5. J.E.B. Gover, A. Mawer, F.M. Stenton, and F.T.S. Houghton, *The Place-Names of Warwickshire*, English Place-Name Society, vol. 13 (Cambridge: Cambridge University Press, 1936), xiii–xiv.
6. William Camden, *Britain*, trans. Philemon Holland (London: 1610), cited by A. Stuart Daley, 'Where Are the Woods in *As You Like It?*', *Shakespeare Quarterly* 34.2 (Summer 1983), 172–80, cit. 175.
7. Originally the Forêt d'Ardenne was the largest and most ancient woodland in pre-modern northern France, Belgium, and Germany; it was mentioned in Julius Caesar's *Commentaries* which Shakespeare read in school (*Henry VI Part Two*, 4.7.56).
8. A. Stuart Daley, 'Observations of the Natural Settings and Flora of the Ardens of Lodge and Shakespeare', *English Language Notes* 22 (1985), 20–9.
9. *Poly-Olbion*, in *Works of Michael Drayton*, ed. Hebel, iv. stanza 13, ll. 20–3.
10. *Anti-Oedipus: capitalism and schizophrenia* (Minneapolis: University of Minnesota Press, 1983), 145–6.
11. Heise, *Sense of Place and Sense of Planet*, 51–3. Also Buell, *Future of Environmental Criticism*, 64.

12. The idea of privatizing enclosure humorously sharpens class distinctions in *The Comedy of Errors* when Antipholus of Syracuse rebuffs Dromio's overfamiliar jesting by charging him with 'making a common of my serious hours' (2.2.9). On a different scale, Thidias insinuates Octavius's ambitions to absorb Egypt into his nascent personal empire by urging Cleopatra to forsake Antony and embrace the alleged generosity of 'The universal landlord' (3.13.72).

13. *Representations* 16 (Autumn 1986), 50–85, subsequently incorporated in *Forms of Nationhood: The Elizabethan Writing of England* (Chicago: University of Chicago Press, 1992).

14. *Reinhabiting a Separate Country: A Bioregional Anthology of Northern California* (San Francisco: Planet Drum Foundation, 1978), 218, cited in Clark, *Literature and the Environment*, 131; Peter Berg and Raymond Dasman, 'Reinhabiting California', *Ecologist* 7 (December 1977), 399–40, discussed by Buell, *Future of Environmental Criticism*, 83–4.

15. Sale, *Dwellers in the Land*, 27, 77.

16. Watkins, 'The Woodland Economy of the Forest of Arden', 19–36; Skipp, *Crisis and Development*, 10; Sale, *Dwellers in the Land*, 43.

17. Buell, *Future of Environmental Criticism*, 83.

18. Clark, *Literature and the Environment*, 131.

19. Mike Carr, *Bioregionalism and Civil Society: Democratic Challenges to Corporate Culture* (Vancouver: University of British Columbia Press, 2004), 49 and *passim*.

20. Michel de Certeau, *The Practice of Everyday Life*, trans. Steven Rendall (Berkeley: University of California Press, 1984); Henri Lefebvre, *The Production of Space*, trans. Donald Nicholson-Smith (Oxford: Blackwell, 1991).

21. Rebecca Laroche, 'Ophelia's Plants and the Death of Violets', *Ecocritical Shakespeare*, ed. Lynne Bruckner and Daniel Brayton (Farnham, Surrey and Burlington VT: Ashgate, 2011), 211–21.

22. Mabey, *Beechcomings*; Roger Deakin, *Wildwood: A Journey Through Trees* (London: Hamish Hamilton, 2007).

23. Nardizzi, *Wooden Os*, 20 and *passim*; Gabriel Egan, *Green Shakespeare: From ecopolitics to ecocriticism* (London and New York: Routledge, 2006), 79-82.

24. Harrison, *Forests*, 93–7.

25. Thomas Lodge, *Rosalynde*, reproduced in *Narrative and Dramatic Sources of Shakespeare*, ed. Geoffrey Bullough, 6 vols. (London: Macmillan, 1958–76), iv. 158–67. Shakespeare saw in this conflict another version of the stories of Richard of Gloucester, Philip Falconbridge, Don John, or Edmund, in which a younger sibling chafes against an elder brother,

rightly or wrongly, under the exclusionary laws of primogeniture and/or bastardy.

26. Andrew McRae, *God Speed the Plough: The representation of agrarian England, 1500–1660* (Cambridge: Cambridge University Press, 1996).

27. See, e.g., Thomas Tusser, 'The Ladder to thrift', *Fiue hundreth pointes of good husbandrie as well for the champion or open countrie, as also for the woodland or seuerall* (1573; London, 1593), A8v–B5r.

28. Alastair Fowler, 'Georgic and Pastoral: Laws of Genre in the Seventeenth Century', *Culture and Cultivation in Early Modern England: Writing the Land*, eds. Michael Leslie and Timothy Raylor (Leicester and London: Leicester University Press, 1992), 81–8, cit. 83.

29. Watkins, 'The Woodland Economy of the Forest of Arden', 31–2; Steve Mentz, 'Tongues in the Storm: Shakespeare, the Ecological Crisis, and the Resources of Genre', *Ecocritical Shakespeare*, ed. Lynne Bruckner and Daniel Brayton (Farnham, Surrey and Burlington, VT: Ashgate, 2011), 155–71, cit. 157.

30. Compare the agrarian hoarder Sogliardo in Ben Jonson's *Every Man Out of His Humour*, staged, like *As You Like It*, in the opening year of The Globe theatre, 1599.

31. Wendy Wall, 'Renaissance National Husbandry: Gervase Markham and the Publication of England', *Sixteenth-Century Journal* 27.3 (1996), 767–85.

32. Skipp, *Crisis and Development*, 39, 42–78.

33. Thirsk, 'Enclosure and Engrossing', 200–55; Joan Thirsk, 'Tudor Enclosures', *The Tudors*, ed. Joel Hurstfield (New York: St Martin's, 1973), 65–83.

34. Displaced from its former social dominance, pastoral farming became the object of literary nostalgia and sexualized humour, with numerous instances in Shakespeare; e.g.:

> KATHERINE Two hot sheeps, marry!
> BOYET And wherefore not 'ships'?
>   No sheep, sweet lamb, unless we fee on your lips.
> KATHERINE You sheep, and I pasture. Shall that finish the jest?
> BOYET So you grant pasture for me. [*He tries to kiss her.*]
> KATHERINE Not so, gentle beast.
>   My lips are no common, though they several be.
> BOYET Belonging to whom?
> KATHERINE To my fortunes and me.
>
> (*Love's Labour's Lost*, 2.1.218–23)

35. William C. Carroll, '"The Nursery of Beggary": Enclosure, Vagrancy, and Sedition in the Tudor-Stuart Period', *Enclosure Acts: Sexuality, Property, and Culture in Early Modern England*, ed. Richard Burt and John Michael Archer (Ithaca and London: Cornell University Press, 1994), 34–47 cit. 43; *Henry VI Part Two*, 4.10.16–25, and n. to l. 25, ed. Roger Warren (Oxford: Oxford University Press, 2003).

36. Richard Wilson, '"Like the Old Robin Hood": "As You Like It" and the Enclosure Riots', *Shakespeare Quarterly* 43.1 (Spring 1992), 5.

37. Skipp, *Crisis and Development*, 42, 65, 77–80, 84, 88.

38. Thirsk, 'Tudor Enclosures', 81–2.

39. *OED* 3, 4a-b; see Shakespeare's figurative uses: *Henry IV Part* One, 4 3.2.148; *Merry Wives of Windsor*, 2.2.191.

40. Thirsk, 'Tudor Enclosures', 72.

41. This also hints that Silvius is content to be a cuckold if he could have Phoebe.

42. Robert N. Watson, 'As You Liken It: Simile in the Forest', *Back to Nature: The Green and the Real in the Late Renaissance* (Philadelphia: University of Pennsylvania Press, 2008), 77–107.

43. Watson, 'As You Liken It', 90–1.

44. Agamben, *The Open*, 30-1.

45. Hardin, 'The Tragedy of the Commons'.

46. Thirsk, 'Tudor Enclosures', 73, 78; 'Enclosing and Engrossing', 229–31.

47. Tusser, *Fiue hundreth pointes of good husbandrie*, G3r.

48. John Fitzherbert, *The Booke of Husbandrie* (1534).

49. Gervase Markham, *The English Husbandman* (1613); Jim Cheney, 'Nature/Theory/Difference', *Ecological Feminism*, ed. Karen J. Warren (London: Routledge, 1994), 158–78, cit. 174–5.

50. Thirsk, 'Tudor Enclosures', 69–70, 81.

51. Shakespeare might have recalled these practices when, after his retirement in 1614, his tithing interests in land at Welcombe, near Stratford-upon-Avon, were threatened by Lord Ellesmere's enclosure. Shakespeare shrewdly entered into a private agreement with his agents to be compensated for any loss of income, tacitly consenting to the enclosure. Ditches for fences began to be dug, but Stratford and regional townspeople whose livelihoods were at stake, including women and children, defiantly filled them in. At the spring assizes in Warwick, the Stratford Council succeeded in restraining Ellesmere's agents. But one named Combe vindictively engrossed and depopulated the village of Welcombe in the same way that Corin's master has deliberately let his sheep farm decay in anticipation of either selling its valuable land or converting it to more profitable arable husbandry. Ellesmere was rebuked by Chief Justice Sir Edward Coke at

the Lent assizes in 1616, after Shakespeare's death. For discussion of this revealing episode, see Schoenbaum, *William Shakespeare*, 281–5; C.M. Ingleby, *Shakespeare and the Enclosure of Common Fields at Welcombe* (Birmingham: Robert Birbeck, 1885).

52. Carroll, '"The Nursery of Beggary"', 38–9.
53. Skipp, *Crisis and Development*, 54–64; Daley, 'Observations', 28–9.
54. Leopold, *A Sand County Almanac*, 175–8, 203, 212, 216.
55. Thirsk, 'Tudor Enclosures', 77.

CHAPTER 3

1. Geoffrey Parker, *The Military Revolution: Military Innovation and the Rise of the West, 1500–1800* (Cambridge: Cambridge University Press, 1988).
2. In his comprehensive study of Shakespeare's language of weapons and combat, Charles Edelman shows that 'Warfare is everywhere in Shakespeare'. Even in 'the most non-military of the comedies' when characters have no conscious thoughts of war, 'there is a great deal of military imagery'. *Shakespeare's Military Language: a Dictionary* (London: Athlone Press, 2000), 2.
3. Jared Diamond, *Guns, Germs, and Steel: The Fates of Human Societies* (1997; New York: Norton, 1999), 246–7.
4. Resistance to the replacement of longbows in the 1560s spawned a vigorous pamphlet war between traditionalists and modernists which lasted into the next century. See Parker, *Military Revolution*, 19, Charles Oman, *A History of the Art of War in the Sixteenth Century* (1937; Barnsley, S. Yorks.: Greenhill Books, 1997), 380–2.
5. Sharon O'Dair, 'The State of the Green: A Review Essay on Shakespearean Ecocriticism', *Shakespeare* 4.4 (December 2008), 474–92; 'Is it Ecocriticism if it isn't Presentist?', *Ecocritical Shakespeare*, ed. Lynne Bruckner and Daniel Brayton (Farnham, Surrey and Burlington, VT: Ashgate, 2011), 71–85.
6. Roy S. Wolper, 'The Rhetoric of Gunpowder and the Idea of Progress', *Journal of the History of Ideas*, 31.4 (Oct–Dec 1970), 589–98, cit. 590; Carlo M. Cipolla, *Clocks and Culture 1300–1700* (New York: Norton, 1977), 33.
7. Bacon, *Novum Organum*, aphorism 129, cited in Bert S. Hall, *Weapons and Warfare in Renaissance Europe: Gunpowder, Technology, and Tactics* (Baltimore and London: Johns Hopkins University Press, 1997), 1.
8. Richard Eden, Dedication, Joannes Taisnerius [Jean Taisnier], *Of Continuall Motions* (1574), reprinted in Edward Arber, *The First Three English*

Books on America (Birmingham, 1885), xlvi, cited in Wolper, 'Rhetoric of Gunpowder', 592.

9. Michel Serres, *The Natural Contract*, trans. Elizabeth MacArthur and William Paulson (Ann Arbor: The University of Michigan Press, 1995), 10–11.
10. Also *King John*, 1.1.26, 2.1.37, 251, 382, 463.
11. *King John*, 2.1.343–44, 368, 3.2.2–3.
12. Adam Max Cohen's phrase: *Shakespeare and Technology: Dramatizing Early Modern Technological Revolutions* (Basingstoke and New York: Palgrave Macmillan, 2006), 17. I am indebted to Cohen for his discussion of early modern cyborgs and gunpowder in ch. 4, 'Weapons of Fire and Shakespeare's Dramatic Trajectory', 91–126.
13. George Dyson, *Darwin Among the Machines* (London: Allan Lane Science, 1997).
14. George Basalla, *The Evolution of Technology* (Cambridge: Cambridge University Press, 1988), 15, cited in Cohen, *Shakespeare and Technology* 18; Jonathan Sawday, '"Forms Such as Never Were in Nature": the Renaissance Cyborg', *At the Borders of the Human: Beasts, Bodies and Natural Philosophy in the Early Modern Period*, ed. Erica Fudge, Ruth Gilbert, and Susan Wiseman (1999; Basingstoke and New York: Palgrave Macmillan, 2002), 171–95, cit. 181.
15. *Anti-Oedipus*, trans. Robert Hurley, et al. (New York: Viking Press, 1977), 145–6, 195–7; 'Nomad Thought', *The New Nietzsche: Contemporary Styles of Interpretation*, ed. and intro. David Allison (New York: Delta, 1977), 142–9.
16. Edelman, *Shakespeare's Military Language*, 132–3.
17. N. Katherine Hayles, 'The Condition of Virtuality', *Language Machines: Technologies of Literary and Cultural Production* (New York: Routledge, 1997), 183–208, cit. 201.
18. H.R. Schubert, *History of the British Iron and Steel Industry from c. 450 to A.D. 1775* (London: Routledge & Kegan Paul, 1957), 171–2, 247–55; Carlo M. Cipolla, *Guns and Sails in the Early Phase of European Expansion 1400–1700* (London: Collins, 1965), 36–46.
19. Cipolla, *Guns and Sails,* 62–3.
20. Nef, *Rise of the British Coal Industry*, i. 158–62, 196–200; Hatcher, 'From Abundance to Scarcity', i. 31–55.
21. Godfrey, *English Glassmaking, passim*.
22. Richard Winship Stewart, *The English Ordnance Office 1585–1625: A case study in bureaucracy* (Woodbridge, Suffolk: The Royal Historical Society, 1996), 65–88.

23. Geoffrey York, 'Why this Ebola outbreak is a warning sign', *The Globe and Mail*, 3 April 2014.

24. Ulrich Beck, *Risk Society: Towards a New Modernity* (London: Sage Publications, 1992); *World Risk Society* (Cambridge, MA: Polity, 1998); Heise, *Sense of Place and Sense of Planet*, 11, 119–59.

25. Serres, *Natural Contract*, 3–7.

26. Hall, *Weapons and Warfare*, 105, 210.

27. Peter Whitehorne, *Certaine Waies for the ordering of Souldiers . . . And . . . how to make Saltpetre, Gounpouder and diuers sortes of Fireworkes* (1588), Ff4–G3v.

28. Brenda J. Buchanan, '"The Art and Mystery of Making Gunpowder": The English Experience in the Seventeenth and Eighteenth Centuries', *The Heirs of Archimedes: Science and the Art of War through the Age of Enlightenment*, ed. Brett D. Steele and Tamera Dorland (Cambridge, MA: MIT Press, 2005), 233–74, cit. 235–40.

29. David Cressy, 'Saltpetre, State Security and Vexation in Early Modern England', *Past & Present* 212 (August 2011), 73–111, cit. 99; John X. Evans, 'Shakespeare's "Villainous Salt-Peter": The Dimensions of an Allusion', *Shakespeare Quarterly* 15.4 (Autumn 1964), 451–5.

30. All quotations are taken from René Weis's Oxford Shakespeare edition (1997).

31. Stewart, *English Ordnance Office*, 82, citing Public Record Office, State Papers 14/1/64, petition dated April 1603.

32. Anthony Giddens, *The Consequences of Modernity* (Cambridge: Polity Press, 1990), 126–7 and *passim*; Stewart, *English Ordnance Office*, 6, 63–4, and *passim*.

33. Serres, *Natural Contract*, 29–36.

34. James C. Bulman, 'Shakespeare's Georgic Histories', *Shakespeare Survey* 38 (1985), 37–47.

35. Also: 'Your country's fat shall pay your pains the hire'; 'Enrich the time to come with smooth-faced peace, / With smiling plenty, and fair prosperous days. /Abate the edge of traitors . . . Let them not live to taste this land's increase' (*Richard III*, 5.4.237, 5.7.33–38).

36. Isaiah 2.3–40; Virgil, *Georgics* (trans. 1589), books 1–2; Hesiod, *Georgics* (trans. 1618).

37. York's sons George and Edward blandly repeat these promises, oblivious to their responsibility for skewing them (*Henry VI Part Three*, 2.2.163–69, 4.8.60–61, 5.7.3–20; *Richard III*, 2.2.115). Buckingham and Richard ironize the Yorkist harvest theme (*Richard III*, 2.2.102–103).

38. Andrew Wear, 'Making sense of health and the environment in early modern England', *Medicine in England: Historical Essays* (Cambridge: Cambridge University Press, 1992), 119–48, cit. 127.

39. *Henry IV Part Two*, 3.2.251, 259, 262, 271. 'Bounce' (i.e. bang! [3.2.273]) echoes the fashionable word for firepower which the Bastard mocks in *King John*, 2.1.463.

40. Clifford Chalmers Huffman and John H. Betts have examined links between Burgundy's speech and Virgil; respectively: 'Burgundy's Speech on France: A Note on Shakespeare's Sources', *English Language Notes* 9 (1971), 12–18; 'Shakespeare's *Henry V* and Virgil's *Georgics*', *Notes and Queries* 223 (1978), 134–6. See also Gary Taylor's note on the possible echo of *Georgics* in Burgundy's reference to the rusting coulter (*Henry V*, 5.2.43, p. 267). It has long been recognized that Canterbury's analogy between bee and human orders (1.2.187–206) also draws on the fourth chapter of Virgil's *Georgics*. See Bulman, *Shakespeare's Georgic Histories*, 43–4.

41. 'How [much] a good yoke of bullocks at Stamford Fair? . . . How a score of ewes now?' (*Henry IV Part Two*, 3.2.35–36, 46–7).

42. Will Squeal, a Cotswold man 3.2.18; Stamford Fair, Lincolnshire 3.2.36; Hinckley Fair 5.1.21; William Visor of Won'cot and Clement Perks o'th'Hill 5.1.32–33; Goodman Puff of Bar'son 5.3.88–89.

43. Falstaff's recruits have names like Shadow, Wart, and Feeble. Bullcalf's alleged cold reflects the public context of ill-health (3.2.173–75). 'We see th'appearing buds, which to prove fruit / Hope gives not so warrant as despair / That frosts will bite them' (1.3.39–41).

44. Possibly the Folio compositors did not recognize the rural word 'hade' and substituted the spatially general 'head'. Or possibly Shakespeare decided to revise this more 'countrified' vocabulary in the Folio version (*Henry IV Part Two*, ed. A.R. Humphreys [London: Methuen. & Co., 1966] n. to 5.1.12).

45. Plat, *Jewell House of Art and Nature*, G3v–H1v.

46. Leopold, *A Sand County Almanac*, 216–17.

47. Mascall's book was published in at least eight editions between 1572 and 1599 and reissued after the Restoration. William Harrison noted the modernizing interest of English farmers in new hybridization techniques (*Description of England*, ed. Edelen, 269–70).

48. *Henry IV Part Two*, ed. Humphreys, n. to 5.3.2–3.

49. William Major, 'The Agrarian Vision and Ecocriticism', *Interdisciplinary Studies in Literature and the Environment* 14.2 (Summer 2007), 51–70.

50. Heise, *Sense of Place and Sense of Planet*, 50–67, cit. 60.

51. Lawrence Buell, 'Space, Place, and Imagination from Local to Global', *Future of Environmental Criticism*, 62–96.

52. For Deleuze and Guattari, 'reterritorialization' refers to the ways global capital recaptures departures from its own processes of deterritorialization in multilayered economies. In *Sense of Place and Sense of Planet*, Ursula Heise applies their idea to ecological relationships. Shakespeare's plays reflect both kinds of exchange.

53. Wear, 'Making sense of health and the environment', 127.

54. Sale, *Dwellers in the Land*, 27–31.

55. Mary Floyd-Wilson, *English Ethnicity and Race in Early Modern Drama* (Cambridge: Cambridge University Press, 2003), 2. See also Gail Kern Paster, *Humoring the Body: Emotions and the Shakespearian Stage* (Chicago: University of Chicago Press, 2004).

56. Benjamin Bertram, 'Falstaff's Body, the Body Politic, and the Body of Trade', *Exemplaria: A Journal of Theory in Medieval and Renaissance Studies* 21 (2009), 296–318.

57. York places greater emphasis on the country's moral health, whose sins he believes war will purge. But his imagery is similar: '. . . we are all diseased, / And with our surfeiting and wanton hours / Have brought ourselves into a burning fever, / And we must bleed for it.' (*Henry IV Part Two*, 4.1.54–57).

58. Morris Palmer Tilley, *A Dictionary of Proverbs in England in the Sixteenth and Seventeenth Centuries* (Ann Arbor: University of Michigan Press, 1950), S918.

59. Nick de Somogyi, *Shakespeare's Theatre of War* (Aldershot: Ashgate, 1998), 20–1.

60. E.g. 'The Tuscan service . . . may serve / A nursery to our gentry, who are sick / For breathing and exploit' (*All's Well That Ends Well*, 1.2.14–17).

61. Gascoigne's report was well-known to London readers both in itself and its spin-offs; e.g. *An Historical Discourse of Antwerp* (1589), and *A Larum for London*, a jingoistic anti-Spanish play performed by the Chamberlain's Men at the Globe in 1599 and published in 1601/2, when the Elizabethan government was negotiating an end to the war with Spain.

62. The Spanish watchword for attacking Antwerp was 'Fuora villiaco' [= afuera bellacos = come out you villains]. Andrew Cairncross noted that Old Clifford uses this phrase (possibly garbled by the typesetter) to persuade Cade's followers to abandon him: 'Methinks already in this civil broil / I see [the French] lording it in London streets / Crying "*Villiago!*" unto all they meet' (*Henry VI Part Two*, ed. Humphreys, n. to 4.9.44–46). Earlier Suffolk tries unconvincingly to frame his approaching death as heroic by arguing that 'Great men oft die by vile Bezonians' (4.1.135), a

name Gascoigne first used in *The Spoil of Antwerp* (C3r). By 1596–97, the bombastic Pistol shows that it had become a dramatic cliché (*Henry IV Part Two*, 5.3.112). Shakespeare adapted Gascoigne's play *Supposes*, the first prose comedy in English, for the subplot of *The Taming of the Shrew*, which was written about the same time as *The First Part of the Contention* (later *Henry VI Part Two*) was being performed at the Rose in 1590–91. *Richard III* suggests he almost certainly also knew Gascoigne's blank-verse tragedy *Jocasta*, based on Euripedes's *Phoenician Women*. Both classical plays were written for the 1566 Gray's Inn revels, the same festivity for which Shakespeare wrote *The Comedy of Errors* in 1594.

63. Coriolanus echoes Henry's idea: 'You common cry of curs . . . whose loves I prize / As the dead carcasses of unburied men / That do corrupt my air' (*Coriolanus*, 3.3.121–24).
64. Serres, *Natural Contract*, 39.
65. Serres, *Natural Contract*, 11.
66. Wolper, 'Rhetoric of Gunpowder', 597–8.
67. The quotation in the heading of this section is from Michel Serres, *The Natural Contract*, 11.
    All quotations are taken from Nicholas Brooke's Oxford Shakespeare edition (1990).
68. Harry Berger Jr, 'The Early Scenes of "*Macbeth*": Preface to a New Interpretation', *Making Trifles of Terrors: Redistributing Complicities in Shakespeare* (Stanford: Stanford University Press, 1997), 70–97, cit. 79.
69. Robert N. Watson, '"Thriftless Ambition," Foolish Witches, and the Tragedy of *Macbeth*', *Shakespeare and the Hazards of Ambition* (Cambridge, MA: Harvard University Press, 1984), 83–141, cit. 94.
70. 'The Origins of *Macbeth*', *Muriel Bradbrook on Shakespeare* (Brighton: Harvester Press, 1984), 143–60.
71. Contrast the fears of the gunpowder-wary Talbot about his son's coming-of-age in battle (*Henry VI Part One*, 4.4).
72. Bill McKibben, *The End of Nature* (1989; New York: Random House, 2006) 51, 83–4, 100.
73. Serres, *Natural Contract*, 9, 12.
74. Bernice Kliman, *Macbeth: Shakespeare in Performance* (Manchester: Manchester University Press, 1988); Stephen Orgel, '*Macbeth* and the Antic Round', *The Authentic Shakespeare, and Other Problems of the Early Modern Stage* (New York and London: Routledge, 2002), 159–71.
75. Lawrence Danson, *Tragic Alphabet: Shakespeare's Drama of Language* (Yale, 1974), 124, cited in *Macbeth: An Arden Critical Reader*, ed. John Drakakis and Dale Townshend (Bloomsbury, 2013), 37.

76. The *OED* associates 'filthy' only with air and clouds, citing the two Shakespearian uses discussed here. This limited definition appears to have been influenced by phrase 'filthy weather', in use from the nineteenth century onwards.
77. Serres, *Natural Contract*, 41–3.
78. Ronald Wright, 'Fool's Paradise', *An Illustrated Short History of Progress* (Toronto: Anansi Press, 2006), 73–107.
79. 'Thriftless ambition, that will raven up / Thine own life's means' (2.4.28–29); Serres, *Natural Contract*, 36.
80. Harrison, *Forests*, 104.

CHAPTER 4

1. Lawrence Danson, *Shakespeare and Genre* (Oxford: Oxford University Press, 2000), whose work Mentz draws on in 'Tongues in the Storm", 155–71. Also Mentz, 'Shipwreck and Ecology: Toward a Structural Theory of Shakespeare and Romance', *Shakespeare International Yearbook* 8 (2008), 165–82.
2. In *Pericles, The Tempest*, and other romance-framed plays such as *The Comedy of Errors* and *Twelfth Night*, physical modes of dwelling extend beyond land-attachments to seas and oceans. See Further Reading.
3. Buell, *Future of Environmental Criticism*, 44, 62.
4. Buell, 'Space, Place, and Imagination from Local to Global', Heise, *Sense of Place and Sense of Planet*, 6–9, 28–49; Clark, 'Questions of Scale: the local, the national and the global', *Literature and the Environment*, 130–40.
5. Jonathan Bate, *Romantic Ecology: Wordsworth and the Environmental Tradition* (New York: Routledge, 1991); *The Song of the Earth* (Cambridge, MA: Harvard University Press, 2002). Clark discusses Bate in 'Old World Romanticism', *Literature and the Environment*, 26–34.
6. Which does not mean, as Timothy Clark clarifies, 'collapsing the trivial and the catastrophic into each', and reducing environmental action to 'shopping or lifestyle decisions' (Clark, *Literature and the Environment*, 136).
7. See the map of Global Forest Change between 2000 and 2012: <http://earthenginepartners.appspot.com/science-2013-global-forest>
   According to a related BBC News article, between 2000 and 2012 'the Earth lost a combined "forest" the size of Mongolia, enough trees to cover the UK six times'. <http://www.bbc.co.uk/news/science-environment-24934790>
8. E.g. John Gillies, *Shakespeare and the Geography of Difference* (Cambridge: Cambridge University Press, 1994); and John Gillies and Virginia Vaughan Mason, *Playing the globe: genre and geography in English Renaissance drama* (Madison: Fairleigh Dickinson University Press, 1998).

9. Roger Warren reproduces Forman's account in his Oxford edition (1998), 4. All quotations from the play are taken from this edition.

10. Scientifically, nested patterns consist of 'specialists interact[ing] with species that form perfect subsets of the species with which generalists interact' (J. Bascompte and P. Jordan, 'Plant-animal mutualistic networks: The architecture of biodiversity', *Annual Review of Ecological Evolutionary Systematics* 38 [2007], 567–9, cit. 575; 'Food Web', 'Complexity and Stability', n. 77: <http://en.wikipedia.org/wiki/Food_web>

11. Heise, 'Ethics of proximity', *Sense of Place and Sense of Planet*, 28–34.

12. See Google Map's interactive map of Global Sea Level Rise <http://geology.com/sea-level-rise/>

13. Coppélia Kahn, 'Paying Tribute to Rome,' *Roman Shakespeare: Warriors, Wounds, and Women: Feminist Readings of Shakespeare* (London and New York: Routledge, 1997), 163.

14. <http://en.wikipedia.org/wiki/Resilience_(ecology)>

15. I am grateful to Rachel Bryant for these observations.

16. Eric Heinze, 'Imperialism and Nationalism in Early Modernity: The "Cosmopolitan" and the "Provincial" in Shakespeare's *Cymbeline*', *Social and Legal Studies* 18.3 (2009), 273–396.

17. Ulrich Beck, *The Cosmopolitan Vision* (Cambridge MA: Polity Press, 2006), 21, cited in Clark, *Literature and the Environment*, 131.

18. This is not to suggest that *Cymbeline* validates imperial conquest. The invading Romans kill each other in 'friendly fire' amid the disorder of their retreat from the British resurgence led by Posthumus (5.2.15–16). This recalls the battlefield confusion in *All's Well That Ends Well* (3.6.48–50). Shakespeare's battle scenes are always marked by details that challenge an uncritical celebration of the warrior ethos.

19. Peggy Muñoz Simonds, *Myth, Emblem, and Music in Shakespeare's Cymbeline: An Iconographic Reconstruction* (Newark, NJ: Delaware University Press, 1992), 308.

20. Richard Dawkins, *The Selfish Gene* (1976; Oxford: Oxford University Press, 2006), 12.

21. Ulrich Beck, *What is Globalization?* (Cambridge MA: Polity Press, 2000), 11.

22. Leopold, *A Sand County Almanac*, 188–201, 204.

23. Buell, *Future of Environmental Criticism*, 83.

24. Clark, *Literature and the Environment*, 118.

25. Huw Griffiths, 'The Geographies of Shakespeare's *Cymbeline*', *English Literary Renaissance* 43.3 (2004), 339–58. Garrett A. Sullivan Jr argues similarly that 'England's conception of Britishness... involves not the confirmation but the eradication of a distinctive Welsh identity' (*The Drama of Landscape: Land, Property, and Social Relations on the Early Modern Stage*

[Stanford: Stanford University Press, 1998], 127–58, cit. 146). Belarius's cave is close to the politically resonant site of Milford Haven. As Shakespeare's English history plays showed, the Lancastrian and Tudor regimes began with overseas invasions of England through Milford. During Elizabeth's and James's reign Milford continued to represent a site of possible invasion from Catholic Spain and Ireland. *Cymbeline* mobilizes these paradoxical associations of vulnerability and regeneration by having Lucius and the Romans land there to confront the British forces.

26. Griffiths, 'The Geographies of Shakespeare's *Cymbeline*', 352.

27. Clark, *Literature and the Environment*, 130–2.

28. Harrison, *Description of England*, ed. Edelen, 124.

29. Gibson, *Visual Perception*, 127–43.

30. Danta and Vardoulakis, 'The Political Animal', *SubStance* 117 (37.3), 2008, 3–6; Bruno Latour, *We Have Never Been Modern* (Cambridge, MA: Harvard, 1993); Shannon, *The Accommodated Animal, passim*.

31. Gibson, *Visual Perception*, 42.

32. Gibson, *Visual Perception*, 135; Montaigne, 'Apology For Raymond Sebond', discussed by Erica Fudge, *Brutal Reasoning: Animals, Rationality, and Humanity in Early Modern England* (Ithaca and London: Cornell University Press, 2006), 95–7.

33. David Abrahm, *The Spell of the Sensuous: Perception and Language in a More-than-Human World* (New York: Pantheon Books, 1996). See also Caesar's account of Antony: 'The barks of trees thou browsed' (*Antony and Cleopatra*, 1.4.66).

34. 3.3.73–67, 98, 107; 3.6.29; 4.2.2.

35. John Vaillant, *The Tiger: A True Story of Vengeance and Survival* (New York and Toronto: Alfred A. Knopf, 2010).

36. Erica Fudge, 'Becoming Animal', *Brutal Reasoning*, 59–83.

37. Henno Martin, *The Sheltering Desert* (London: William Kimber, 1957); cit. Vaillant 176.

38. *OED*'s first citation of this definition of 'forked' in 1611 makes this addition to the usual sense, 'two-legged', possible.

39. Posthumus's Sicilius states that same combination of genetics and environment determined his son's physiology: 'Great nature like his ancestry / Moulded the stuff so fair' (5.3.142–43). This is also the dual significance of Jupiter's revelation to Posthumus on his tablet (5.3.232–38). See also Steven Pinker, *The Blank Slate: The Modern Denial of Human Nature* (New York and London: Viking, 2002).

40. Jodi Mikalachki, 'The Masculine Romance of Roman Britain: *Cymbeline* and Early Modern English Nationalism', *Shakespeare Quarterly* 46 (1995), 301–22; Kahn, 'Paying Tribute to Rome', *Roman Shakespeare*, 163.

41. Edward I. Berry, *Shakespeare and the Hunt: a social and cultural study* (Cambridge: Cambridge University Press, 2001).

42. Griffiths, 'The Geographies of Shakespeare's *Cymbeline*', 350–1.

43. Eugene Waith, 'The Metamorphosis of Violence in *Titus Andronicus*', *Shakespeare Quarterly* 10 (1957), 39–49; Roger Warren, *Cymbeline: Shakespeare in Performance* (Manchester: Manchester University Press, 1989), 5–6.

44. Roger Warren remarks: . . . 'as the speech proceeds, the language and rhythms convey a haunting impression that the body is itself becoming a part of the natural world evoked, especially in the final lines, where the body is covered with the protective moss of the winter landscape' (ed. *Cymbeline*, 24).

45. Guiderius depreciates the 'stinking elder', grief, in favour of the patience of the 'increasing vine'. But Shakespeare later insists on their symbiosis representing marital prosperity; e.g. Posthumus: 'Hang there like fruit, my soul, / Till the tree die' (5.4.263–64). Also *The Comedy of Errors*, 2.2.176–79.

46. Warren suggests that the fact that Belarius insists Fidele's head must be laid 'to th'east' emphasizes the pagan world of the play, 'since Christian custom is to bury people *facing* east' (4.2.356–57 and Warren's note). But the ambiguous 'laid to' could be read the opposite way, and the echoes of the Bible and the burial service which Warren notes in 'Fear no more the heat o'th'sun' could support a culturally syncretic interpretation.

47. William Barry Thorne, '*Cymbeline*: "Lopp'd Branches" and the Concept of Regeneration', *Shakespeare Quarterly* 20.2 (Spring 1969), 143–59, cit. 157.

48. Jacobean audiences' understanding of the Roman army's defeat may have been shaped by the fact that it is composed not of regular soldiers but militia lacking the experience of legion-disciplined forces (3.7).

49. Greg Woolf, *Rome: An Empire's Story* (New York: Oxford University Press, 2012).

CHAPTER 5

1. André Voisin, *Better Grassland Sward: Ecology—Botany—Management* (London: Crosby, Lockwood & Son, 1960), 304–5.

2. Margreta de Grazia focuses on the mole to trace the still-dominant image of Hamlet as the iconic hero (or anti-hero) of sovereign consciousness and inward self-determination back to the Romantic reinterpretation of *Hamlet* as a play of autonomous individual character rather than Aristotelian or historically derived action (an image popularized by Harold Bloom's *Shakespeare: The Invention of the Human* [1998] and Michael Almereyda's

feature film starring Ethan Hawke [2000]). Philosopher G.W.F. Hegel later used Hamlet's image of his revenant father as a mole to figure the progress of human consciousness in the modern world, and Romantic poets and critics projected this philosophical ideal back on to Hamlet. Karl Marx—an admirer of Shakespeare's insights into emergent capitalism in *Timon of Athens*—then adopted the mole, contra Hegel, as the embodiment of revolutionary dialectics. Although Jacques Derrida's *Specters of Marx* does not refer to either of these symbolic moles, it does examine the transformation of Marx's teleological narrative into a post-metaphysical condition of eschatological haunting comparable to the Ghost's challenge to *Hamlet*'s untested self-awareness. See de Grazia, 'Teleology, Delay, and the "Old Mole"', *Shakespeare Quarterly* 50.3 (Autumn 1999), 251–67; '*Hamlet* before its time', *Modern Language Quarterly* 62.4 (December 2001), 355–75; Derrida, *Specters of Marx: The State of Death, the Work of Mourning and the New International*, trans. Peggy Kamuf (London and New York: Routledge, 1994).

All quotations are taken from G.R. Hibbard's Oxford Shakespeare edition (1987).

3. Edward O. Wilson, *The Social Conquest of Earth* (New York: Norton, 2012). See Chapter 3, pp. 21–32.

4. Stefan Herbrechter and Ivan Callus, 'Introduction: Shakespeare ever after', *Posthumanist Shakespeares*, ed. Stefan Herbrechter and Ivan Callus (Basingstoke and London: Palgrave Macmillan, 2012), 1–19.

5. Agamben, *The Open*, 14–38; Höfele, *Stage, Stake, & Scaffold*, xi and *passim*.

6. Linda Woodbridge, *English Revenge Drama: Money, Resistance, Equality* (Cambridge: Cambridge University Press, 2010); Ania Loomba, 'The Imperial Romance of *Antony and Cleopatra*', *Shakespeare, Race and Colonialism* (Oxford: Oxford University Press, 2002), 112–34.

7. All quotations are taken from Michael Neill's Oxford Shakespeare edition (1994).

8. Mary Thomas Crane, 'Roman World, Egyptian Earth: Cognitive Difference and Empire in Shakespeare's *Antony and Cleopatra*', *Comparative Drama* 43.1 (Spring 2009), 1–17, cit. 3.

9. Michel Serres, *Natural Contract*, 1–3; *Biogea*, trans. Randolph Burks (2010; Minneapolis: Univocal Publishing, 2012), 79, 113–19 and *passim*; Janet Adelman, *The Common Liar: An Essay on Antony and Cleopatra* (New Haven: Yale University Press, 1973).

10. Daniel C. Dennett, *Darwin's Dangerous Idea: Evolution and the Meanings of Life* (1995; New York: Touchstone, 1996).

11. *Antony and Cleopatra*, ed. Neill, notes to 5.2.58, 270, 310, 306, 318, 321.

12. Hunter, 'Biological Diversity',13; <http://en.wikipedia.org/wiki/Charis matic_megafauna>

13. Darwin first presented his ideas in an 1837 paper, 'On the Formation of Mould', to the Geological Society of London. After extended observation and experiment, they evolved into the final 1881 monograph. Adam Phillips, *Darwin's Worms: On Life and Death Stories* (1999; London: Basic Books, 2000), 42–52.

14. Modern scientists have shown that the earthworm population of the Nile valley is one million per acre, and their recycling rate up to one thousand tons of castings, or earthworm manure, per acre (Amy Stewart, *The Earth Moved: On the Remarkable Achievements of Earthworms* [Chapel Hill, NC: Algonquin Books, 2004], 10).

15. Charles Darwin, *The Formation of Vegetable Mould, Through the Actions of Worms, with Observations on their Habits* (London: John Murray, 1881), 243, 258.

16. Darwin, *Vegetable Mould*, 97, 312; Stewart, *The Earth Moved*, 12–18.

17. Darwin, *Vegetable Mould*, 312. Earthworms possess a primitive brain, 'two almost confluent cerebral ganglia', in the third segment of their bodies (Darwin, *Vegetable Mould*, 19; Stewart, *The Earth Moved*, 67).

18. Clark, *Literature and the Environment*, 15–21.

19. E.g. Mercutio's 'They [the feuding houses of Capulet and Montague] have made worms' meat of me' (*Romeo and Juliet*, 3.1.107).

20. *Hamlet*, ed. Harold Jenkins (London and New York: Methuen, 1982), 550–1. Besides connections to *Hamlet*, de Granada's two chapters are suggestive of passages in *Henry VI Part Three* and *Richard II*.

21. Aa8r-v, Cc2v, Cc3v, Cc5r.

22. On worms as omnivores, see Darwin, *Vegetable Mould*, 30, 35–6.

23. Raymond Williams, 'Tragedy and the Tradition', *Modern Tragedy* (London: Chatto and Windus, 1969), 15–44; Philip Sidney, *An Apology for Poetry*, ed. Geoffrey Shepherd (London: Thomas Nelson and Sons, 1965), 135; Rebecca W. Bushnell, *Tragedies of Tyrants: Political Thought and Theater in the English Renaissance* (Ithaca: Cornell University Press, 1990), 1–8. Bushnell argues that the political and moral meanings of much early modern English tragedy are complicated by the ambivalent affects of stage violence.

24. Amy Stewart, 'Intestines of the Soil', *The Earth Moved*, 45–64.

25. Biologists would define the relationship with human bodies as commensual: one organism benefits while the other is unharmed.

26. 'Trophic levels', in 'Food Web': <http://en.wikipedia.org/wiki/Food_web>

27. *On the Origin of Species*, ed. William Bynum (London: Penguin Books, 2009), 20, 427.

28. Edward J. Geisweidt, 'The Nobleness of Life: Spontaneous Generation and Excremental Life in *Antony and Cleopatra*', *Ecocritical Shakespeare*, ed. Lynne Bruckner and Daniel Brayton (Farnham, Surrey and Burlington, VT: 2011), 89–103.

29. Paster, *The Body Embarrassed*; Floyd-Wilson, *English Ethnicity and Race*; *Reading the Early Modern Passions*, ed. Gail Kern Paster, Katherine Rowe, Mary Floyd-Wilson (Philadelphia: University of Pennsylvania Press, 2004).

30. Jonathan Dollimore, *Radical Tragedy: Religion, Ideology, and Power in the Drama of Shakespeare and his Contemporaries* (Chicago: University of Chicago Press, 1984), 2–3.

31. Egan, *Green Shakespeare*, 110.

32. Thomas Crane, 'Roman World, Egyptian Earth', 9.

33. Floyd-Wilson, *English Ethnicity*, 2.

34. Richard H. Grove, *Green Imperialism: Colonial expansion, tropical island Edens and the origins of environmentalism, 1600–1860* (Cambridge: Cambridge University Press, 1995), 16–17.

35. Woodbridge, *English Revenge Drama*, 217.

36. Or bawdy house; more figuratively, sterile sexuality and infanticide.

37. Timothy Morton, *Ecology Without Nature: Rethinking Environmental Aesthetics* (Cambridge, MA: Harvard University Press, 2007): 'Ecological art is bound to hold the slimy in view' (159).

38. Darwin, *Vegetable Mould*, 313.

39. 'It is interesting to contemplate an entangled bank... (*Origin of Species*, 426–7).

40. Phillips, *Darwin's Worms*, 58–9.

41. Ewan Fernie, 'The last act: Presentism, spirituality and the politics of *Hamlet*', *Spiritual Shakespeares*, ed. E. Fernie (London and New York: Routledge, 2005), 186–211, cit. 209.

42. Harrison, *Forests*, 29–30, 53.

43. Stewart Cole, 'Empires of the Self: Property and Power in *Antony and Cleopatra*', *The University of New Brunswick Journal of Student Writing* 28 (2006), 33–55, cit. 38.

44. Steve Mentz, '#Rising Waters, Pirate Utopias, *Antony and Cleopatra*', paper given at the 2014 meeting of the Shakespeare Association of America.

45. Michael MacDonald, 'Ophelia's Maimed Rites', *Shakespeare Quarterly* 37.3 (Fall 1986), 309–17; *True Rites and Maimed Rites: Ritual and Anti-Ritual in Shakespeare and His Age*, ed. Linda Woodbridge and Edward Berry (Urbana and Chicago: University of Illinois Press, 1992); David Beauregard, '"Great Command O'ersways the Order": Purgatory,

Revenge, and Maimed Rites in *Hamlet*', *Religion and the Arts* 11.1 (2007), 45–73.

46. Close observation was one of Darwin's most admired, and self-cultivated, skills.

47. Richard Halpern, 'An impure history of ghosts: Derrida, Marx, Shakespeare', *Marxist Shakespeares*, ed. Jean E. Howard and Scott Cutler (Florence, KY: Routledge, 2000), 31–52: 'If the skull represents a seemingly more solid and less paradoxical materiality than does the Ghost, it is nevertheless in the slow process of disappearing once and for all' (45).

48. See note to 5.1.193–205, Arden 3 *Hamlet*, ed. Anne Thompson and Neil Taylor (London: Thomson Learning, 2006).

49. E.g., 'cork into a hogshead', *The Winter's Tale*, 3.3.90–91.

50. Ewan Fernie, 'Introduction: Shakespeare, spirituality, and contemporary criticism', *Spiritual Shakespeares*, 8–9.

51. To the First Thief's uncomprehending objection, 'We cannot live on grass, on berries, water, / As beasts and birds and fishes', Timon replies 'Nor on the beasts themselves, the birds and the fishes; / You must eat men' (14.422–25). The issue is not what may be eaten, but the outstripping of available resources.

52. Joseph Meeker, 'Hamlet and the Animals', *The Comedy of Survival: Studies in Literary Ecology* (New York: Scribner, 1974), 60–78.

53. Darwin, *Origin of Species*, 313; Phillips, *Darwin's Worms*, 58–9.

EPILOGUE

1. Reviews by Michael Billington, *The Guardian*, 10 August 2006; Alastair Macaulay, *Financial Times*, 10 August 2006; Dominic Cavendish, *The Daily Telegraph*, 10 August 2006; Maxwell Cooter and Pete Wood, *WhatsOnStage*, 10 August 2006; Kate Bassett, *The Independent*, 13 August 2006; Christopher Hart, *The Sunday Times*, 13 August 2006; Quentin Letts, *Mail on Sunday*, 13 August 2006.

2. Deleuze, 'Desert Islands'; Geraldo de Sousa, 'Alien Habitats in *The Tempest*', *The Tempest: Critical Essays*, ed. Patrick M. Murphy (New York: Routledge, 2001), 439–61.

Further Reading

Although Timothy Clark's *Cambridge Introduction to Literature and the Environment* (Cambridge, 2011) does not discuss Shakespeare, I have found it the most useful recent survey for orienting his work towards contemporary concepts and issues in literary environmentalism. Also valuable are Lawrence Buell's *The Future of Environmental Criticism: Environmental Crisis and Literary Imagination* (Oxford, 2005); Gabriel Egan's *Green Shakespeare: from ecopolitics and ecocriticism* (London and New York: Routledge, 2006); Greg Garrard's *Ecocriticism* (New Critical Idiom series), 2nd edition (London, 2011); and Ursula K. Heise's *Sense of Place and Sense of Planet: The Environmental Imagination of the Global* (Oxford, 2008). Heise's trenchant 'Science and Ecocriticism', *American Book Review* 18.5 (1997), 4–6, makes the case for integrating greater scientific knowledge into ecocriticism, partly to detach it from idealist and symbolic conceptions of nature, and partly to create an interdisciplinary practice that will address ecological problems that demand integrated cultural and ecological action. Bruce R. Smith clarifies the conceptual range of recent scholarly approaches in 'Shakespeare @ the Limits', part of a Forum on Shakespeare and Ecology in *Shakespeare Studies* 39 (2011), 104–113. Julian Yates and Garrett A. Sullivan Jr present a theoretically illuminating Introduction (23–31) to the Forum's eight essays, as do Lynne Bruckner and Daniel Brayton for their excellent representative collection, *Ecocritical Shakespeare* (Farnham, Surrey, and Burlington, VT, 2011). (See also Greg Garrard's elegant Foreword and Simon Estok's politically engaged Afterword to the same volume, respectively xvii-xxiv, 239–46.) A now somewhat older but still helpful survey of ecocriticism for the period is Karen Raber's 'Recent Ecocritical Studies of English Renaissance Literature', *English Literary Renaissance* (2007), 151–71.

The governing theory of much recent ecocriticism is the scientific shift from steady-state to non-equilibrium ecology. This changeover embraces continuous non-catastrophic environmental disturbance and change as ecologically and evolutionarily normative, and so corrects Romantic views of nature as balanced and harmonious when it is separated from human culture. See: S.T.A. Pickett and P.S. White in *The Ecology of Natural Disturbance and Patch Dynamics* (Orlando and London, 1985); Daniel Botkin, *Discordant Harmonies: A New Ecology for the Twenty-First Century* (Oxford, 1992); Richard T.T. Forman, *Land Mosaics: the ecology of landscapes and regions* (Cambridge, 1995). The related concepts of biodiversity and ecological resilience are described by: C.S. Holling, 'Resilience and the stability of ecological systems,' *Annual Review of Ecology & Systematics* 4 (1973), 1–23; L.H. Gunderson, 'Ecological Resilience—In Theory and Application', *Annual Review of Ecology & Systematics* 31 (2000), 425–39; and Malcolm J. Hunter, Jr, *Fundamentals of Conservation Biology* (Cambridge, MA, 1996).

Contemporary non-equilibrium ecology suggests analogies with early modern speculation about the causes of environmental disturbance, and with emerging empirical and materialist outlooks that challenged providentialist worldviews. John F. Danby originally showed how Shakespeare represented these opposing 'two natures' in *Shakespeare's Doctrine of Nature: A Study of King Lear* (London, 1949). Gabriel Egan and Steve Mentz respectively update Danby's discussions in 'Supernature and the weather: *King Lear* and *The Tempest*', part of his book, *Green Shakespeare: From ecopolitics to ecocriticism* (London and New York, 2006), 132–71, and 'Strange weather in *King Lear*', *Shakespeare* 6.2 (June 2010), 139–52.

Shakespeare's plays engaged with a variety of early modern environmental controversies. One was forest and woodland management. Oliver Rackham's magisterial *Ancient Woodland: its history, vegetation and uses in England*, 2nd edition (Colvend, Kirkcudbrightshire, 2003) provides essential scientific and historical information. Two excellent cultural anthropologies are Robert Pogue Harrison's *Forests: The Shadow of Civilization* (Chicago, 1992), and John Perlin's *A Forest Journey: The Role of Wood in the Development of Civilization* (New York, 1989). The philosophical implications of Pogue Harrison's ideas are opened up by Ben De Bruyn's 'The Gathering of Form: Forests, Gardens, and Legacies in Robert Pogue Harrison', *The Oxford Literary Review* 32.1 (2010), 19–36. In terms of Shakespeare, Vin Nardizzi has interwoven materialist and cultural studies perspectives in *Wooden Os: Shakespeare's Theatres and England's Trees* (Toronto and London, 2013), while Lynne Bruckner combines physical and political studies in '"Consuming means, soon preys upon itself": Political Expedience and Environmental Degradation in Richard II', *Shakespeare and The Urgency of Now: Criticism and Theory in the 21st Century*, ed. Cary DiPietro and Hugh Grady (Basingstoke and New York, 2013), 126–47. Jeffrey S. Theis discusses Shakespeare's woodland and pastoral environments and their reception by seventeenth-century writers in *Writing the Forest in Early Modern England: A Sylvan Pastoral Nation* (Pittsburgh, 2009).

Because England's early modern economy was dominantly agricultural, changing methods of land-exploitation directly affected most of the population, including Shakespeare. Two of the most contested practices were enclosure and engrossing. Their historical scholarship is vast, but Joan Thirsk provides accessible and authoritative overviews in 'Enclosing and Engrossing', *The Agrarian History of England and Wales*, ed. H.P.R. Finberg and J. Thirsk, 8 vols. (Cambridge, 1967–2000), iv. 221, 233, and 'Tudor Enclosures', *The Tudors*, ed. Joel Hurstfield (New York, 1973), 65–83. Christopher Hill's *Reformation to Industrial Revolution* (Harmondsworth, 1971) and Roger B. Manning's *Village Revolts: Social Protest and Popular Disturbances in England, 1509–1640* (Oxford, 1988) discuss subsistence crises and political protests related to shifting land ecologies. They are the framework for: Richard Wilson's '"Like the Old Robin Hood": *As You Like It* and the Enclosure Riots', *Shakespeare Quarterly* 43.1 (Spring 1992), 1–19; Jane Elisabeth Archer, Richard Marggraf Turley, and Howard Thomas's 'The Autumn King: Remembering the Land in *King Lear*', *Shakespeare Quarterly* 63.4 (Winter 2012), 518–43; Hillary Eklund's 'Revolting Diets: Jack Cade's "Sallet" and the Politics of Hunger in *2 Henry VI*', *Shakespeare Studies* 42 (2014), 51–62 and James R. Siemon's economically focused 'Landlord Not King: Agrarian Change and Interarticulation', *Enclosure Acts: Sexuality, Property, and Culture in Early Modern England*, ed. Richard Burt and John Michael Archer (Ithaca and London, 1994), 17–33.

There are, to my knowledge, no environmentalist studies of the relationships between early modern war and industrial militarization of the kind observed by Shakespeare and George Gascoigne, although Bruce Boehrer's *Environmental Degradation in Jacobean Drama* discusses a wide range of related controversies, including land-uses and mining (Cambridge, 2013). The latter is also the subject of John Jowett's 'Timon and Mining', *SEDERI: Yearbook of the Spanish and Portuguese Society for English Renaissance Studies* 14 (2004): 77–92. On wartime resource exploitation, suggestive modern analogies are presented by: Susan D. Lanier-Graham, *The Ecology of War: Environmental Impacts of Weaponry and Warfare* (New York, 1993); Jurgen Bauer, *War and Nature: The Environmental Consequences of War in a Globalized World* (Lanham, MD and Plymouth, UK, 2009); and Barry Sanders, *The Green Zone: The Environmental Costs of Militarism* (Oakland, Edinburgh, and Baltimore, 2009).

Relationships between European imperialism, ecological disturbance, and environmental degradation are discussed by Alfred W. Crosby, *Ecological Imperialism: The Biological Expansion, 900–1900* (Cambridge, 1986), and Richard H. Grove, *Green Imperialism: Colonial expansion, tropical island Edens and the origins of environmentalism, 1600–1860* (Cambridge, 1995), which has a section on *The Tempest* (32–39). Simon Estok explores related instrumentalist attitudes to nature in *Ecocriticism and Shakespeare: Reading Ecophobia* (Basingstoke and New York, 2011). Globalization and domestic consumption are the subject of Lisa Jardine's *Worldly Goods: A New History*

of the Renaissance (New York and London, 1996). Deborah Harkness
studies the effects of New World discoveries on London's nascent scientific
community in *The Jewel House: Elizabethan London and the Scientific Revolution* (New Haven, 2008).

Relationships between early modern voyaging, natural history, and postcolonial
environmentalism overlap with ocean, river, and water ecologies. See: Steve
Mentz, *At the Bottom of Shakespeare's Ocean* (New York, 2009), which has an
outstanding bibliography, 'Reading the New Thalassology', 101–12;
'Toward a Blue Cultural Studies: The Sea, Maritime Culture, and Early
Modern English Literature', *Literature Compass* 6.5 (September, 2009),
997–1013; 'Shakespeare's Beach House, or the Green and the Blue in
Macbeth', *Shakespeare Studies* 39 (2011), 84–93; Daniel Brayton, 'Shake-
speare and the Global Ocean', *Ecocritical Shakespeare* (cited above), 173–92;
Shakespeare's Ocean: An Ecocritical Exploration (Charlottesville and London,
2012); Lowell Duckert, *Enter, Wet: Composing with Water in Early Modern
Drama and Travel Literature* (Minneapolis, forthcoming).

Early modern English and overseas environments, physiological responses,
and changing cultural outlooks are discussed in: Keith Thomas, *Man and
the Natural World: Changing Attitudes in England 1500–1800* (Oxford,
1983); Mary Floyd-Wilson, *English Ethnicity and Race in Early Modern
Drama* (Cambridge, 2003); *Reading the Early Modern Passions: Essays in the
Cultural History of Emotion*, ed. Gail Kern Paster, Katherine Rowe, and
Mary Floyd-Wilson (Philadelphia, 2004); Daryl W. Palmer, 'Hamlet's
Northern Lineage: Masculinity, Climate, and the Mechanician in Early
Modern Britain', *Renaissance Drama* 35 (2006), 3–25; *Environment and
Embodiment in Early Modern England*, ed. Mary Floyd-Wilson and Garrett
A. Sullivan Jr, (Basingstoke and New York, 2007). Environmental agency
in the Shakespearian theatre is explored by: Gail Kern Paster, *Humoring the
Body: Emotions and the Shakespearean Stage* (Chicago, 2004); Tim Fitzpatrick,
*Playwright, Space, and Place in Early Modern Performance: Shakespeare and
Company* (Farnham, Surrey and Burlington, VT, 2011); Cary DiPietro,
'Performing Place in *The Tempest*', *Shakespeare and the Urgency of Now*, ed.
C. DiPietro and Hugh Grady (London and New York, 2013), 83–102.

Essays by Michel de Montaigne such as 'On Cruelty' and 'The Apology for
Raymond Sebond' (*The Complete Essays*, trans. M.A. Screech [1991; London,
2003]), both known to Shakespeare in John Florio's 1603 translation and
possibly earlier in French, are a starting point for investigating the early
modern rediscovery of classical scepticism towards separating human and
non-human animals that anticipates animal studies and post-humanist
scholarship today. For animals, see: Keith Thomas's *Man and the Natural
World* (cited above), especially Chapter 4, 'Compassion for Brute Creation',

143–91; Erica Fudge, *Brutal Reasoning: Animals, Rationality, and Humanity in Early Modern England* (Ithaca and London, 2006), particularly Chapter 4, 'Being Animal', 84–122; Bruce Boehrer, *Shakespeare among the Animals: Nature and Society in the Drama of Early Modern England* (Basingstoke and New York, 2002); *Animal Characters: Non-Human Beings in Early Modern Literature* (Philadelphia, 2010); *At the Borders of the Human: Beasts, Bodies, and Natural Philosophy in the Early Modern Period*, ed. Erica Fudge, Ruth Gilbert, and Susan Wiseman (Basingstoke and New York, 2002); Erica Sheen, '"Why should a dog, a horse, a rat, have life, and thou no breath at all?", Shakespeare's Animations', *Renaissance Beasts: Of Animals, Humans, and Other Wonderful Creatures*, ed. Erica Fudge (2004); Andreas Höfele, *Stage, Stake, and Scaffold: Humans & Animals in Shakespeare's Theatre* (Oxford, 2011); Laurie Shannon, *The Accommodated Animal: Cosmopolity in Shakespearean Locales* (Chicago, 2013); Scott Maisano, 'Rise of the Poet of the Apes', *Shakespeare Studies* 41 (2013), 64–76. For post-humanism, environmental materialism, and object-oriented ontology, see: Adam Max Cohen, *Shakespeare and Technology: Dramatizing Early Modern Technological Revolutions* (Basingstoke and New York, 2006); Jane Bennett, *Vibrant Matter: a political ecology of things* (Durham and London, 2010); *Posthumanist Shakespeares*, ed. Stefan Herbrechter and Ivan Callus (Basingstoke and New York, 2012); *The Indistinct Human in Renaissance Literature*, ed. Jean E. Feerick and Vin Nardizzi (Basingstoke and New York, 2012); Stacey Alaimo, 'Sustainable This, Sustainable That: New Materialisms, Posthumanism, and Unknown Futures', *PMLA* 127.3 (May 2012), 558–64, as well as other essays in the Sustainability cluster in that volume; Julian Yates, *Error, Misuse, Failure: Object Lessons From The English Renaissance* (Minneapolis, 2002); *Prismatic Ecology: Ecotheory Beyond Green*, ed. Jeffrey Jerome Cohen (Minneapolis and London, 2013).

Scientifically, connections between human and non-human organisms are explained by the modern synthesis of evolutionary biology and genetics, of which phylogeny is the study of molecular relationships and lineages. See Richard Dawkins, *The Selfish Gene*, 30th Anniversary edition (Oxford, 2006); Jan Sapp, *The New Foundations of Evolution: On the Tree of Life* (Oxford, 2009). Descent with modification, symbiosis, and gene transfers outside of sexual reproduction suggest affinities with older ideas of metamorphosis and transmutation familiar to Shakespeare. See Lewis Thomas, *The Lives of a Cell: Notes of a Biology Watcher* (New York, 1974); Lynn Margulis, *Symbiotic Planet: A New Look at Evolution* (Amherst, MA, 1998); Jan Sapp, *Evolution by Association: A History of Symbiosis* (New York and Oxford, 1994); Michel Serres, *Biogea* (Minneapolis, 2012); Rebecca Stott, *Darwin and the Barnacle: The Story of One Tiny Creature and History's Most*

> *Spectacular Scientific Breakthrough* (London, 2003); *Darwin's Ghosts: In Search of the First Evolutionists* (London, 2012), especially 'Leonardo and the Potter—Milan, 1493; Paris, 1570', 61–85.

The politics and ethics of environmental philosophy and criticism are usefully outlined by Andrew Dobson, *Green Political Thought*, 4th edition (London, 2007), and Patrick Curry, *Ecological Ethics: An Introduction*, 2nd edition (Cambridge, 2011), 92–134. For their relationship to theoretically 'presentist' approaches to Shakespeare, see: Sharon O'Dair, 'Slow Shakespeare: An Eco-Critique of "Method" in Early Modern Literary Studies', *Early Modern Ecostudies: From the Florentine Codex to Shakespeare*, ed. Thomas Hallock, Ivo Kamps, and Karen L. Raber (New York, 2008), 11–30; '"To fright the animals and to kill them up": Shakespeare and Ecology', *Shakespeare Studies* 39 (2011), 74–83; Todd A. Borlik, *Ecocriticism and Early Modern English Literature* (New York and London, 2011); Simon Estok, 'A Progress Report on Shakespearean and Early Modern Ecocriticism', *Revista canaria de studios ingleses* 64 (2012), 47–60.

Index

Aelian 6

Agamben, Giorgio 28, 135

Alaimo, Stacey 44

Allen, Giles 1

All's Well That Ends Well 16, 93, 112, 119

Animal and human relations. See human nature

Antony and Cleopatra 9, 13–14, 20, 29–30, 134–65

anthropocentrism (human exceptionalism) 8, 29, 108, 126, 135, 137, 158, 160, 167

Arden. See forests

Arden, Robert 35

Ariosto, Ludovico (*Orlando Furioso*) 63

Aristotle, chain of being 6

Armaments (artillery, cannons, firearms) 21–2, 78–88, 101

Artemis (Diana) 29, 120, 132

Artificial selection. See evolution.

As You Like It 4, 9–14, 17–20, 24–5, 29, 34–8, 55–78, 81, 89, 93, 95, 101, 115, 121

Augustine: book of nature 6, 24 theory of war 98

Bacon, Francis 25–6, 80, 119

Basalla, George 83–4

Bate, Jonathan 34, 113

Beck, Ulrich: 23, 86, 117–19 methodological nationalism 117–18 reflexive modernization (environmental risk) 23, 86–7, 100, 102–3, 109

Berg, Peter 60

Berger, Harry 101, 103–4

biocentrism 8 (defined), 44, 56, 60–2, 66–7, 70, 91–3, 126, 130, 138, 140–50, 159

biodiversity 4, 7–8, 19, 23–7 (defined), 53, 56, 65, 74, 112–16, 130, 133, 136–7, 148, 151, 163–4

biodynamic farming 4, 19, 66–7, 73–7, 91–4, 149

bioregionalism 9, 19–23 (defined), 27–8, 37, 55–79, 89–100, 107, 115, 121–7, 138, 147–8, 157

biosphere 9, 105–9, 112–33. See also nested biological relations

Blackfriars Theatre 1

Bleach, Julian 170–1

Book of nature. See also Augustine

Boyd, Michael 69, 72–3

Brayton, Daniel 167

Brundtland Commission (sustainability) 43–6

Buell, Lawrence 113

Bulman, James C. 89

Burbage, Richard and Cuthbert 1

Cadle, Giles 167–8

Camden, William (*Britannia*) 58

Cannons. See armaments

Carr, Mike 60

Carroll, William C. 68

Carrying capacity 12–16 (defined), 40–2, 89–91, 100, 150

Carson, Rachel (*Silent Spring*) 105–6

Cecil, William (Lord Burghley) 39

Certeau, Michel de 61

Chamberlain's Men 1, 14, 36, 133

Chases 33, 36, 47

Chimneys (fireplaces) 2, 14–16, 38, 40, 53, 85

Church, Rook 41, 51

Cimolino, Antoni 117

Clare, John 113

Clark, Timothy 113

Climate change 2–6, 9–11, 16, 32, 78–9, 83, 89, 110, 113, 166–7

Coal. See sea coal

Cogan, Thomas (*Haven of Health*) 94

Coke, Sir Edward 43

Printed and bound by CPI Group (UK) Ltd, Croydon, CR0 4YY